John Smith
ON THE SIDE OF
THE ANGELS

'In the 1980s actions speak louder than words.
On the back of John Smith's Harley
there's more action than in most places.
Truly a preacher to the convertible ... his
message is for people who want to do more
than just listen.'

BONO
U2

John Smith
ON THE SIDE OF
THE ANGELS

JOHN SMITH and
MALCOLM DONEY

A LION PAPERBACK
Tring • Batavia • Sydney

This book is dedicated to:

My parents who taught me there was more to life than pleasure, particularly to Dad who taught me how to think and to feel with integrity.

Grandma and Grandad Smith who taught me that wit and wisdom survive far outside the university and the academy.

My wife Glena who has taught me that life is like a rough diamond which requires cutting and polishing, and that love is a subtle mixture of commitment and romance, fantasy and reality, spirituality, adoring love and determination to do, as well as to say.

Paul, Kathy and Lyndal who, like all kids, give true parents their greatest moments of pain and pleasure, and who have suffered much for their father's commitment and who I know will each, in their own way, grow to be anything but boring people.

Copyright © 1987 John Smith and Malcolm Doney

Published by
Lion Publishing plc
Icknield Way, Tring, Herts, England
ISBN 0 7459 1328 8
Albatross Books Pty Ltd
PO Box 320, Sutherland, NSW 2232, Australia
ISBN 0 86760 919 2

First edition 1987

Printed and bound in Great Britain by
Cox and Wyman, Reading

CHAPTER ONE

He was big, greasy and drunk. I couldn't tell, as he shambled towards me with an almost empty flagon of cheap port in his huge fist, whether his intentions were friendly or dangerous.

I was new to the bike scene, but had learned already that you could never predict what reaction you'd get when you first made contact with a group of outlaw bikers. I stood under the street lamps only too conscious of my leathers, still shiny from the shop, and my own club colours emblazoned on my back. 'God's Squad, Melbourne' they read in mock gothic script.

I'll tell you later how I, a thirty-year-old preacher's son whose idea of fashion adventure was to wear a tie with a stripe in it, came to be in this get-up. But for the moment I was more concerned for my safety.

This character had turned up in town with his mates because he'd heard this group of 'religious' bikers had arrived and were willing to talk. But bikers are very tribal and very territorial, so I couldn't be sure whether he wanted to shake me by the hand or smack me in the teeth. I think either would have been preferable to what actually happened.

I wasn't exactly street-wise and I had no idea if I was sending the right signals, but concealing my innocence in silence, I tried to appear both fearless and welcoming at the same time.

As he drew nearer, a blast of foul breath would have made the prim teetotal maiden aunt who once lurked inside me wilt in revulsion. Rotting teeth and cheap Aussie plonk are a formidable combination. I stayed my ground. He shifted his bottle from right to left hand and threw his meaty fist towards me. He *did* want to shake hands.

We stood facing each other, me with my relatively new beard and hair recently grown long, he with well-worn leathers and Levis which gave new dimensions to the word 'grime'. We shook hands, thumbs interlocked as if we were about to start a bout of arm wrestling. This is the biker tradition. I knew that much at least.

I was about to start off a conversation along the lines of, 'How ya goin' mate?' when he stepped, or rather stumbled, forward and wrapped his arms around me in a friendly, alcoholic bear hug. It had been a warm day as far as I recall and this particular biker had obviously not heard of Right Guard. But it was a welcome and I was glad of it. I had been accepted.

I responded, beating him on the back in a friendly way. Then, all of a sudden he planted his lips on mine. Even worse, his tongue snaked into my mouth in a slobbering male French kiss! I recoiled in horror and repulsion. My whole being went rigid and my jaw clamped shut. It was pure instinct. I was so stunned I couldn't think what to do.

We stood there locked for what seemed an age, and then the guy pushed himself away from me. He stepped back and looked at me, his bleary eyes a mixture of sadness and confusion. It was as if he was saying, 'You came to us. We accepted you. So why have you rejected me?' Then he shrugged in that offhand, take it or leave it way bikers have and walked off into the night.

I should say that there was no homosexuality in the big man's action. He didn't fancy me in the least. Bikers (not just people who like motorcycles, but those who line themselves up with outlaw bike clubs like the Hell's Angels and the many others which live in the same tradition) are given to these unconventional physical gestures of affection. It tends to happen mostly when they've had a few drinks. That kind of tongue kissing is rare these days, but it was a way of declaring brotherhood in a manner sometimes chosen for its shockingness to 'polite' society.

I still wonder about that incident. If I had been prepared for it, if I knew then what fourteen years of experience of meeting with bikers have taught me, would I have reacted differently? The fact is, I don't know. It doesn't say anywhere in the Bible, 'Thou shalt not touch tongue with tongue,' and different cultures have their own time-honoured means of greeting. But it revolted me then, and if I'm honest, it still revolts me now. What makes me feel worse though, is that through my own naivety I effectively gave him the cold shoulder. He knew I was a Christian and that, as far as our attitudes went, we were poles apart. Despite that, he had been prepared to come more than half-way to meet me. More than that, he was telling me I was OK by him.

But as I say, even though I was almost thirty, I was still a raw recruit. I had all the right gear. I had the leathers, the boots and what was then an acceptable machine in most of the club scene, a Honda 500cc four cylinder (Japanese bikes are now sneered at in the outlaw circles — but more of that later). At that stage though, I was only a biker on the outside. On the inside I was a sort of born-again hippie, and a pretty new one at that.

It was hard to believe that just a few years earlier I had stood in a pulpit, the shortness of my haircut leaving my ears open to the breeze, dressed in a sombre suit of conservative cut. During my message I had delivered a stinging diatribe against the black American civil rights leader Martin Luther King. I claimed he was a dangerous communist bent on the destruction of American society. And I believed it.

Yet here I was, covered in badges bearing hip Christian slogans, looking like a well fed Rasputin in black leather and hanging around at night in a small-town high street with a group of people generally regarded as the scum of the earth. What had happened?

I'd changed a lot, that was for sure. And, as is evident from this incident, I had to change some more, and learn to avoid hurting the very people I so desperately wanted to befriend — people society called 'outcasts'.

I suppose I was on a kind of pilgrimage — a journey I'm still part way through. In geographical terms, it's taken me across most of my home country, Australia, and has also led me to Europe and the United States. Physically, spiritually and emotionally it's been a voyage of exploration during which I've met some extraordinary people. I've found myself debating with professors one day and sitting with winos in the gutter the next. I've had a fair share of pain, especially as a kid. That's something I've learned to thank God for because it's made me a stronger person, and also because it has helped me identify with the pain and suffering that surrounds us all. In particular it has enabled me to understand something of the feelings of the many people I've met whose lives have been shattered by the blows they've been dealt in their struggle to survive our often hostile world.

It hasn't been a lone journey. I've had the company for many of those years of my wonderful wife, Glena, my marvellous kids and a host of good mates.

But above all — and this isn't as glib as it sounds — there's God. He started me off on my explorations. He's the goal of my pilgrimage and he's been my constant guide and companion throughout. Don't get me wrong. This is no pie-in-the-sky when you die story. Irrelevant religious smugness gets right up my nose. But it is a search, and the only search worth embarking on. One person's quest to make real contact with his maker and to become more fully human.

I guess I'd better start at the beginning.

CHAPTER TWO

I was a rebellious, argumentative little shaver, but deep inside, dead scared. I'd do things, or mostly say things, without thinking and then worry myself witless about the consequences. My schooldays, as I recall, were characterized by me opening my big mouth before attaching it to my brain, and then having to face the repercussions. One of the most difficult but rewarding developments for me has been the maturing since then of what Martin Luther King called 'a tough mind and a tender heart'. A fast mouth is a great gift if under that kind of direction.

I wouldn't want to saddle my parents or my grandparents with the blame for that part of my nature. But there is a history of stubborn wills and argumentation in the family. And not just that. We don't mind getting up on our hind legs and letting the world know what we've got to say. I'm now the third generation of preaching Smiths. But it took me some time before I got going.

I was born in Melbourne, in the state of Victoria, Australia, on 7 April 1942, just three years before the end of World War II.

Melbourne's fine, just as long as you don't come from Sydney. And I don't. Since almost the earliest days of the British settlers, these two south-eastern cities have been intense rivals. But I spent my earliest years in Melbourne and I love the place. Which is why I live there now. It has a vibrant, cosmopolitan inner-city life with many safe bay beaches with acres of yellow sand. Within one or two hours' drive, there is a wild open coastline with wind-scarred volcanic rocks. Melbourne sprawls over 6,000 square kilometres, built on a grid road system reminiscent of many American cities.

For most of the first nine years of my life we lived in a simple, rented one-storey house with a pokey back yard, in the inner-city district of Preston. My father, Kenneth, worked for the Victorian Railways as an adding machine mechanic. My mother, Nancy, stayed home and looked after the house.

On the surface, we would seem to be a normal Melbourne working class family. But we weren't. My parents were evangelical Christians of the old school. On religious principle they would neither drink, smoke, gamble, dance, go to the cinema, nor listen to popular music. I'm not knocking their principles, though I don't hold to these rules of abstinence myself, but they were an essential part of my background.

It has to be said that what might seem a rigid code, was found in the context of a warm, loving and sincere faith, well thought out and intelligently presented. They were not mere legalists, but rather possessed a faith typical of the old world Methodists — very socially active in concern for broken people or any in distress.

In fact, my earliest memories of home are full of people — people who would come to our house and feel they could relax. My parents would particularly welcome young men and women in their twenties, who would be invited around for an evening of what church people call 'fellowship'. This would include singing hymns and Christian choruses, tea, soft drinks and biscuits; often concluded by a short, informal message given by Dad.

I especially remember the evenings my parents hosted for young men and women in the armed forces. It must have been in the period following armistice, when these people, just returning from active service were billeted in the city before their demobilization came through. I was really too young to understand what was going on, but I can still feel the emotional warmth of those evenings. There is something haunting and humane about genuine faith — something in strong contrast to the secular barrenness of spirit so apparent in our post-Christian culture of the eighties.

So I grew up, not only with the strictness of non-conformist Christianity, but also with its genuine warmth and humanity. It was a bit of a mystery to me, but I got the feeling that Mum and Dad were involved in something bigger and more important than the routine daily realities of earning a living and running a home.

Their concern for people showed itself in other ways, too. From the earliest days of their marriage, Mum and Dad would take in people who were facing problems and who needed a shelter from the storm. For instance, even though this was a time before the advent of common drug addiction, they took in at least one nurse who had become dependent on drugs through using substances filched from the hospital she worked at. They took in other girls too, who had family or other problems. Our home became a real haven for people like these.

Mum and Dad were also involved in what were known as 'the Fitzroy Drives'. Local church people would tour the inner-city areas of Melbourne and pick up the winos and homeless to give them a good feed at the Fitzroy Mission, which would be followed by a Christian service. The Drives had begun in the depression of the thirties, but had been carried over into the immediate post-war years.

It was a common practice in those days, though one that's frowned upon now. It is said that there's no such thing as a free lunch and that this is a prime example; such Christian do-goodery has a religious price tag. But these people, my parents included, realized that human beings are more than simply bodies which need to be fed. Besides — the food was not simply a way to sell the religious propaganda — they genuinely loved and wanted to feed the hungry.

I have since done enough work with alcoholics and junkies to know that alcoholism and drug addiction are almost always symptoms of an inner lostness. But our society gears itself only to treat symptoms. It tries to dull the pain in our

11

world by supplying aspirin in the form of money, food, sex or other benefits without dealing with the underlying causes.

Paying for a fleet of ambulances at the bottom of a cliff is far more expensive and less effective than erecting warning signs and a fence at the top of a cliff. Preventative medicine is superior in the physical realms of life. If only we recognized the principle in relationship and moral areas of life.

Christians have a duty to do more than feed people who have found themselves at the bottom of the heap. If our Christianity means anything at all, then we are morally bound to say to these people, 'There is a way you can find belief, meaning and a structure to your life. There's no need to resort to escape, especially a false escape like drink or drugs which ultimately mean slavery and the inability to look after yourself.'

You can't separate physical, emotional and spiritual needs. I have no more time for the kind of secular religion which refuses to meet the transcendant needs of people, than I have for the kind of doctrinaire Christianity that refuses to meet the physical and social needs of humanity. OK, so in the old fundamentalist days there were patronizing overtones. But they did what they did out of a genuine concern to help those who were no longer able to help themselves. And my parents were very much part of that. Secular fundamentalists frequently ignore the spirit and soul with a narrow bloody-mindedness of their own.

Growing up in an atmosphere of care and concern like this has had the strongest possible influence on me. A foundation was laid here for so much of what was to become real to me much later on. These were some of the ideas that first set me on my path.

I would probably never have got past the first bend in the road if it hadn't been for my Dad. Humanly speaking, he has probably been the single biggest influence on my life. Dad is not a big man, he stands about five foot six, slightly built but absolutely resolute. Very much his own man. He has always come across as a man of firmness and principle, but I believe this has been part of a deliberate choice; for beneath the tempered steel exterior he has fabricated, he is a warm man with deep feelings.

Ironically, one of the things he taught me, for which I'm eternally grateful, is the ability to cry. Weeping has never been high on the macho Aussie male's scale of virtues, yet despite his reserve, my father was not afraid to shed tears if he felt something deeply. These demonstrations of human emotion did two things for me. They showed me he wasn't as unyielding as he would have the world believe. Also, his example gave me the strength not to be afraid or ashamed of my own emotions. And, as those who know me even slightly will confirm, when my feelings boil over — as they're apt to — tears are often the result. And the ability to help liberate other men to the point of tears has in recent years been one of the best gifts I've exercised.

Dad was trained as a fitter and turner before he joined the railways and has always been a hard and conscientious worker. He dressed soberly and neatly and always hated anything that could remotely be called flashy or dandified — even a moustache he considered suspect.

When he wasn't working, he was putting his prodigious energies into the local Methodist church, where he was a lay preacher. He had been converted to Christianity at the age of ten. And while that may seem young to make such a life-changing decision, he never once regretted it and lived unswervingly in the service of God and humanity from that point onwards. His was a stern and uncompromising faith, based on the belief that the Bible was 100 per cent true.

My Grandad was a remarkable character and a rugged individualist. Jack worked in a boot-making factory in the city and, as was normal, joined the bootmakers' trade union. He was later elected President of the union. He retained this role for three of the union's most difficult years during the depression. He then became the Federal Secretary but was ousted after three months, as he tried to reconcile the left and

13

right factions within the movement.

He was blacklisted by the union and wasn't able to carry on his trade. He became a door-to-door salesman of Rawleigh's products. This was in the days before the kind of chemist shops we have now, and so his visits were valued, unlike those of the encyclopedia salesmen and other unwanted doorsteppers today.

What impressed me was that Grandad always worked on the basis of service rather than profit. He became a friend to many of his regular customers. There was always a twinkle in his eye, along with a quick-witted observant gleam. He was always straightforward, with an open, even-handed friendliness that appealed to people. I loved him. His sense of humour was incorrigible — hilarious jokes given with a classic poker face.

With only five years to go before retirement, he left it all behind to join an organization called Open Air Campaigners, whose task was to preach to the people of Australia — going where they lived and worked rather than expecting them to come to church and be preached at. It was a bold move for a man of his age.

I saw him in action a number of times. And he was worth watching. He was a natural stump orator. He'd go to a factory yard at midday where men would sit eating their lunch. He'd be heckled from the very start. But this was meat and drink to Grandad, who had a marvellous, sharp-witted way of turning an off-the-cuff comment into a positive point. He was as funny as a circus, too, disarming the men he spoke to with his dry humour. While his beliefs were traditional his images and language were secular and realistic.

Mum had talent. She danced the lead at the Tivoli Theatre junior ballet when she was a kid and could sing up a storm. She'd had some voice training and sang with great emotion in operatic style.

She had got into a fairly wild bunch of kids at school and she and her mates would take delight in trying their best to disrupt the gatherings of the small Christian group which

14

met at her school. Religion wasn't exactly high on her agenda. But through a teacher who befriended her and took her away to a Christian convention one summer, she decided she wanted to become a committed follower of Jesus.

She had a hard time convincing her parents that this was a genuine change of heart, and there was some animosity at home for a while, but she remained firm in her resolve. It was as a young woman that she met Dad and married him.

Mum was short — less than five feet tall — and plump. She wore no make-up on principle and dressed in plain simplicity, partly because she thought it was right and partly because of a meagre budget. We weren't a rich family. Like my father, she was a strong-willed, resolute person of iron convictions who saw things in distinct black and white. This meant that whatever she undertook to do, she did, and would brook no denial.

I have a mixture of feelings about my mother. We clashed often. She was a perfectionist and I felt I could never match her standards for me. And since I was a rebellious soul, things weren't always easy between us. She had a firm (I thought then, inflexible and vindictive) sense of discipline, and a stern way about her, which I interpreted as a lack of affection. There were times when I really hated her, and would nurse my grievances like a child holding tight to a teddy bear.

That was how I felt then, but I have since had more time, more information and, I hope more maturity, to reflect on Mum and her way of doing things. I found out, for instance, that her own parents were the kind of people who found it difficult to express affection and that was reflected in her treatment of her own children. She had no role model to follow. I also discovered that she had been sexually abused when quite young, though not, I must stress, by anyone in the family. These incidents left a painful legacy and also made her reticent about displaying her softer feelings, and meant that she was often more tense than she might have been.

Finally, she was a sick woman for a long time. When she died tragically at the young age of forty-two, it was because of a massive, and by then inoperable aneurysm (a dilated artery) in the brain. The evidence suggested that Mum had been suffering from this condition for years. She must have been in considerable pain at times, which would inevitably have affected her temper and her state of mind.

But as a child, I reacted to what I saw as unfairness in anger and rebellion. I found it very difficult to accept discipline from her — especially the slaps around the face which she gave when she was angry.

But there was a remarkable counterpoint to her apparent coldness. She treated the visitors who came to our house with genuine warmth. Whenever she was involved in what she considered to be her ministry — her service before God — she was a different person. She had a way of making people feel at home — helping them feel they weren't so much guests as family friends.

If Mum felt unable to express deep feelings in everyday family life, she made up for it when she sang. Mum had a resonant soprano voice. She often sang solo when Dad preached, and as she launched into those old hymns, you could almost touch the emotion, it was so tangible. It was as if this heartfelt sacred music was the only vehicle she felt free enough in, or perhaps thought worthy enough to let everything she had inside her go. But for whatever reason, when my mother sang, she was transformed. Her music was often accompanied by a tearful eye.

With parents who were such firm Christians, it was inevitable that I should be introduced to church at an early age. The Methodist tradition, as it was in many Western churches, is for the children to be tolerated only when they are absolutely silent. You dared not so much as wriggle, since any fidgeting drew angry glares from parents and fellow members of the congregation alike.

I had a love/hate relationship with the place. Most of the

16

time it bored me rigid. Just now and then I'd get a flash — sometimes when my Dad preached — that he was in touch with some bigger outside reality. I felt the same about the revival prayer meetings my parents took me to when I was still quite small.

We'd meet in a crowded room and pray with great fervour. The atmosphere was intense. One after another would stand up and plead with God for revival to sweep over Australia, for a movement of God across the world. I can remember sitting there with a sense of holy wonder at all this. Here was I, part of a small group of people huddled together in this room, normal in every way, yet they believed that they were in touch with the almighty Creator of the Universe.

But when the meeting was over and we had to leave the physical and emotional warmth and cohesion of that place, my attitude changed. We had to travel some way home, sometimes on a cold winter's night, in a tram with no doors. In my little shorts I froze, and resented it deeply. I would fall asleep whimpering, only to be woken when we reached our stop to walk the quarter of a mile home.

I don't want this to sound like an 'I was the poor, repressed child of fanatical fundamentalists' story, however. My parents were strict, but they loved me as much as they loved each other. There has never been any doubt about that. They wanted the very best for me, and in their terms that meant that I should be brought up to be a child of God. They followed the biblical command to 'bring (your children) up in the nurture and admonition of the Lord,' as the old King James version of the Bible puts it. And they did so according to their own understanding of what that meant.

I certainly needed a firm hand. I don't subscribe to the romantic belief that children are pure and innocent, and that, left to themselves, they will grow up good, kind and generous members of society. Humans are selfish; from their earliest days they demand 'Me first!' It is only a combination of generous love and firm discipline which will teach children that others have legitimate needs too, and that we

17

often have to temper our own desires in the light of those.

I'm grateful to my parents for the discipline they gave me, though I didn't like it at the time. Dad was always scrupulously fair. He would never lash out; he was predictable in the best sense of the word. I always knew exactly why he was punishing me, and I accepted it. That's not to say that I was always immediately obedient to his commands. Quite the opposite. It was a habit of mine always to test any command. If my Dad said, 'Don't do that', I would go straight off and do it — I suppose to see whether he really meant it. He invariably did.

One Sunday, I remember, I was being a real pain in church. I can't recall exactly what I was up to, but Dad was beginning to get annoyed. He leaned over to me and whispered threateningly, 'If you don't start behaving right now, I'm going to take you out of here and give you a hiding'. I heard the warning in his voice, understood exactly what he meant, and carried on what I was doing. He took me outside.

There was an alleyway down the side of the church, and rather than clout me in public view, he took me here for a discreet walloping. While justice was being administered, a woman's voice shouted out behind him.

'What do you think you're doing to that boy? Stop this minute. I'm calling the police!' It turned out that there'd been someone molesting children in the area. She'd seen my Dad in what must have looked very suspicious circumstances and bravely stepped in. He was extremely embarrassed, which pleased me, but he explained to the woman that I was his son and I was getting my just deserts, so I didn't escape the conclusion of my hiding, despite her intervention.

One day my Dad decided I was old enough to know a bit more about the human condition, something beyond applying the board of education to the seat of learning! I reckon I was about four and a half. I was quite precocious in religious terms, having been brought up to it from my mother's breast. And I had, quite self-motivated, started asking a lot of questions about God and shown a genuine interest in

18

wanting to know more about him.

It was evening, and I had been particularly uncontrollable at church. I had been rather full of myself, largely due to the fact that I was wearing a brand new pair of shorts of which I was inordinately proud. I had strutted around thinking I was Mr Wonderful, and had been thoroughly objectionable.

Dad sat me down in the lounge room and gave me a talk which has lived with me ever since. 'You've got a brand new pair of trousers on, and you look pretty good. To look at you, anyone would say, "What a nice little boy". But let me show you something.'

He stepped over to the glass-fronted cabinet by the wall and picked up the apple which lay on top. It was a lovely, polished apple without visible flaw. Dad showed it to me.

'There,' he said. 'Looks good doesn't it?' Then, taking out his pocket knife, he sliced it in half. He opened the apple up and showed me the inside. It was literally rotten to the core.

How he knew it was like that I don't know. There must have been some small, tell-tale mark on it somewhere. But the effect on me was dramatic. He did not need to say much more, and as far as I can recall, he didn't. I was struck by an overwhelming sense, even at that young age, that my inward self had to be dealt with. I felt ashamed.

A lot of people would say that this was a cruel, heartless gesture for a parent to make. That he was loading me up with a sense of inadequacy and personal guilt which could cripple me for life. Certainly the image has stuck with me for years, but I'm glad.

Dad didn't give me a huge moralistic lecture. He just showed me the apple and made the point. If there was a weight on me, it was one I took upon myself. I know that you could say he was an adult and that as an infant, I had no defences. But I don't feel that way about it, even now.

Our culture deals far too much with externals. On the outside you can seem totally acceptable to the rest of society, yet on the inside be a complete mess, full of hate and selfishness.

19

And in any case this example didn't simply have the effect of making me feel bad. Much more, it made me desire goodness. It's a desire that has been pilloried in the twentieth century, but it is a wonderful motivation. There's nothing that feels better than knowing you've done something genuinely good and right without ulterior motive.

And there's nothing so magnificent, as we look back at history, and even at our own generation, as the character and courage of those who do good. Despite the disintegration and sickness there is in our society, most people will admire people like Mother Teresa, Martin Luther King and Desmond Tutu — people whose lives are dominated by the desire to do good for its own sake.

What I sensed at that moment, but could never have expressed, was that religion was not so much about escaping hell or going to heaven. It was about becoming more fully human; more like the person God intended us to be. It makes me warm to something Mother Theresa once said about God: 'Oh that there was no heaven to gain and no hell to shun, that I could love him only for himself.'

I knew even then that there were some areas of John Smith's life that could be destructive of others and himself. In my heart I cried out to God for a sense of moral liberation, some kind of victory over anger and self-absorption. I'd made an important discovery about myself. Having taken that small step, I had to take more.

The next major occurrence in my life ended up teaching me more about other people than it did about me.

CHAPTER THREE

Life in Melbourne wasn't all prayer meetings and austere discipline. Dad could be serious, but he could be a lot of fun too. We were great companions. I especially used to love those Saturday mornings when we'd go off hunting rabbits.

Because Australia is such a young country, its people are probably nearer to their rural roots than those whose nations have a longer history of industrialization. The frontier-busting days when a family had to make their living from the bush are not that far away. So there's a great romantic feel for hunting and fishing, for camping out and cooking over an open fire.

My Dad had the same spirit within him. So have I. And in those early post-war days money was tight, so some extra meat for the pot was luxury.

Dad had a rifle, and sometimes we'd shoot for our supper, or we'd take a ferret and a net. Dad bred a few ferrets which he kept in small hutches of his own making in the back garden. They're curious creatures, easy enough to domesticate, but difficult to tame completely. They have an innate viciousness which you can't quite get rid of, and they can quite easily give you a nasty nip, despite the fact that you've been handling them since they were tiny. And they smell pretty bad too. Ours were a dull brown, though they are often a creamy yellow colour. They look a bit like an otter.

Dad, like his father, was good with his hands, and if he could make or mend something rather than buy it new, he would. He knotted and repaired the nets we used to catch the rabbits with.

We'd set off very early in the morning while it was still

dark. We had no car in those days, so we would catch a train to the hills to the north of Melbourne — places like Hurstbridge or Wattle Glen. We'd arrive in the half-light of early dawn and make our way to the places where we knew rabbits could be found.

More often than not these spring and summer mornings would be shrouded in thick mist. We'd negotiate the prickly patches of gorse bushes until we found a likely-looking warren and settle down until the mist lifted in the morning sunshine.

I was too small to shoot, so when we took the rifle, I'd be more of a spectator. But it was exciting nonetheless. Waiting for the rabbits to appear, then the tense moments, staying silent and downwind so as not to disturb our prey. Dad would lift the rifle to his shoulder and take aim. Then, 'Crack!' followed by the smell of cordite and usually (Dad was a good shot) a rabbit to take home to Mum.

Those expeditions were probably the happiest times of my early childhood, out there among the tall stately gums, with the early morning alarm call (in truth, more of a maniacal cackle) of the kookaburras ringing in our ears. With the strengthening sun warming our backs, we'd listen out for the warning thump of a rabbit, beating his back feet on the ground to let his mates know something was up.

If we'd brought a ferret, we'd slip him down one of the holes to drive the rabbit through and wait with the net by the other end of the burrow. We had to take a shovel with us when we went ferreting, because sometimes the ferret would catch the rabbit rather than chase it out, and then he might take it into his head to stay down there to feed on it. You can't afford to lose your ferret in the wild, so we'd have to go in after him and dig the creature out.

This time-honoured practice might seem barbaric to some, but if it's any consolation, we weren't out there simply for the sport, though there is an undeniable thrill in the chase. We were there to get food for the family. I love animals, domestic and wild, and I find no pleasure in the moment of their death. But I'm not a vegetarian and can't see any difference in substance between eating meat that someone else has killed and eating meat that I have.

There is satisfaction, though, in the sense of achievement that comes from completing any skilled job. And if you're going to eat meat, there is more reality in hunting, killing and bringing home your own than there is in buying it off the butcher's slab.

On these trips, Dad and I would be equally content talking or drifting into a companionable silence. In those moments I was content. But such simple pleasures were overshadowed by an event whose consequences were to affect me for a long time.

We had a wash-house at home — a primitive version of today's utility room. Here stood the copper, a large copper galvanized water tank raised on brick over a wood fire. This monster heated the water for all our household needs.

Its main drawback was that it was a self-contained system. You could heat the water in the tank but you couldn't run it off anywhere. If anyone wanted a bath (or any hot water for that matter) then you had to take off the lid, which was made of wooden slats, and scoop the water out with a dixie.

As a little boy, I was always poking my nose into the wash-room. While the water was heating up it was the warmest place in the house. And I used to love looking at the fire under the copper. One day, when I was five years old, I squatted down to peer into the flames, engrossed in the pictures I could see among the glowing logs.

What happened next is a bit of a blur, but it went something like this. Mum told me to move away from the fire. She was concerned lest I fall, and was looking at me instead of concentrating on anything else. Her elbow slipped and shifted the wooden lid of the copper. The lid knocked a dixie that stood on the top of the tank and which Mum had just filled to the brim with boiling water.

The dixie was pushed off the top of the copper and a sheet

of scalding water poured over me, drenching my left side, arm, back and part of my leg. I don't remember the pain, just the shock. This was not just hot water. It had been taken direct from the bubbling copper and had no time to cool down. The boiling water cooked my five-year-old flesh.

My mother acted quickly and sensibly. She ripped off my clothes and wrapped me in a cool sheet. We now know to pour cold water on burns, but that was not common knowledge at the time. She did everything in her power and knowledge and then rushed me to hospital.

I had third-degree burns and was suffering badly from shock. At five years old that combination could easily have killed me, and I think it was touch-and-go for a while. But even after getting through the first twenty-four hours or so, my problems weren't over, by any means. I was to stay in hospital for four months.

It was a long struggle and I was very low, physically and emotionally, during that time. If I don't remember, or have blocked out the pain of the initial incident, the pain that was to follow is all too real in my memory. It became a stark daily terror for almost the whole of those four months.

Burn treatment by the late 1940s had advanced considerably since pre-war days. The need to treat the many burn victims of the fighting had, by necessity, led to advances in plastic surgery. But even so, skin-graft techniques and other aspects of the treatment of burns were not nearly so sophisticated as they are today.

The surgeons took skin from my thighs to make pinch grafts on my back and arms, but they didn't all take. Areas of burnt flesh became septic under the new grafts, and every morning the dressings would have to be changed.

It was this morning routine which terrified me. The pads and gauze bandages with which they dressed my wounds would stick to the scabs and the sloughing skin, and the staff would patiently have to soak off the dressing before putting on fresh bandages. Despite the real care the nurses took, it was still extremely painful. I would scream and yell, and would often have to be held down.

The nursing staff used a liquid called eusol to soak the bandages off; it has a distinctive smell, rather like chlorine. A number of household cleaning products contain the same stuff and smell similar as a result. Whenever anyone uses them in the washing or to clean the bathroom, the smell takes me back with a sense of chill to the pain and fear I experienced as a small child in that hospital ward.

That's not all there is to remind me of the incident. I left the hospital with disfiguring scars down the length of my left arm and the left side of my back. Skin has grown over the burn area, but it looks as if the flesh beneath has been twisted and wrinkled. Not a pretty sight.

Those scars are still there. As a child, I was always self-conscious about them and tried whenever possible not to show them to anyone. And by the time I reached adolescence I was deeply ashamed of them. As I developed an interest in girls (and therefore became preoccupied with my own appearance) I tried to conceal the scars at all costs.

Australians are fanatical about their sun tans. Only the USA compares as a nation of sun worshippers. The fanaticism has been tempered a bit recently when it was revealed that, as a result, Australia is the skin cancer capital of the world. But in my youth you were nobody unless you had a good tan. With most Aussies living within reach of a beach, there's always been ample opportunity.

I would sit on the wide, white, sandy beach in a shirt with the sleeves buttoned at the wrists, while my mates would strip down to their trunks and plunge into the surf. I'd sit there as the sun beat down, reading a book or watching the girls, trying to look casual as if to say, only idiots run around like that. If you're really cool, you sit on the beach fully dressed like me.

Mates would sprint up from the blue-green, white-capped surf, the sun gleaming off their sea-soaked tans, shake their dripping hair on me and say, 'Come and have a swim, Smithy!'

I would turn back to my book and mutter as airily as I could, 'No thanks, I'm not really interested.' Deep inside I desperately ached to be able to strip off as unself-consciously as they did. But I knew my burns would cause comment even if they didn't cause the laughter of ridicule. I stayed where I was.

If I was reluctant to show my scarred arms to blokes, think what I felt like with girls. Perhaps because I felt I wasn't getting my share of warmth from my mother, I craved female affection, gentleness and warmth long before adolescence. That's not my definition of womanhood — but it was what I thought women represented at the time.

I believed that if a girl saw my scars, she would be revolted and go off me for ever. I couldn't see any girl wanting to go out with someone whose body was so ugly. I would talk to girls and ask them out, but carrying around my guilty secret didn't do a lot for my confidence. In one case I went out with a girl for eighteen months, and she never saw my scars. I felt so insecure. I really believed that even though we had a good relationship going, it would end the day I took my shirt off.

If I had any doubts about what reaction women might have to my burns, my worst fears were confirmed one summer day at school. I must have been about fifteen and was sitting in French class. We had a good-looking young French teacher and some of the guys quite fancied her. But she didn't like me, and I didn't like her. She was very aggressive towards me, which may have had something to do with my being the classroom pest — I still had a big mouth.

We were living in a district called Gippsland in south-east Victoria and there was a heat wave. The temperature had been in the hundreds for days. So for once, the discomfort of long sleeves overcame fear and I rolled them up to my shoulder to cool off.

The teacher came over to me and looked at my arm. Then, in front of the whole class, in a voice that everyone could hear, she said, 'Cover that revolting thing up, Smith. It makes me sick!'

26

I died, or wished I could have. Even now it makes me tremble with rage and humiliation at the injustice and callousness of the treatment. You're never at your most secure or self-confident at fifteen in any case. But to be humiliated in such a way in front of all my peers was torture.

The incident reinforced what I'd felt deep inside. My scars were so hideous that no woman would ever want me. I was sure from that point on, until I was out of my teens, that I would never marry. I was an imperfect specimen in a world which was telling me you had to be in decent shape to be acceptable.

I still bear the scars, which have mellowed with age, but they don't bother me now in the least. Apart from age and the feeling I no longer have to compete in the ritual Australian summer wonderful-beach-boy contest, a couple of instances helped me come to terms with them.

When I was twenty-one, I came to a point where Christianity suddenly became real for me. I was reading some words in the Bible found in 1 Corinthians 15. The passage was talking about how, in the future, after we have died and been brought into the presence of God, we will be recreated — given 'glorious bodies'. It's a picture of the healing of all things that God brings. Suddenly I realized that I was just one more person who longed for that time when all things would come together. Since that time a concern for wholeness and healing and a longing for the restoration of the Universe has been very personal.

The other instance came soon after I met Glena, my wife to be. We had been going together for a short while when she first saw my scars. She wasn't horror-struck, she wasn't rendered speechless and forced to think up some understanding remark to cover her embarrassment. She reacted with the pure, loving instinct that is her hallmark. She simply ran her hand tenderly down my arm and said in a voice full of gentleness and warm sympathy, 'Oh, you poor guy.'

It was the best therapy I could ever have received. The

27

touch, the sensitivity and the acceptance made me feel like a million dollars. I no longer felt the need to hide my blemishes. They were part of who I was and Glena was prepared to accept me as a whole, scars and all. It's difficult to describe how good that felt. It just needed someone to demonstrate it.

I hope the feelings and experiences I've had as a result of those burns have taught me to understand other people's sensitivities. We've had to face the question at home when my youngest daughter, Lyndal, suffered a badly-cut face at the age of six when we were involved in a car smash. She had to have more than 250 stitches in a miracle six and a half hours of micro-surgery which saved her pretty looks. She still bears visible marks which, in those sensitive teenage years, she is successfully coming to terms with. I guess I know a bit of what she feels like, having been there before.

Personal experience is no guarantee of understanding, however. There was an occasion some years later when, after I'd preached, a number of people stayed behind because they wanted to become Christians, or needed advice concerning their personal problems. They came up to the platform where I was standing with a number of people who were there especially to counsel enquirers. A queue was forming in front of me as I spoke quietly to those who came up to me, and passed them on to one or other of the waiting counsellors.

Then, in the line, I spotted a woman whose face was covered with vicious burn scars. I didn't want to look, partly because I didn't want to embarrass her and partly because the scarring was so horrific. Yet my eyes were drawn to her ravaged face. By a kind of mental reflex action I decided to shuffle her off to one of the other counsellors; her face made me feel too uncomfortable. But as this thought came into my head, I forced myself to think again. I was making the same response to her that others had made to me. Here was I, someone who knew, if only a tiny bit, something of what she felt. Yet I was fending her off because she made me feel uneasy. With a sense of shame, I welcomed her as she came up and we spent time talking together.

What suffering must be provoked in those who are disfigured when the extravagant TV and glossy magazine adverts for cosmetics come to their attention. Maybe that immortal book and subsequent movie *The Hunchback of Notre Dame* should be compulsory viewing for the Dynasty generation.

I visited Amsterdam some years ago, and because of the relationship I had developed by then with the biker community in Melbourne, I visited the Amsterdam chapter of the Hell's Angels. I met a guy there whose face was all but demolished by burns. It was just one mass of scar tissue. He must have suffered the most terrible third-degree burns. He had no eyebrows, no eyelashes, and his mouth was simply a gap beneath a blob of a nose, with no lips to speak of. He looked like something out of a 1940s horror movie.

He spoke no English and I spoke no Dutch, but I tried to communicate with him through his eyes. As our eyes met, I saw in his such bitterness, hatred and violence, it shook me and filled me with distress at what he must have felt. He was a Hell's Angel probably because there he would be accepted as an outcast among outlaws.

In Brisbane some years ago I met a neo-Nazi who I understand was involved in a bombing incident in the city. He was a bitter, violent outlaw biker. He spotted me in a pair of swimming trunks and, seeing my scars, blurted out, 'Hey man, look at those scars. What class!' Out of that meeting came many hours of fruitful counselling concerning his bitter past and consequent violence. His life was changed through that meeting.

It made me reflect on what different responses people can make to their scars; and I don't just mean physical scars. Increasingly, it seems in our society, people grow up battered and bruised, damaged and hurt, bearing psychological and emotional scars as well as the marks of physical pain. There is nothing more ugly than the soapy TV bitch whose cosmetic beauty hides a shrivelled, viciously scarred personhood. How I long for inner soul beauty and attractiveness. There is no plastic surgery available for the soul, though I believe I've often seen inner transformation and personality healing through faith.

So much of the so-called civilized world seems to be falling apart at the seams. The permissiveness that the prophets of the sixties thought would bring us freedom and a release from repression, has brought in its wake a flotsam of broken relationships, shattered families, damaged trust and a hard and bitter cynicism about humanity. On top of that, the AIDS epidemic, itself a result of promiscuity, threatens to engulf us. The scars of this society are no longer cosmetic but profound and internal.

In the 1980s we have to face that legacy. Ours, in many ways, is a broken generation. And its individual members deal with their scars in different ways.

Some, like the Amsterdam Angel, take their scars and make them into weapons with which they avenge themselves for the misfortune they believe the world, or cruel fate, has dealt them. Many others, failing to come to terms with what's happening to themselves and those around them, look for escape. They find it in a million different ways: money and possessions, sex, work, drugs, drink, sport, even the family. And for the Woody Allens of this world, collecting analysts.

Alternatively, you can take your scars and use them as a basis for tenderness and understanding — as a means of identifying yourself with the struggles your fellow humans are going through. In the end, this is the toughest response of all. And it's not because I think I'm good at it that I suggest it. But this was Jesus' reaction. He was rejected by many, mocked by others, hated and reviled by the authorities of his day. His response was one of tenderness and compassion.

But you have to have something going for you to do that. No one can hope to overcome their scars unless they can be sure what they're on this Earth for. That's one of the reasons my faith is so important to me. Life itself has a meaning and a purpose, scarred or not. Without it I think I would be a bitter man.

Following a study I once gave, an elderly Jewish man accosted me at the front of the hall. He cried, 'I've been searching all over Melbourne for you. I believe you care and I respect you, but I have a question for you.'

With tears streaming down his worn features, he dropped his trousers without warning. He wore no underclothes. His thighs and lower torso were hideously scarred with geometric patterns of a bizarre kind. He had been used by Adolf Hitler for experimental surgery. With young students and others standing agape around us, he poured out his bitterness and inner scarring at the irrationality of his suffering under Nazi Germany.

'I know there must be a God to make sense of it all — but tell me, my friend, why did you bastard Protestants do this to us Jews.'

In the face of such a question no neat theological or religious clichés make any sense. One can only say that cruelty and inhumanity in an absurd and meaningless cosmos is unbearable. If there is a meaning however hidden at this moment, if there is significance to our human existence and to human love, then the wordless tears I shared with my Jewish brother on that night bring healing within reach. The Bible tells us that Jesus wept at the funeral of his friend. If Jesus is who he claimed to be — God and a human being — then God and humanity weep together at the insanity of our perversion of free will and its awful dehumanizing consequences.

Another Jewish businessman once called me to his office to discuss evidence of corporate crime in our city. Before laying before me some horrendous documentation of corruption, he said, 'Before I trust you, I want to tell you something and then ask you a question.

'Before the war, I thought I was a Catholic. When Hitler

31

invaded my country, it was discovered I had Jewish ancestry. One hundred of my relatives — mother, father, brothers, sisters, aunts, uncles, cousins, were herded off to a concentration camp. The weak ones were sent straight to the gas chambers. The stronger ones were preserved for a little while. At the end of the war I was the only one left alive out of 100 relatives. Tell me, young man, would you believe in God if that had happened to you?'

I was again stunned by the images of insanity spewed up by modern human history. I burst into tears of empathy and distress and said, 'How can I answer it? I've never suffered so. But I think I would need his love all the more and would want to know that somewhere in the Universe there lies justice, meaning and hope.'

He replied, 'Young man, the only thing that made it worth going on was the belief that there had to be a higher meaning. Faith is the only strength at such a time. But I wish I had a personal faith like yours. You have answered right.'

I think in this respect the following words of Robert McAfee Brown ring so true to me. He was speaking at the ruins of the crematorium at Birkenau, the death-camp of Auschwitz. 'We are standing on ruins the Germans tried (unsuccessfully) to obliterate, to hide evidence that six million Jews had been shot and gassed and burned in such places, solely because they were Jews. I reflect: if Golgotha revealed the sense of God-forsakenness of one Jew, Birkenau multiplies that anguish at least three and a half million times. For the rest of my life, this crematorium will represent the most powerful case against God, the spot where one could — with justice — denounce, deny, or (worst of all) ignore God, the God who was silent.

'Of what use are words at such a time? So many cried out to God at this spot and were not heard. Human silence today seems the only appropriate response to divine silence yesterday.

'We remain silent. Our silence is deafening.

'And then it comes — first from the lips of one man, Elie

32

Wiesel (standing in the camp where thirty-five years earlier his life and family and faith were destroyed), and then in a mounting chorus from others, mostly Jews, the great affirmation: *Shema Yisroel, Adonai Elohenu, Adonai echod,* Hear, O Israel, the Lord our God, the Lord is One.

'At the place where the name of God could be agonizingly denied, the name of God is agonizingly affirmed — by those with most reason to deny. I shake in the tension between my impulse to deny and their decision to affirm.

'Because of having stood at Birkenau, it is now impossible for me to affirm God in the ways I did before.

'Because of having stood at Birkenau with them, it is now possible for me to affirm God in ways I never did before.'

I didn't realize at the time (if I had, I would probably have given up altogether), but getting burnt was just the first in a whole chapter of accidents. It was a suitably dramatic launch into an accident-prone life.

Accidents are a bit like greatness. You either achieve them because you're doing something dangerous (in which case they're an occupational hazard), or else they're thrust upon you. Mine were almost always thrust upon me. Though of course my responses have been a matter of meaningful choice.

The next calamity after the burn was the police car. We have trams in Melbourne, and they're quite bulky, so they tend to block your view of the traffic a bit. Anyway, I did the typical kid's thing: ran out behind a tram and smack into a police car. I was unconscious for a day or so. I remember waking up in hospital. The first thing I saw was a policeman. I thought, oh no, what's a cop doing here? Have I done something wrong? It turned out he was there to make sure I was all right. Which I was, soon enough.

I also had the ordinary childhood knocks and scrapes, and one or two that were a bit out of the ordinary. One of those happened when I tried my prowess at the triple jump. It would have been more sensible to try it outdoors, but I reckoned the house was big enough. According to my calculations, I could start my run up at one end of the lounge-room, hop and step in the kitchen and then launch into the jump which would take me down the two steps from the kitchen and (negotiating a slight, angled change in flight) out into the wash-house.

I wound up the run through the lounge, I thought, with surprising acceleration over such a short distance. The hop and the step went magnificently; I landed just exactly right on the take-off board in the kitchen doorway. With my eyes on the two-step drop and the angle into the wash-house, I threw myself into a prodigious leap, gaining just enough height to smash my head straight against the lintel of the wash house door! I landed in a crumpled heap on the ground with my head split open and blood pouring out. Yet another trip to the hospital.

On another occasion (I must have been twenty-one), I was fooling around on Dad's car outside the church where he was minister. He started off without me so I threw myself across the bonnet. Dad never plays practical jokes, but for some reason he decided he'd have a laugh and drove the car across the grass around the side of the church.

This would have been fine but for one thing. When he decided to dump me on the grass by slamming the brakes on, he forgot that the ancient Holden he was driving had a chrome-plated mascot with sharp outstretched wings. As the car ground to a halt, instead of rolling off the bonnet, I lurched forward and was impaled on the wings of the mascot. That really was a narrow escape because it went straight into my stomach, left its mark on my colon and narrowly missed the liver. After some concerned exploratory surgery, I was released with yet another significant scar.

So you can see, this claim of accident proneness is no idle boast. It took a hand again later on when I managed to tread on a stone fish. I was in the semi-tropical waters off Queensland, but it was rare even then to find these creatures that far south.

34

The stone fish looks just like a mossy rock and has thirteen poisonous spikes along its back. If it's disturbed, it raises these spines upright. I was stung on the toe, which may seem a trifle, but its poison is deadly. As soon as I felt the sting, not knowing what it was, I made for the beach. You have to take that kind of precaution in these waters. Within seconds I was writhing in agony on the beach, the pain was so intense.

Dad bundled me in the trusty old Holden, and I think he sat on about ninety miles an hour, the fastest the old girl would go, in the direction of the hospital. I was in a real state. You could feel the pain spread in a matter of seconds, through the foot up the leg to the groin. By the time we arrived at the casualty department the toe which had been stung was black. They gave me morphine to attack the pain but it merely took the edge off.

I hadn't seen the fish so I couldn't help the doctor identify the problem. I sat there in a daze while he sat with an open medical textbook in front of him, trying to work out what might have got me. He was looking somewhat indecisive when the battle-axe of a charge nurse took a hand.

'You idiot, what are you looking at that book for!' she exclaimed. 'Look at the man's eyes. The only thing that could do that is a stone fish. And if you don't pull your finger out, Doctor, you're going to have a dead patient!'

I'm for ever grateful for her strident interjection, because the doctor leapt into action and put me on oxygen (they have to because the stone fish's poison is very toxic and causes the central nervous system to pack up). They then found there was just one anti-denine shot — the antidote — in the hospital. This they gave me, and there was almost immediate relief. The nurse was right. It was a stone fish. It had been a close run thing.

Later, as a student, I was a passenger in a car when another driver came straight through a red light and cleaned us up. The passenger door swung open and I landed on my head in the middle of the road. For a while, I couldn't string more than five words together in a row. I was flown home to

35

Queensland. Memory beyond a few words remained elusive for three months. For a born talker, the anguish and fear of such a period of incapacity was extremely distressing both mentally and verbally.

These are just a selection of Smith-type disasters. If it's taught me anything, it is that God's not ready for me to go yet. I'm not suggesting I'm anything special; that would be unfair and insensitive to the relatives of people who've been through those sorts of situations and died. Nevertheless, I'm personally grateful to God that I'm still here when it could have been curtains on more than one occasion.

John Wesley's escape from a burning manse in childhood left him with the sense of being 'a brand plucked from the burning'. Sometimes I do feel a sense of destiny about the near escapes of my life. I feel responsible to do the job since being apparently spared so many times.

On the other hand, it's incredible, if not laughable, that someone with an accident record like mine should find himself riding a powerful motorbike.

Of course, that's some way ahead. We started this chapter when I was a nipper. And I was not much more of a nipper when we moved house away from the city. It was an important move for us all. But we might easily have moved somewhere a great deal more exotic.

CHAPTER FOUR

The church began to take up more and more of my parents' time. Their commitment to Christianity grew to the extent that they began to think seriously about Dad leaving the railways and becoming some kind of full-time Christian worker.

For a long time, they were convinced God was telling them he wanted them to work for him among the people of the Congo, in Africa. They were accepted as candidates by a mission society who sent workers out to that part of Africa. They began to learn French, and all seemed to be going ahead. But complications arose through no fault of their own, and they were unable to raise the finance they needed. They had to abandon the plan.

It was a severe blow. But Dad was able to put the collapse of the plans for the Congo behind him. Instead, he explored other avenues of full-time Christian mission. As I have said, he was already a Methodist lay preacher. He applied to become a fully-fledged minister, was accepted and, in 1951 was given his first church.

So, at nine years of age I moved with Mum and Dad to the town of Raywood, not far from Bendigo, about 100 miles north of Melbourne. From that age I grew up as a child of the manse.

I can't remember a time when seeing Dad in the pulpit was anything but normal. It was almost as everyday as it would be for any kid to see their father at work. Dad had been a very active preacher for some years before we moved to Raywood, and it didn't seem to me to be a dramatic change of direction. If I think about it, it must have been quite a shift from the daily trip to the Victorian Railways offices.

I have vivid memories of Dad preaching. He wasn't one of those academic ministers who would stand stock still and deliver a written text. Instead, he would have his arms around, grip the lectern and make sure he had eye contact with his congregation. At times he would be strong and dominating in his delivery, speaking sternly to his flock about their responsibilities. But when the occasion demanded he could be tender and understanding. I think he was at his best when he told stories. Not Sunday school tales, but instances from real life as examples of what he had to say.

Despite his reserve, he had deep feelings and, just as my mother felt free to express the depth of her emotion in praise to God, so my father seemed more able to disclose what was on his heart when he was in the pulpit than at home. I have seen him moved literally to tears in the pulpit; tears of sorrow at the sufferings of Christ in the Garden of Gethsemane, and tears of gratitude when he spoke of God's willingness to forgive us however little we deserve it.

Even as a kid I caught something of that intensity of belief. It was something I aspired to and empathized with, but it was not something I had yet truly experienced.

My mother was no mean preacher either. She took the local Methodist preachers' course when she was in her thirties, became an accredited local preacher and would sometimes be invited to other congregations in the district.

The heated arguments in Australia about the ordination of women these last few years provoke in me old Methodist memories of strong women preachers in that tradition.

They say William Booth's daughters in early Salvation Army days, preached in pubs and made strong men quake and weep.

For my parents, these changes in job and location were a matter of degree. They were part of a continuing development in their Christian lives — they already had a ministry based around home and church. But it was a dramatic experience for me, because we moved from the city to the country. This change of location opened up a new world of beauty and fascination which has left an enduring passion, not only for the landscape of the Australian bush and outback, but also for the detail of plant and animal life.

This part of northern Victoria has its own kind of beauty. It's not, by any means, the standard picturesque countryside of rolling greenery, but I love it just the same. The region is very flat and was given over to wheat and sheep farming — immense farms of thousands of acres. In the summer you could see great plains of wheat shimmering in the sun, while in the distance small stands of eucalyptus trees would break the skyline. After harvest these would change to become vast tracts of wheat stubble. I have an abiding impression of miles and miles of this terrain marked out by red gum posts and endless strands of wire.

Gums (also called eucalypts) are majestic trees, some with tall, often sturdy trunks awkwardly reaching skywards with their aromatic leaves clustered on branches right at the top, looking a bit like giant broccoli. There are about 600 varieties of gum. They range from small, sprawling mallees three or four metres high to majestic mountain ash, growing well over 100 metres. Some ironbarks have rugged, pitch-black bark, while ghost gums have stunningly smooth white trunks and branches. They are peculiar to Australia and are wonderfully adapted to the conditions of the country. An area that has been devastated by bush fire can, in a matter of only a few years, be covered by healthy gums.

The eucalypts have another survival tactic. In a dry season they will drop superfluous branches so they can make the most of the moisture available.

As often as not you'd find, stuck in the middle of one of these immense paddocks, a solitary old red gum. Its pale, mottled bark and branches have a way of reaching out in all directions, as if to say, I'm living, organic. I'll grow the way I choose.

Closer to the main town of Bendigo, you could find clumps

of ironbark whose wood is as hard as its name. They survive on poor soil and wherever you see the ironbark, slimmer than the red gum and with characteristic furrowed bark, you know the earth around won't be very good.

When a gum drops a branch, it leaves a hollow in the trunk, ideally suited for nests. The delicate pink and grey galahs (somewhere in between a cockatoo and a budgerigar), and the more brightly coloured cockatoos or parrots can be found all over this area, twittering and squawking high up in the trees. Unlike human beings, they don't reproduce until they have an appropriate home well staked out — and they mate for life.

The biggest town in the district is Bendigo. Gold was discovered here in the heady gold-rush days of the 1850s. The district is littered with abandoned mines. As a result there is another highly visible feature of the landscape: mullock heaps. These tall mounds of yellow clay were excavated from the mines and left standing, some of them for a hundred years or more.

The mines themselves had mostly been long abandoned and a good many of them filled in. But now and again you'd hear of someone who'd come to grief down a disused shaft, and we were warned to keep away from them. I didn't. There was something mysterious and frightening about these dead places.

The mullock heaps were a great source of adventure for kids. For one, they give you a terrific vantage point from which to survey the surrounding territory. But also the steep sides of the heap would become corrugated by the rain and, with a bit of old tin and some string to help steer, you could toboggan down this smoothed-off surface. I fondly believed you could find gems in these dead heaps of clay. More than once I'd come home with a lump of iron pyrites, absolutely convinced I'd found a nugget of gold.

The mullock heaps were also the home of one of Australia's most exquisite birds, the bee-eater. They are almost swallow-like in their shape, and have two beautiful feathers growing out of their backs, very similar to the honey-eaters that can be found in Latin America.

These beautiful creatures would dig long, shaft-like holes in the soft clay. I would spend hours watching them flying in and out, feeding their young. And it was the bee-eaters which gave me my first real public platform. Dad kept bees for a while so I became particularly interested in them. At that time the Australian Broadcasting Commission did a country broadcast from Bendigo, and in the junior section they gave time for some kids to talk about their interests. I did a quarter of an hour talk on bee-keeping.

Another legacy of the gold-rush years were the peppercorn trees. These had been imported by the Chinese who came to Australia in that period, mostly as underpaid coolies or chefs. The peppercorn is now very common in northern Victoria. They are big rambling trees with what botanists call bipinnate leaves — lots of feathery leaflets growing out at an angle from each main leaf. They were great to climb, except that they oozed a very strong-smelling white sap. I got into severe trouble with Mum or Dad several times because the sap would get all over your clothes and then leave a dark sticky stain which would, in turn, attract every morsel of dirt or dust that went near it. It was terrible stuff to get off, especially when you think that in the 1950s washing meant hard scrubbing by hand.

The peppercorn trees had an additional charm for me because they were the home of the emperor gum moth, a large beautiful soft pink-grey moth, with magnificent painted eyes central to their wings, and wide feathery feelers. I discovered a metaphor for life from the emperor gum moth when I was young, which I still think holds true. Its caterpillar creates a very hard grey-brown cocoon, similar to that of a silkworm. When it's time for the moth to emerge, you can hear it scratching inside. It has its own cutting gear which it uses to carve an escape hatch from its hard casing. As a boy, I'd take pity on one of these poor, struggling creatures and help it on its way to freedom by slitting the cocoon with a razor blade. But I only succeeded in crippling the moth. A by-product of its struggle to escape was that the moth would pump juices into its wings, which enabled it to fly once it was free. By interfering too much with the natural process, I prevented this from happening and rendered it unable to cope with the world outside. Observation has since taught me that people are a bit like that. You can be over-protective. People need to be buffeted a bit by the world in order to grow. Painful experience is essential to the development of maturity.

As Scott Peck in his psychology book, *The Road Less Travelled*, observes, 'Life is a series of problems. So we want to moan about them or solve them. As Benjamin Franklin said, "Those things that hurt instruct". It is through the pain of confronting and solving problems that we learn (and grow). Problems are the cutting edge that distinguishes between success and failure. Problems call forth our courage and our wisdom.'

Raywood was a marvellous place to grow up. I was never stuck for things to do. Dad had grown up in a suburb of Melbourne called Eltham which, when he was a nipper, was mostly bush. There, as a fairly lonely kid, he'd learned to observe nature. He now passed that on to me. I'd spend hours out in the fields and in the woods.

I found you could catch fish in the most unlikely places. In the middle of the wheat and sheep area lay Dingee, a small dairying area where the wheat fields were often irrigated by narrow canals. These canals contained small native fish as well as European carp (now a pest, having done a great deal of damage to our waterways). After a particularly rainy season, the water would flood over the sides of the canals and lie in the long reedy grass which sprang up, and you could often find small fish flapping about there. After really heavy rains, you could even find them in the gutters in town.

Frogs abounded in these canals. To this day I love the sound of frogs singing. I'd collect the frog-spawn and take it home to watch the tadpoles grow, develop legs and lose their tails. Then I'd release them back into their original habitat. They weren't the only things I brought home either. Fish, blue-tongued lizards, the occasional goanna — they'd all be brought back and cherished for a while. In my time, I've kept an extraordinary number of pets. There have been several dogs, a bat with a broken wing which used to eat beetles from my fingers, lizards, snakes (including several species of python — one of them over six metres long), goats, many different birds, and much later on, a dingo.

I was, and am a great collector of things. As a kid I had an insect collection, a butterfly collection, then lizards and animal skulls. More recently I have been collecting seeds and gum nuts as well as geological samples.

Reptiles have always fascinated me, and therefore became something of a specialization. In my early twenties I had a formidable collection of snakes, many of them venomous. I'd give lectures on reptiles (with a sackful of living examples) at rotary clubs in Queensland, where I was living at the time. I was only bitten once, and that after I'd milked the snake's venom; even so it made me quite unwell for a day or two.

My wife Glena's first photo of me was taken with a python around my neck and a handful of writhing serpents. My love of snakes is one of the few things not shared by Glena, and before we were married, she quite understandably asked me to get rid of them.

Dad caught me my first ever snake, a copperhead which he almost trod on when we were out one day looking for rabbits. He held down its head with the butt of his rifle and called me to fetch the tool box from the car. He picked up the snake behind its head with a pair of multi-grips and then lowered it into the tool box, and that was how we brought it home.

Much later, when I was working on a sheep station for a short while, I caught the biggest brown snake I've ever seen. The brown snake is deadly, growing up to seven feet long. This particular specimen was found in the grounds of the school where I was teaching in Queensland. The children couldn't play outside while it was still around, so I caught it, killed it and preserved it in methylated spirits. I still have him in a large onion jar in my study, along with myriad other bits of flora and fauna and the like. I have a theory that he's a record-breaking size — some two and a half metres. I'd love to measure him, but I'm afraid he'd disintegrate if he were removed from the jar. Record or not, he's a magnificent specimen.

This sense of wonder at the beauty and mystery of creation was born in me in Raywood from nine years old and onwards. The child-like curiosity about God's world is still with me. But I never felt a rapacious sense of domination over nature. Even in those early days I kept nesting sites secret from other kids to protect them from egg collectors. And if I did kill a specimen for my collection, then I made sure its termination was as swift and painless as possible, and would make sure that taking it would not jeopardize the survival in that area of that particular species. I'm only too aware of the United Nations report which says that by the 1990s we will have wiped out 500,000 species of plants, animals and birds this century. That kind of destruction is an obscenity.

In response to such statistics, I have felt the need to work hard at discovering a Christian way of thinking which takes in our responsibility to preserve the balance of nature. I was delighted, but not surprised, to find that the Bible is far from silent on the issue. Job, in the Old Testament, lists before God the things he has done which are right and proper: 'If my land cries out against me and all its furrows are wet with tears, if I have devoured its yield without payment or broken the spirit of its tenants, then let briers come up instead of wheat and weeds instead of barley.'

Furthermore, in the Jewish order of the Old Testament, it was set down that the land had to be rested. You couldn't rape it. Yet in my lifetime I have seen in my own country too much land destroyed. Places like the peninsula areas west of Adelaide are a tragic picture of how self-defeating eradication of the natural order created a stark barrenness of the environment in the wheat areas of that state.

Human beings are the most wonderful creatures. I believe that we are made in the image of God — that we are in character and potential pale reflections of him. This makes us the most wonderful creations on the planet. People must not be allowed to starve. Therefore we must have farms and to do that we must clear land. But in Australia we have done that in such a way as to all but wipe out our natural heritage. And it seems we are hell-bent on doing further damage.

The picture is the same the world over, but in Australia, for instance, we still have some of the rarest rain forest in the world, but it is receding fast under commercial pressures. To me that is an issue of the Christian faith. We must not destroy this wonder and miracle which God has done.

I'm not, however, an 'if it stands still conserve it' person. There is a tendency among the green lobby to worship nature, to put it on an equal footing with humanity. I believe in worshipping the Creator, not the creation. I also believe that since he has made humans significantly different from other animal and plant life, people's genuine needs (not their every desire) take precedence.

Christians believe that God in his creation has revealed something of himself to us. He teaches us lessons through nature. The Bible is full of natural metaphors. I am constantly discovering biblical parallels in the bush.

The seventeenth chapter of the Book of Jeremiah, for example, says, 'Cursed is the one who trusts in man, who depends on flesh for his strength and whose heart turns away from the Lord. He will be like a bush in the wastelands; he will not see prosperity when it comes. He will dwell in the parched places of the desert, in a salt land where no one lives.'

There are living examples of this kind of terrain in the west of Australia. In some of the parched desert land, you'll get rain which will now and again sweep through and dormant wild flowers spring up and carpet this otherwise bleak

45

landscape. It is unbelievably beautiful. But the Australian salt bush doesn't react that way. Unless you're interested in it botanically you'd find it dull and grey. Whatever changes occur, it never ever flourishes. It just carries on in its own semi-lifeless fashion.

But Jeremiah continues: 'But blessed is the man who trusts in the Lord, whose confidence is in him. He will be like a tree planted by the water that sends out roots by the stream. It does not fear when the heat comes; its leaves are always green. It has no worries in a year of drought and never fails to bear fruit.'

I've seen dry river beds out west which haven't flowed with water for five or six years. You can tell where these are, even from the air, because there are thousands of flourishing red gums marking their routes. These gums have their roots deep in the soil, tapping an artesian watercourse running below the desert. On the surface it looks as though these majestic trees could never survive in their blitzed surroundings. Yet they have hidden resources.

These aren't glib illustrations either. They say something powerful about what we are. One of the significant truths about Christianity is that those who believe in Jesus have resources beyond themselves which enable them not only to withstand the difficulties life throws at them, but to flourish in the midst of them.

Despite my avowed love of nature, in particular my love of animals, I like to hunt and fish. People often ask me how I can justify this apparent contradiction. My first defence is one that has been mentioned before. Animals are not the equal of human beings. The Bible teaches that and my eyes observe it. There is a worshipfulness, a creativity in a human being not to be found in any other animal on the planet. I'm not about to get confused between the feelings of a human being and a goat.

I'm not a vegetarian. I have nothing against eating meat, but I don't believe in being cruel. When I hunt or when I fish

I do so for food and I use equipment which makes for the kindest and quickest death possible. I taken no pleasure in the act of killing, though I admit to satisfaction in personally providing for the family from my own effort and skill. It seems better than a plastic bag of meat from a chain-store supermarket.

Some people rightly point out that living in a modern city I have no need to hunt; all the meat and fish I might want are available from the butcher or fishmonger. I have to confess to an element of romance or nostalgia for a past I never experienced. I like playing the role of the traditional hunter-gatherer. And perhaps it's part of my conditioning as an Australian male that makes me feel that way.

Certainly this whole idea of 'going bush' is a real trait among Aussie men. Though tragically, sensitivity to nature is not! I'm appalled at the free-wheeling attitude of 'if it moves, shoot it — if it don't, chop it down!' The obsession with the bush is peculiar really, because most white Australians for most of the country's history have been city dwellers, even if we earned our money off the sheep's back. But this old myth about mateship, facing adversity with toughness and refusing to cry however many times you get knocked down, comes from our notion of outback life. It's the *Crocodile Dundee* story all over.

I love to spend time in the more remote regions of Australia. I like the toughness that genuinely is bred out in those places. It's a great antidote to the cushioned life and hectic pace of the city; almost another reality. This affinity can all be traced back to Raywood. I've hunted and fished now since I was very small. I've shot, skinned and eaten wild goat and feral pig (dangerous beasts who rush out at you from the bush with no warning and maim or even kill you with their tusks). I've even killed kangaroo, but only when it's been necessary to cull an over-abundant population in areas where they were a serious threat to sheep pasture — and then once again only for meat and for hides which I've used as an amateur leather worker.

47

I've certainly seen some dreadful travesties done in the name of hunting which make me feel ashamed: blokes going out in four-wheel drives armed with axes or sledge-hammers to smash in the skulls of kangaroos for sadistic and perverse pleasure. Or guys coming out from Sydney, blasting off their guns at anything that moves, leaving crippled animals crawling along the ground in anguish. I take no part in that 'sport' and continue to denounce it. Nevertheless, I maintain that it's possible to hunt prudently and from the right motives while retaining a profound respect for nature. It's strange the inconsistency of intellectuals who decry any such paradox for me, yet support hunter-gatherer societies such as Australia's Aborigines.

Fishing is another of my great loves. Dad taught me almost all I know about the pursuit; to this day he knows far more than I do. From as early as I can remember, we had family holidays in a place called Kilcunda, south-east of Melbourne. We'd take our patched and weathered old army tent and cook what we caught on an open fire.

Kilcunda is part of a rocky peninsular heading out into the Tasman sea. The great waves of the ocean smash against the rocks here with that sense of tireless energy and power peculiar to the sea. I loved to watch the storms from Kilcunda — you could see them sweeping across the water, hear the growl of distant thunder and the forked tongues of lightning slicing up the sky. I loved it as much as the countryside; it's just that there was a different quality to the elements and so I experienced a different feeling of awe.

I'm not excited by the endless debates between 'creationists' and 'evolutionists' about what particular nuts and bolts were used in the creation of this world. When you read the Bible, you get the impression of much bigger concerns. As it says in the Psalms: 'When I consider your heavens, the work of your fingers, the moon and the stars, which you have set in place, what is man that you are mindful of him?'

You find there what you experience when you look at the ocean: the wonder, the magnitude of the creation compared to the tiny apparent insignificance and fragility of human life. Regardless of how you think the Universe was made or who or what was behind it, the comparison is always daunting, and yet exciting and exhilarating.

I draw comfort and perspective from the fact the Bible also teaches that we as people have the unique possibility of a special relationship with the person who made us all. That made sense to me when I was a child, but later, when I lost my sense that God was there, I was left only with the naked forces of nature. Me and them. It was a horrendous and frightening experience intellectually and emotionally.

Dad and I would stand on some rocky outcrop, chosen by Dad not only for its fishing potential but also for its safety, since it would have been easy to have been swept off by a freak wave and sucked into the pounding surf. Even here there was still a sense of risk which thrilled me as a boy. The occasional wave would soak us and if you looked down from our rocky eyrie, you could scare yourself by imagining what would happen to you if you fell in the (what looked like) boiling water below.

Dad always knew what bait to use for the right fish on the right occasion. When I saw other people struggling for a bite, it made me terrifically proud to see my Dad in action, pulling fish after fish out of the waves. It's good for a kid to know his Dad's smart.

The best eating fish you could catch at Kilcunda was sweep, a beautiful swallow-tailed creature which took speed and skill to catch — they'd dart and zig-zag everywhere. Then we'd catch blue-nose which is a bit like a parrot fish but more edible. We'd eat parrot fish a lot, though I don't know how. Their flesh is so coarse, I can only think Dad must have been a good cook or else we must have been really hungry. Sometimes we'd manage to catch leatherjackets. These have got skin like emery paper and you actually need to skin them, but they tasted very good.

Those years at Raywood, like the early years of any child

who is just waking up to the wonder of the world, were very important to me. It's the reason why I sometimes screech my bike to a halt by the side of some remote road and scuttle off into the bush because I've seen a rare species of Australian wattle. And it's what makes me pack the family into our large Toyota four-wheel drive and head out for the open bush to live by what we catch and to contemplate the greatness of God's creation.

I'm glad my mind was opened up at such an early age to such a rich area of investigation. And I'm grateful that living close to nature gave me such good times. Because these were comparatively rare moments in my childhood, and so all the more to be cherished.

There was an early intellectual root to all this. Dad gave me the old classic on cosmology, Sir James Jeans' *The Mysterious Universe* to read when I was about ten years old. I was an avid reader, but it was still heavy going. Somehow a sense of wonder and mystery concerning the stars was born in my heart. To this day, I grieve at the loss of wonder and delight in the bored, arrogant kids born of the post-technological wilderness. I long for what C. S. Lewis described as the miracle of the common things of life.

CHAPTER FIVE

I wasn't an only child any more. My sister Faye was born in 1949, eighteen months before we moved to Raywood. After we moved there, my brother Colin was born, eleven years my junior. A short while later we were joined by Joy at two years of age. She was the daughter of someone Mum and Dad had helped, but who was no longer able to look after her child. Joy became my adopted sister. I've never felt any different about her. She always felt just as all the others to me — my blood sister. Some years later Beverley was born, closely followed by Beth — by which time I was twenty.

We weren't particularly close, because of the age difference. I was very much the big brother. I used to referee the fights between the younger ones, and in an arrogant adolescent fashion tell Mum and Dad where they were going wrong in bringing up the kids.

By the time we left Raywood in 1955, I had three siblings, but they weren't really playmates for me. I would be off on my own most of the time. Already a fairly solitary child, I was beginning to develop into a lonely one. This isn't meant to be a sob story, but there were factors which meant I found it difficult to make friends.

Loneliness is one of the biggest diseases of our century. I didn't know it at the time, and have only in my adult years come to understand why. But the preparation was laid down as a kid, helped by the fact that I became seriously ill for quite a long while.

It started in January 1952. I was ten years old. My joints began to ache, particularly my ankles which started to swell. My temperature would soar and I had to have time off school. Our doctor, not the most up-to-date man in the medical profession, told my parents I was suffering from growing pains. For this mythical ailment there was of course no treatment.

The trouble grew steadily worse and I was sent for X-rays. It was thought I might have tuberculosis of the bone. Nothing was found. In May, five months after the symptoms had first appeared, I woke up one night in so much pain that I got out of bed and crawled — because it was too painful to walk — to my parents' bedroom.

Inevitably they were concerned and sent me to Bendigo hospital. There they discovered that all this time I had been suffering from a severe case of rheumatic fever. They kept me in. I wasn't to return home properly for about two years.

The fever continued, giving me dramatic temperatures right through to February the next year. At this point I was moved to the local children's hospital, where I began to make some progress. But I still had to have penicillin injections every three and a half hours, which left my arms and my butt constantly sore. It was all a bit hard for a ten-year-old to take.

It became clear, because the disease had gone so long undiagnosed, that it was going to take a long fight to wrestle it into submission. But things began to look up, and before long I was sent to a rehabilitation home at Hampton to recuperate before re-entry into the hurly-burly of school life.

It was a vain hope to expect a bunch of kids who were feeling better after long illnesses to rest quietly. We took every opportunity to do just the opposite. One day my mother came visiting and found a crowd of us poor invalids, all of whom had been ordered to complete bed rest, roaring around the dormitory, feathers flying, in a raging pillow fight.

That October, eighteen months after I'd first been hospitalized, I was struck by a second attack, more severe even than the first. I was taken back into hospital and began to deteriorate, losing two pounds in weight a week. I failed to respond to any of the treatment offered.

I developed chorea, commonly called St Vitus' dance. It gets its name from the involuntary muscle spasms that occur quite without warning. These twitches meant that I was unable to guide a fork to my mouth with any success, so I had to be spoon-fed, which was pretty humiliating for a kid going on twelve. I couldn't control my speech properly either; I would slur my words badly, which was equally frustrating.

It was a terrible time for my parents, who had to stand aside, powerless to do anything to arrest my decline. By now I was suffering heart murmurs, and the doctors discovered my heart had what they described as extensive pericardiac scarring and diseased valves.

Eventually they told my parents there was nothing more they could do for me. They'd run out of options. I continued to deteriorate, growing skinnier by the day; if nothing happened soon, then I would die. They were stunned.

Mum, I think, always believed I'd pull through. Somewhere deep inside her she had a conviction that I would do what she had never been able to do, and that was become a missionary. She was sure that was God's plan for my life, and therefore I would be spared. Dad didn't know what to believe.

Having been told by the doctors that there was nothing more that he could do, he returned home, took his shovel, went out to the backyard of the parsonage and began to dig up some potatoes in his small vegetable plot. What happened then was very simple, and to my understanding, miraculous. Sceptics will say, rightly, that what later happened could be explained in other ways, but my experience tells me different.

On that spring day in 1954 he leaned on his shovel and spoke to God. He said something like, 'Lord, there's nothing else the doctors can do for John. It's all up to you now.'

Dad tells me he was immediately overwhelmed with a sense of peace and assurance that all would be well. He went straight indoors and told Mum I was going to be OK.

The medical records indicate that I began to respond to treatment from that day. I gradually picked up, put on weight and, though I was still pretty weak and was forbidden to play any contact sports, I was discharged from hospital in October 1954, at the age of twelve. The doctor stated that I was, under no circumstances, to be emotionally excited. For me that was as good as a death sentence.

I've already mentioned how reserved my father was, but on the way home from hospital that day he pulled the car over to the side of the road, got out and ran into the bush with no explanation. I thought he'd gone crazy. Moments later he came running back with an old cow's horn in his hand. He stood there in the middle of the road and trumpeted a fanfare of celebration. He was delighted. I was coming home at last.

I had to take things slowly, and was cotton-woolled for a while, but despite being told that I would never be able to swim, and that I would never be able to participate in sport, I made good progress. The damage to my heart still placed a question mark over my long-term well-being, and deep down I was scared of what might happen. But no problem arose.

One holiday when I was about fifteen, Dad — without my realizing what he was doing — gave my fitness a real test. We went off to Wilson's Promontory, a beautiful rugged peninsular east of Melbourne, much of it national parkland covered by a wilderness-like dense scrub.

Dad decided we would walk to a place called Sealers Cove for a spot of fishing. It was a good hike — many walkers would expect to give the trip a whole day, with a break at the Cove, for the two-way journey. We did the outward leg in four hours, which was respectable going, considering the thick vegetation and the often mountainous terrain.

But carrying our fishing tackle and a couple of dozen mullet we'd caught, we decided to push the pace on the way back. We'd trot some of the way and scramble up the tracks, treating it like an obstacle course. We made it in two hours forty minutes, and that really was some going. I was tired but suffered no ill effects. I'd passed the fitness test with room to spare.

The trek did a lot for my confidence. I had, for some time after leaving the hospital, felt I was sentenced to an abnormal life, kept apart from other kids my age because I couldn't properly join in with them for fear of ruining my fragile health. There was also the problem of my damaged heart. That cast a shadow of uncertainty over my future. Now I felt a little more able to face the rigours of the world.

But I was to receive another scare about a year later, when I began to get severe chest pains. I ended up in hospital yet again. The doctor, looking through my medical records and reading about my heart, told my father, 'It looks like your son is suffering serious heart pains. If this is the case, then with his history I'm afraid there's not much chance for him.'

Dad came to my bedside. He told me as gently but as straightforwardly as he could that it seemed like my heart was packing it in. 'In that case,' he said, 'it looks as if you may not have long to live.' I couldn't take it in. Was this it? The end?

The answer, as you'll have guessed, was no. Once the doctors looked a bit closer, they discovered I had pneumonia and some pleurisy in the left lung, giving me pains close to the region of the heart. Another reprieve.

Having recovered from that, I re-entered everyday life, but the shadow of my problem heart was still there, growing and diminishing in size according to my mood. The cloud was to loom large one last time when, as an adult, I had to go for a medical examination as a young teacher. Because of my medical history, the education board refused to allow me to enter the superannuation scheme. I had a number of inconclusive check-ups, before my local doctor sent me to a heart specialist for a final verdict.

I went to this examination with a sense of foreboding. But there was nothing I could do to influence the result, so I had to sit patiently while I was wired up for cardiac tests. Now is the time, I thought to myself, when I find out whether the old ticker is on its last legs. I felt sure he would tell me I only had a limited time to live.

I watched the needle on the chart rise and fall. Unable to decipher the meaning of these frightening, jagged contours, I was inclined to believe the worst. And the doctor gave me no reassurance as he pulled the graph paper through his fingers in ominous silence, his eyes intent on the reading my heart had given.

He looked up seriously and embarked on a short technical lecture. He's preparing me for the worst, I thought. He pointed out that with rheumatic fever, if it isn't treated early enough, and if you don't rest during critical stages of the disease, the heart valves can become damaged and there is pericardiac damage from the scar tissue around the heart.

'Of course in your case, Mr Smith,' he continued, 'we would expect the symptoms to be very clear.'

What does he mean, I screamed inside. Then he looked up with a faint smile. He said, 'I have no understanding of the precise details of your previous medical record, but all I can say to you is that, according to this test, which I believe is the most accurate means we have to assess your condition, you have a clinically perfect heart. I will recommend to the Education Department that there should be no further delay in granting you full status for superannuation, nor should there be any hindrance to you taking any life assurance you wish to. All things being equal, you should live to be a fine old man.'

I ran out of the surgery with tears streaming down my face. I scampered down the street, leaping in the air and praising God. People must have thought I was nuts. The sense of relief and release was indescribable. For the whole of my adolescent years I had lived knowing there was an enemy lurking not far away, and that any day death could come knocking at my door. Now that fear had been banished.

I'm sceptical about claims to miracles. I have an aggressive mental attitude towards investigating truth. I really couldn't hold to a faith which didn't stand up to some rational examination. On the other hand, I am terribly aware of the mighty mystery of God. Time and again I have seen evidence of his hand in the lives of people around me. In this particular instance I will take a lot of persuading to believe that God's own healing processes were not at work in me. I can find no other logical explanation.

Within months of leaving hospital, the family was on the move again. Dad was transferred to a church in Gippsland, east of Melbourne, to a town called Trafalgar. The countryside here was different again. Whereas northern Victoria could be occasionally very dry, Gippsland was a rich green, even in summer. We used to say that it rained nine months of the year and water dripped off the trees for the other three.

The school I went to there was some way off, and we had to take a roundabout route to pick up all the kids in the far-flung rural districts. We'd set off at seven-thirty in the morning and wouldn't reach school till nearly nine. I loved the journey because it gave a great opportunity to observe the countryside we passed through.

The gentle green valley of Gippsland was fringed by the Strzlecki Ranges, smooth rolling hills with steep sides. Up there in the steep valleys, where the slope prevented cultivation, you'd find dense, almost tropical vegetation. There would be giant tree ferns eight feet high and monkey vines as thick as your wrist which in spring were covered in millions of white star flowers. The tall mountain ash grew here alongside various cool, temperate eucalypts like the white and blue gum. These trees all had pale trunks which would grow straight up like a telephone pole, perhaps twenty feet before the first branch. Now and then, if you were quiet, you might see a goanna, a long lizard which can grow up to six foot, and can shoot up one of these trunks like reverse lightning. It was a wonderful, almost primeval place — you could easily imagine dinosaurs stomping their way through the bush.

Down in the valley the rainfall meant there was a plentiful supply of creeks. And although some of them were barely eighteen inches deep, they ran fast. You could still catch yourself a two-pound trout, either with a line or by tickling them. There were plenty of snakes, of course; black snakes, brown snakes and the dangerous copperhead. If you were very lucky you'd catch a glimpse of a lyre bird, with the most beautiful set of tail feathers you ever saw, from which it earned its name. A male lyre bird's mating dance — with his feathers spread out on display — is a magnificent sight.

The valley region was known for dairy farming. There were jerseys, friesians and shorthorns, and the ever-present smell of cow manure — a delightful smell! We had enough ground around the manse of Trafalgar to keep our own cow, which I used to enjoy milking. I used to race myself against the clock, trying to fill the gallon bucket in three and a half minutes.

The milk our old cow gave was a valuable supplement. We were no better off on a minister's stipend than we were when Dad worked for the railways. A lot of people were very good to us during that time, but others could be positively mean. There is a myth that says being a minister is a cushy number. You get all your accommodation supplied and you only work one day a week. There's an even more insidious belief that says ministers are comfortably off for cash. Of course, it's rarely true, and it certainly wasn't so in my parents' case. Often we were dependent on others, especially having had to pay out hospital bills for such a long period. There are good things about being supported by the community, but there are disadvantages too.

Back in Raywood district there'd been a rich local land-owner who drove around his holdings in a magnificent limousine. He turned up to our house one day with an air of gracious condescension and a bag of quinces. He told my mother, 'We've got a lot of quinces this year. I've given them away to everyone I can think of and we've still got some left. Would you like some?'

I burned with the injustice of this treatment. It was as if my parents had been thrown a last bone as an afterthought. But Mum and Dad were humble and skinned enough to take the gift. And did we use those quinces! We had quince jam, quince jelly, stewed quinces and boiled quinces. It was difficult to look one in the eye after a while, but in our circumstances we had to take what we could.

That landowner was the only man on the church committee who always fought any attempt to raise ministers' wages. Dad was actually getting less than the meagre probationary ministers' stipend. It reminds me of the joke about the Baptist finance committee who read the Bible verse: 'a poor and humble spirit God will not despise'. So they prayed, 'Lord, you keep him humble, and we'll keep him poor.'

The Australian minister, from the Tasmanian Roman Catholic Priest on $50 per week to the Salvation Army officer on a reduced salary, is certainly not in it for the money. In the USA it may be different, perhaps especially for evangelists, but in Australia, ministers are dedicated heroes in my book.

A minister's life is a very public one. In many ways you're owned by the community you serve. In my parents' case that meant having to cope with a committee that wanted to decide what curtains you could hang up in your lounge room. And you can be sure no extravagance was allowed.

My father never minced his words in the pulpit. He was not one of those preachers whose sermons are full of generalities. He would name sins, expose greed and selfishness and proclaim the absolute authority of the Bible. However, this isn't the classic way to win friends and influence people. I've seen church officials shaking their fists at Dad. That made me angry and wish I could protect him.

There was one incident after we moved to Trafalgar when, at the age of sixteen, I had to do just that. It started between the Rotary Club and our calf. There had sometimes been a conflict of interest between church and Rotary; there were people who were officials of both bodies and sometimes bookings of the church hall would clash, producing heated exchanges.

On this particular occasion, the Rotary had booked the hall on a free night; there were no arguments. That is, until our cow's calf got loose. This was to be the Rotary's big night of the year. Dinner was laid on; Rotary members and their wives were all invited. The hall was cleaned scrupulously and decked out for the big occasion.

It was then that the calf got free and decided to investigate the hall. What you have to remember is that if a calf gets inside a strange, enclosed space and starts to panic, the fear makes its bowels work overtime. It began racing around the hall, splattering its droppings everywhere. The organizers were understandably furious.

One of the guys, a leading figure in the town, stormed out of the hall and grabbed hold of me since I was the nearest member of the Smith clan he could find.

'Go and get your old man,' he demanded.

'But he's away preaching,' I replied.

'Well, tell your old man he ought to rustle his butt back here and look after his flamin' calf! He's only a preacher, and if he's got nothing better to do than that, he should be here looking after his bloody animal.'

I was good and mad at him accusing Dad of being some kind of parasite with time on his hands. I knew only too well how committed he was. He was no bludger; he visited, he preached, he was for ever seeking out people who needed help. I blew my stack.

'It's all right for fat cats like you,' I blurted out in my rage. 'You can sit back on your butt while everyone does your work for you to make you your millions (a slight exaggeration). My Dad works hard and gets paid peanuts. You've got no right to go shooting your mouth off about what he should or shouldn't do!'

It was a very high-handed response to get from a teenager, and he was understandably livid. But then so was I. He stalked off.

But that wasn't the end of the incident. I should point out that the wood-frame hall was built in three sections. There was the main meeting area with two extensions attached at either end — a porch at the front and a kitchen at the back.

That evening, after the place had been cleaned up and

everyone had arrived and sat down for the meal, a storm blew up. This was no ordinary tempest, more of a cyclone. The wind blew so hard that it lifted the main section of the building off its footings and dumped it down again, slightly askew. It was only a few inches out, but it jammed the main doors. The lights had gone out as the mighty wind wrenched the building out of true, and there was a general panic inside. The only way out was through the windows.

One of the members of the party, a stern critic of my father, was the first to a window. He pushed the sash up and ushered his wife forward so she could make good her escape, giving her a helpful heave to send her on her way to safety. There was a strangled cry and a big splash. In their eagerness to leave the building, no one had remembered that the water trough where our cow drank was positioned directly under the window! The lady was not happy. But I'm afraid to say that I was ecstatic. Anthony Quayle is right. There's a touch of evil in all of us. And maybe a touch of justice too!

It's obvious that I admired my father greatly. But he was a hard act to follow. He seemed to me to be so honest, so upright, so resolute and certain. His language was without blemish and he was impatient with weakness. Probably because I was their first child, they had great aspirations for me. Dad says now that they both probably asked too much of me, and because I never quite came up to scratch, they dished out more brickbats than praise. I expected a lot of myself as a result. But I never got near the target, and having failed so often, felt I wasn't up to much. As my father says now, I was a pretty discouraged kid.

Don't reach for the Kleenex, but it's never easy being a preacher's kid, because other people demand an unreasonably high standard of behaviour from you. It's all right for other kids to get into trouble, but when it happens to you, somehow it's a big issue. It's easy to resent that.

It's difficult too to find your own faith. When your parents are so much part of the church, somehow your beliefs aren't

61

quite your own. I'm not at all surprised to find just how many ministers' children grow up and throw Christianity aside. I don't think it's a statement about the weakness of the Christian faith so much as an illustration of just how important it is for people to find independently their own form of belief. Australia is a nation riddled with outstanding figures brought up in manses, with much they owe to their parents' faith and commitment, but themselves lost from the personal implications of their past. Bob Hawke, Australia's Prime Minister, is a prime example.

Your mates are a bit shy of you too, when your old man's a man of the cloth. There's a suspicion that you're not quite normal — that somehow you must be an apprentice parson yourself. I remember vividly one time when the American evangelist Billy Graham came to Australia and caused quite a stir with his mass evangelistic rallies. I got off the school bus to find a bunch of kids waiting for me. They had a soap box all set up and they dragged me over and physically lifted me up on to the box in front of a crowd of schoolkids and bowed down, yelling, 'Give us a sermon, Billy Graham!' It made me feel branded by my father's occupation, like some farm animal.

It wasn't just being a preacher's kid that made me feel like an outsider. I was that peculiar beast, the loud introvert. My father recently told me a teacher said I was one of the most argumentative children he'd ever taught. But I was all front. Inside was an uncertain swamp of introspection. And it was frighteningly lonely in there.

I found it really difficult to make friends. My early accident with the boiling water had taken me out of school for a while, and the subsequent scars set me apart a bit. I had to make new friends in Raywood but was then out of the running for two and a half years.

Moving home shortly after leaving hospital meant moving schools too. Still delicate from my operation I argued with one of the school bullies and ended up being badly beaten up. So I was moved to another, twelve miles away, and I could seldom see friends from school at the weekend. What's more, I was forbidden to take part in sports, so that avenue of friendship was blocked off. And I was a preacher's kid. It wasn't the best recipe for making and keeping mates. So I spent a lot of time by myself, off with my dog, tickling trout or catching freshwater crayfish in Sunny Creek.

I'm fairly philosophical about it now, in fact I understand the whole problem of loneliness better because of my experience of it. But I felt pretty desperate about it at times. You begin to think things will never ever be different.

But life wasn't meant to be lonely, although you'd scarcely believe it to look around any average city today. I know it's a bit of an old cliché, but in Melbourne, London, New York, Amsterdam, you can be physically near millions and yet feel totally stranded and alone. As one sociologist put it, 'We have proximity without community'.

The popularity of phone-in problem shows on radio and TV are evidence of the rampant loneliness that surrounds us. I've guested on a number of these programmes and have been constantly surprised by the intimate and bizarre stories people are prepared to tell to a radio audience of many thousands that they wouldn't dare tell their best friend or closest relative.

Recently, I was invited to host an evening radio talk-back show in Melbourne for a week while the popular Hal Todd was away on holiday. A woman rang in to say that she had a spare room at her home and a car available for anyone who would just come over and live with her — male or female. She sounded a warm person, able, caring and plain nice. She said, 'I'm just so lonely.' I offered to send her a book entitled *Escape from Loneliness*. She replied 'I don't want a book. I want a person!'

Some while back in my home country, someone started a telephone service which charged people just to listen to their problems. No advice was given, just a sympathetic ear. The people running the service said the callers didn't want advice, just someone to bounce their decisions or difficulties off. They felt unable to talk to their friends or family about it. They felt much more comfortable with a stranger. The program I recall was a raging success.

Prostitutes I've met say they often spend hours with men who aren't really interested in sex, they just want someone who'll listen. In fact, I know someone who was facing bankruptcy because he'd spent so much money on prostitutes for the want of any other sympathetic listener.

Perhaps the most curious thing to observe about loneliness is that it often affects the most successful, outwardly well-adjusted people. They seem to have absolutely no reason to be lonely, yet deep inside they're crippled by their inability to make real friendships. And loneliness is a social disease afflicting youth in droves.

But this kind of social loneliness is only one manifestation of the disease. And it is the kind that is most easily cured. This kind of loneliness can be overcome often by learning social and communication skills or by making the effort to join a church or a club or society in order to make friends.

Our society encourages loneliness and that must be combated. We literally put up fences between ourselves and our neighbours and we must break those down by being willing to open ourselves to the people who live close by. We have also been encouraged from birth upwards to see ourselves as competitors. When we feel we're competing with schoolmates or work colleagues, that pushes us apart. It works against the formation of friendships and the sharing of ideas. We must be more willing to be vulnerable with one another.

Beyond the social and structural loneliness I've just described lies a darker menace, what I call scientific loneliness. For this we can blame, you've guessed it, the scientists. Or at least a minority of them. There is a general impression among people that science has dismissed God. This is not true. A survey some years back among European scientists indicated that more than 70 per cent believed there was an active mind behind the Universe. But the weight given to the views of prominent scientists who don't believe in God has made it appear as though their opinion is the consensus.

The Nobel Prize-winning biologist, Jacques Moneaux, said, in his book, *Chance and Necessity*, 'Man is alone in the universe's unfeeling immensity, out of which he emerged only by chance. Chance alone is at the source of every innovation of all creation in the biosphere. Pure chance, absolutely free but blind, is at the root of the stupendous edifice of evolution.'

What does that say about loneliness? I don't believe scientific fact or psychological feelings square with Moneaux's statement. Everything I read points to a beginning, perhaps a big bang, and everything begs the question: who started it?

Pink Floyd's album *The Wall* asks, 'Is there anybody out there?'. The answer seems to come back, 'No.' If that is really the reply then what are we left with? Pink Floyd make their own conclusion, 'All we are is another brick in the wall'. Our schools and our families are therefore of no use to us.

Numerous popular songs of the last decade speak of this inner cosmic loneliness — often in sexual terms. 'Help me make it through the night', 'We've got tonight babe', 'I don't want to be lonely tonight'. And then there is a song by Sting that includes the line: 'Everyone I know is lonely and God seems so far away'.

All this indicates a new form of religion and loneliness. They also support psychotherapist Viktor Frankl's theory that, in a society with no meaning to life, libido (sexual desire) will run rampant in the search for pain killers or emotional analgesics.

Without really thinking about it, people in our society have absorbed this kind of scientific philosophy. They haven't recognized where it comes from, but they get the feeling that life is entirely up to them to make what they can of it. This results in a kind of cosmic loneliness which is far more serious than feeling you don't have many or any friends.

It's important to take people this far back in their thinking. I'm not trying to be clever, but the basic question of whether our Universe is an accident or whether there's a mind behind it makes a world of difference in how we feel about ourselves and those around us.

If you believe in God, the magnificence of the stars and the trees and the waves all simply increase our own sense of importance. The world is so enormous and powerful, yet God loves us. On the other hand, without God, nature daunts us, we seem so small and insignificant in comparison to the vast tracts of the cosmos. One of the great Australian poets, Adam Lindsay Gordon, having lost his faith, went to Brighton beach and, listening to the waves, feeling they spoke of an uncaring universe, blew his brains out. It was on the day that his most celebrated work, *Bush Ballads and Galloping Rhymes*, was published that he took his life. To him the waves were like Matthew Arnold's poem, 'Dover Beach'.

In contrast, the writer of one of the psalms felt wonder and self-worth when he looked at the mystery of the Universe. He felt self-worth because God was mindful of him.

Finally, I've discovered that loneliness is not just a legacy of a certain branch of science. It is a deep spiritual problem. However many friends we have, however close we might be to them or to our families, no one can deliver what we really need deep inside.

We were made by God, and we will never feel at home on this planet until we have a relationship with him. Our deepest loneliness is a pining for God. I love my wife dearly, but Glena can't meet my loneliness. No woman ever could. The insatiable cry for fellowship in my heart only ever finds sufficient satisfaction in those deep moments of spiritual reality that I've found through Jesus Christ and the Holy Spirit.

In that sense loneliness is a good thing. I sometimes refer to it as the nerve ends of the soul. It makes us feel pain, and that shows we are in danger. People suffering from leprosy can do serious damage to themselves because they have lost the feeling in their fingers and feet. They could be bleeding but they would feel nothing. We do feel and we should heed the danger signs.

God has put loneliness in our hearts so that we'll start looking for him. As one theologian put it, 'It is as though God made us for himself and we shall not find rest in our hearts until we find it in him.' Our society has no real faith. It has lost sight of God and meaning and purpose to life. We have everything materially — but nothing to live for. As a result, there is an epidemic of loneliness. And it will increase as long as we persist in assuming so arrogantly that we can take on the world ourselves.

One of the *advantages* of being a bit of a loner is that you get time to think and to read. My father taught me to do both. I learned to read quite early for my age, and Dad kept pushing me — giving me books to read, saying, 'I bet you couldn't read that.' So I would. Some of the stuff I read as a nipper has stayed with me ever since. It has shaped my thinking, or at least I responded to the ideas and atmosphere of those books and in some cases have made connections between different areas of my thinking.

My father had a fair-sized library, which included a lot of theological tomes, but also books of sermons from the great preachers of the past. I used to love to read the sermons of the eccentric American preacher, Billy Sunday. He was a converted baseball player with a dramatic way of putting across his message. He used to have a sixty-foot platform which he would use to the full. He'd be talking about the race of life, for example, and run the length of the stage before falling flat on his face.

Billy Sunday's language was visual and working class — it used to upset the more genteel of his audiences. In preaching against the ills of tobacco chewing, he'd conjure up a picture of the town louts lounging on the corner and spitting on the sidewalk. He'd say, '. . . and they'll spit out enough tobacco juice to drown a rabbit.' Strong, slang images like that have stuck in my mind. And though I don't take Billy Sunday's wild-man style too seriously, his ability to use colourful and colloquial language has definitely caused an echo in my own approach to preaching.

A long love affair with North America began through my reading too. My father introduced me to *From Log Cabin to White House*, a romanticized version of the story of US President Garfield, the first president to be assassinated. Around the same time I read the life story of Abe Lincoln. Both books stirred in me a sense of the great dream of struggling through from humble country roots to a position of greatness and fame.

But it wasn't really so much the political side of the States that attracted me so much as the country itself — particularly the old West. I read stacks and stacks of westerns, especially when I was in hospital. Books with titles like *Yankee Saddle*, and *Green Grasses of Wyoming*. There was a whole series of books by Edward T. Ellis about an Indian brave called Deerfoot. I liked them, not only because the image of frontiersman was one I warmed to because of my love of the outdoor life, but because these were pro-Indian. Deerfoot was a lot more than a target for cowboys' bullets. He was shown to be a brilliant tracker, with a great understanding of his environment. I just wish we had a similar kind of literature in Australia that treated the aboriginals with the same degree of dignity.

I read Dickens, too. The whole lot, even the ones that no one reads any more. I was moved by Dickens' moral outrage at the injustices of his time. I was most profoundly affected by *A Tale of Two Cities*. The idea that someone could take the rap for someone else out of love and idealism as Sydney Carton did in that story meant a lot to me. His thoughts on the scaffold, 'It is a far, far better thing that I do, than I have ever done; it is a far, far better rest that I go to, than I have ever known,' instilled in me a yearning for that kind of courageous heroism — the ability to make a great gesture.

Perhaps the most influential book of all was Victor Hugo's mammoth work *Les Miserables*. I struggled through it in answer to a challenge from my father. In many ways it's a crazily romantic tale, almost moral propoganda rather than novel. Briefly, the story hinges on the willingness of an elderly French Bishop of the eighteenth century, Monseigneur Bienvenu, to show love and trust to a complete outcast, a brutalized and embittered criminal, Jean Valjean, whose anti-social condition was the clear result of a vicious and unjust system.

Valjean is eventually transformed by the encounter, yet his past dogs him in the shape of a legalistic and merciless policeman, Javert, whose obsession with the law blinds him to any possibility of forgiveness. *Les Miserables* sowed a number of intuitive feelings in my heart that many years later I have picked up on and which are central to my thinking.

Firstly, it sowed a seed of dissatisfaction with social injustice; secondly, a dissatisfaction with the legal processes that are biased towards those who have power and privilege. Thirdly, it gave me a sense of the right place for a proper religious response to social problems. I felt that besides there being theological bureaucrats and obsessive legalists in the church, there could also be men and women whose graciousness reflects the goodness of Christ in the midst of a corrupt and unjust social order.

The fourth thing Hugo taught me was that the anti-social person is not necessarily simply a sinner. It has now become a major part of my preaching to point out that, while every human being has done wrong, they are often as much sinned against as sinners. I have come to realize that unless you understand this you have an inhumane form of religion. I learned that you have to see past the ugliness of a person's behaviour and to examine the social and religious causes in their life.

Fifthly, and lastly, *Les Miserables* revealed to me that there is an answer to the ancient question of the Bible, 'Can a leopard change its spots?' And the answer is yes. And that answer is not mere romanticism or optimism. I have an indomitable belief, first prompted by Hugo's book, and later confirmed by experience, that when the Bible offers us hope of moral and social change, it is not offering a crude dream that can only mock us in the reality of life.

Things *can* be changed. It took me a long time to realize that, and I had to have many struggles with my own sense of guilt and later a cold legalism which dehumanized my responses to suffering humanity. In fact the book itself foreshadowed many of those tussles I had in my teenage years.

While reading taught me to think, my father disciplined my thinking. If I'm fond of arguing the toss, he's a great demolisher of argument. He could never be described as a rationalist, but he is certainly rational. By that I mean he didn't believe that logical reasoning was an end in itself — he believed too much in the supernatural for that — but he felt the need to reason out his faith. It had to make sense; it couldn't be for him a blind leap in the dark. And for that he had his own father to thank. Grandad took the same approach.

My father was never a great one for setting out a case. But he was a master at finding holes in a weak one — I know from experience. Essentially, he was a troubleshooter, an analyst. He approached argument the same way he approached a machine that had broken down. He was always quick to locate the source of the problem in our old car or some other domestic appliance. That was his strength.

I had a tendency to run on feelings and intuition. Left to my own devices I would have become the most terrible, mawkish sentimentalist. But Dad disciplined me to be different, and he could be quite brutal. I'd say something I felt deeply but had not really thought through and he'd interrogate me, trying to make me find a rational justification for my position. Sometimes he'd destroy a case I was making, and just when I felt totally beaten, he'd stop and say, 'Well done. That was a good effort. In actual fact, I

70

agree with you.' That used to make me really angry. But it was a good apprenticeship to go through.

We didn't argue about politics so much as about the state of the world in more cosmic terms. By the time I was growing up, my father was more or less non-political. He'd flirted with socialism as a young man when he was working for the railways, but had become disillusioned with the restrictive practices and bloody-mindedness of some unions.

But since he was a great student of the Bible, we used to talk at length about matters like the prophecies in the Bible which foretold the end of the world. In some of the Old Testament prophecies and in the Book of Revelation, all sorts of signs and symbols are mentioned which generations of Christians have tried to figure out in comparison to the events of their own times. So we would debate whether, for instance, the formation of the European Common Market was a sign of the impending end of the world as predicted in Revelation.

It might seem a slightly oddball way of looking at history and current affairs, but what it did for me was to make history a live issue rather than a dead subject. The rise and fall of civilizations were enlivened by the possibility that God was involved, and because humankind had a significant part to play in God's scheme of things.

Intellectually, my father was a hard taskmaster, yet those discussions we had gave me such a fascination for and love of history that I eventually came to teach it in school. And it was only because he put the pressure on to make me work at my studies towards the end of my school career that I eventually got to that point.

Perhaps more significantly, my father's habit of playing devil's advocate helped me to realize that, if I was to believe anything, then I really had to believe it. It was no use picking up on my parents' faith second-hand. Ironically, this was to lead me into unbelief, but not before I'd tried hard to believe. I think sixteen times in all.

71

CHAPTER SIX

I didn't want to be John Smith. I didn't want to have a scarred up body; I didn't want to be a non-sportsman or to be seen as a preacher's kid; I didn't want to be a stupid loudmouth; I didn't want to be lonely. And I didn't want to be called John Smith — the most predictable name in the English world.

There was nothing unusual in that. Zits aren't the only problem you're faced with when you're a teenager. Just as they're the outward signs of inner chemical turmoil, so the odd moods of adolescence are the symptom of a confused mind in the search for identity.

Love, sex, schoolwork, attitudes, ideas, friendships, parental values — they all get thrown up in the air. I was different only in the sense that my background and medical history had a special part to play.

It's always seemed cruel to me that the most crucial time in your school career arrives at a time when you're least able to deal with it. You've got to think about exams when you're not sure who you are, or who you want to be. You're constantly falling in and out of love — relationships or crushes which completely drain you of the ability to think about anything else. You're at war with your parents and at odds with the world.

All that happened to me. I was struggling to find a faith that was mine and not my parents'. I became secretly obsessed with girls, and my work at school was below par. As for my name, it branded me as a nonentity. Once, when I was a new boy, I was caught by the headmaster for some minor offence. He asked me my name. When I replied innocently,

'John Smith, Sir,' he caned me for trying to be funny.

It's not that much easier even now. You can imagine what it's like booking a hotel room in the name of Mr and Mrs John Smith, or handing in a cheque to a bank in that name. I used to dream about changing my name by deed poll, but I'm still stuck with it.

With the expectations of my parents and the teachings of the church as a backdrop, I desperately wanted to be a good kid. But however much I tried, I couldn't. My growing sexual interest made things worse. My mother had fostered in me the idea that God sat up in heaven waiting for you to have a lustful thought. When one arrived, he'd spring to his feet and say, 'Ah-ha. Caught you in the act!' I felt guilty most of the time.

I was brought up on church services where you didn't necessarily just sit as a spectator in the pews. Preachers would sometimes ask you to make a response to the message, there and then. At the end of the sermon, they might ask those who felt they wanted to become Christians to come to the front of the church or hall in a public act of submission to God. Quite often they'd ask if anyone who'd lapsed from their Christianity, or felt they needed to recommit themselves to God, would do the same.

I know plenty of people who first decided to follow the path of Christ after appeals like this. They did so fully understanding what they were doing — and they are still firm in their belief. But occasions like these can sometimes be highly-charged emotional affairs, and people who are simply feeling generally unhappy with themselves can be persuaded to come forward.

The fact that I was young, vulnerable, remorseful and sentimental, meant that I often found myself making my way to the front after an appeal. I think it got to be a bit of a joke among the local church people.

'Look, there goes Smith again. How many times d'you make that?'

Sixteen was the number. Sixteen times I went forward,

each response as thoroughly sincere as the time before. On every occasion I was determined it would be the last.

'This time,' I thought, 'I'll really give my life to God and I'll morally and socially change.'

But somehow after a few weeks, or as little as a few days, I'd be back where I'd started from. It never seemed to take. I would momentarily feel as though I was really a Christian, but it didn't last. It was just a set of beliefs I'd borrowed which would do for the time being.

In the meantime I was in love. Constantly. But I was almost always too shy to do anything about it. There was one particular blonde beauty who stole my heart, my common-sense and almost every other faculty I had.

She lived in a small town about ten miles from where we were. I would tell my parents casually that I was just off for a ride on my bike and then I'd pedal over to her place. But I never went in. I was never invited, because I never even spoke to her. I'd simply ride the ten miles, park opposite her house and sit under the shade of a big old gum tree. I'd stare at her front door like a smitten cow, sighing deep romantic sighs. I'd wait for hours sometimes, just for a glimpse of her, hoping against hope that she'd come out. I'd use the time to work out what words of wit and intellect I'd use to charm her when she appeared.

But the moment she stepped outside her front door, I was covered in such confusion and panic, that I'd hop on my bike and pedal the ten miles back home again. I was such a hopeless romantic, I was almost in love with love. Anyone who was simply nice I'd immediately fall in love with. I caused myself a great deal of entirely futile heartache over these one-sided infatuations.

It was the subject of girls that really brought my relationship with my mother to a head. I'd met a nice Methodist girl for once. But she wasn't perfect, a quality demanded by my mother in me and my friends. Not only did I have to be pure in heart and mind, but the same standard of behaviour was expected of anyone I was to go around with.

Mum had good intentions, and felt she was serving my best interests, but her standards were so unyielding and her discipline so fierce that they were difficult to take. Her habit of ripping into me in front of my friends had already stopped most of them from visiting our house. Now she was turning her attentions to would-be girlfriends.

The girl in question had recently become a Christian and had previously had a reputation as a good dancer. Now I had never been allowed to go to so much as a local hop. In evangelical circles the practice was frowned upon. Any Christian who admitted to liking dancing was definitely not the genuine article.

It's ironic that my mother reacted to her with the same suspicion her mother-in-law had shown towards her. She spied us one evening, sitting together quite innocently at some local Christian rally, and later said sarcastically, 'I see you were with that young chit.' The disapproval in her tone and her dismissiveness towards someone I genuinely liked was the last straw. I exploded in fury and resolved never to trust my mother again.

I brought the shutters down between us, and kept them there for some years, my resentment smouldering slowly into hate. It got so bad that I used to fantasize about her falling off the rocks on one of our fishing trips at Kilcunda. I'd imagine her drowning, caught up in the forty-foot strands of kelp which swirled around the salt water there. Despite my yearning for goodness, I wasn't a particularly pleasant customer. Fortunately that was to change before her premature death.

We stayed in Gippsland until I was seventeen. My last year there was probably the best. I'd settled down to work at last, but only after my father had given me a roasting. He told me that if I didn't get my nose stuck into my books, I'd have to go out and find a job. I was a lazy coot, and the one thing worse than getting down to work at school was growing up and working for my living. But Dad never messed with words.

So when he warned me, and added the rider, 'and I don't mean maybe', I took heed. I did quite well in the end, taking subjects which would have led me towards a career in law — the area vocational guidance tests located as most suited to my abilities and personality.

I had also made my first really good friend, Geoff, a keen sportsman, who later became school captain. We're still friends to this day. I drew a lot of confidence from that friendship and gained kudos too, because he was a popular figure. I was strong enough by then to play sport, and while I was pretty inept and unpractised at games like rugby and cricket, I became a reasonable baseball pitcher. I became very enthusiastic and successful but I eventually had to give it up because of an arm injury. Later I won a few middle and long distance races at school. These small victories made me feel a bit better about myself.

Just as things were improving, we had to move again, this time north to the dry region of western Queensland. Dad was despatched to a church in the town of Chinchilla. At a crucial stage in my academic career I had to shift schools and curriculum. The law-oriented subjects I was taking weren't open to me in Queensland and the education authorities didn't make any great effort to meet my needs. Queensland was notorious for the low priority it gave to education. The best the vocational adviser I was referred to could suggest was that I consider a future as a clerk.

Chinchilla was a dramatic contrast to Gippsland. The manse and the surrounding area in Trafalgar had been so damp that I had begun to suffer badly from sinusitis. Queensland was more like northern Victoria where we'd been before, except more so.

Chinchilla is west of the Darling Downs. The soil on these rolling hills is rich and deep. In places the top soil goes down as far as 150 feet. This relatively loose soil shifts over the years, forming 'melon holes' — deep indentations in the ground, large enough to hide a dozen bullocks. A melon hole that suddenly appeared one year, could be gone five years later.

The area was known as brigalow country after the brigalow scrub which abounds in the region. It's similar to ironbark, but with a rich, red wood — an acacia not a eucalypt. The land is generally flat and is predominantly sheep and cattle country, though they grow a lot of wheat and a grain sorghum known as milo.

My fascination with nature had plenty to focus on here. There were flying phallangers, which are somewhere between a possum and a flying squirrel. They can extend their skin in a sort of canopy between their front and back legs and fly like a kite, from tree to tree. Some can glide up to thirty feet. There were many goannas and plenty of snakes. But one of the most striking sights in this part of Queensland is the great flocks of pea-green budgerigars, thousands of them sweeping across the vast, flat plains.

The waterways were different, too. The creeks in Gippsland were so crystal clear you could drink from them. In our part of Queensland we had the Condamine river, a sluggish, muddy brown affair. But it was exciting nonetheless because it was connected to the Murray river. The Murray and its tributaries play host to the Murray cod, known nowhere else in the world. These magnificent fish have been caught weighing as much as eighty pounds.

There were many narrow, cracked and bumpy roads: the bitumen would never stay on the shifting dirt surface. Local drivers quickly learnt to get off the road when another vehicle was coming the other way, or else stones would shatter their windscreens. There was one particular stretch that became known as the crystal highway — on one occasion we counted 120 smashed windscreens.

Dry country does something to you. It breeds that kind of tough stoicism Aussies are renowned for. When the drought comes, you see the country suffer, the animals suffer and the people too. The feeling you get when you see dark rain clouds roll over a parched landscape, dropping nothing, is close to despair. As a teenager, I can remember week after week watching these dark clouds pass over; maybe you'd feel two or three drops. But the most disheartening thing was to see these clouds lift over the distant ranges and pour their contents away. Living in those circumstances has helped me understand the tough, bloody-mindedness of the outback Australian. His dogged self-reliance and bitter humour is built to survive disaster. It breeds a healthy cynicism about unproven promises from man or nature. But sometimes it robs people of healthy or reasonable hope.

When the drought broke, the Condamine would sometimes break its banks and the flood water would lay in stagnant pools, a breeding ground for sand flies. These are nasty little blood-sucking creatures the size of a pin head, which can give you a vicious bite. The irritation lasts for days, often followed by angry red pussy sores which ceaselessly invite you to scratch — a bit like chicken pox.

In these conditions dense clouds of the blighters would rise up from the river banks. They were such a menace to cattle that in a bad season, farmers would knock down a few old trees, bulldoze them together in the paddock and set fire to them. The cows and horses would be prepared to stand, coughing, in the middle of the smoke to avoid their bite.

Effective insect repellent for these was little known in 1960, and mosquito coils were a rarity. So if there was a bad sand-fly plague, we'd simply drag a four-gallon oil or kero drum into the middle of the house, fill it with dried cow dung and burn it. The stench was definitely preferable to the vicious sting of the sand fly!

With the help of correspondence courses I managed to complete my secondary education successfully enough to be given a place at a teachers' college in Brisbane.

During my last years at school, what faith I had in God began to disintegrate. Deep inside I knew that all these years I'd simply been living on borrowed faith and personally untested theories. In our schoolroom debates during science periods we'd discuss the origin of the Universe and whether or not there was a God. In those days, British astronomer

Fred Hoyle was the hero of classroom atheists. That was before the Big Bang theory showed itself to be backed by almost overwhelming scientific evidence. And before Robert Jastrow, a NASA agnostic, admitted that it was a logical and inevitable question to ask, 'Who lit the fuse?' I was still the vigorous defender of the faith. But it was a case of argument weak, shout louder. I knew all the classic arguments, they just didn't convince me anymore.

From that time on there was a steady, if gradual, decline in my belief. Now and then I'd hear a preacher or Christian teacher who'd make me feel safe in the fold of Christianity. But as I became increasingly aware of the critical arguments against the Christian faith being bandied about — arguments largely ignored or vilified, but rarely seriously addressed within the church — I had this sinking feeling that I couldn't defend what I once thought I believed.

The traditional defence for Christian belief was to make a convincing case for the resurrection based on the evidence. Or alternatively, people pointed to the experience of individual Christians who could say, for instance, 'I was a junkie until I became a Christian and now I'm off heroin.' Either might be seen as a convincing reason for taking Christianity seriously.

But the growing generation of the sixties didn't think the same way. People began to operate much more on how they felt, or what worked for them. So you could prove to someone three times before breakfast that Jesus rose from the dead and they could still say, 'So what? Maybe he did, I dunno. It doesn't make any difference to me, and it doesn't prove to me he's the Son of God.'

Similarly, if you said, 'Becoming a Christian got me off drugs', there was always someone else who could say yoga or Buddhism got them off drugs. That's not the uniqueness of Christianity.

In the absence of a consistent experience of God, I found I had no compelling answers. That worried me. Besides this, the rationalists were beginning to give me a hard time. I began to ask the same questions they did. Is the Universe really the consequence of God's act, or is it just the random product of the same forces that ripen corn and rust iron?

Leaving school and moving away from home accelerated the process of unbelief. The factors that influence what we think, I've found, aren't always to do with reason or logical processes of thought. We adopt attitudes and positions that justify the way we happen to be living. To some degree this happened to me.

I met and fell in love with a girl who we'll call Anne. We were both struggling to come to terms with our own backgrounds and our own beliefs and we drew comfort from one another. Before long, we began sleeping together. With my upbringing, this was close to an unforgivable sin. Sex or even sexual intimacy outside marriage was forbidden territory.

We thought we cared for one another, but in the end we used each other to dull the pain of our own insecurity. Ours was a dark and uncomfortable secret, which ultimately made us feel worse, not better. This was my first real sexual encounter and was therefore very exciting, but it left a bad taste, because the love affair became inextricably tangled with my own internal struggles.

I know for certain that the end of the relationship left Anne desperately hurt. To this day I feel remorse at what I put her through. When we use relationships to work through our own hang-ups, people always get damaged.

I was being torn apart by my own hypocrisy. No one else knew. All my social life support systems were good. How could I wound those who cared by revealing I was no longer really one of them? The events and times become confused here, not through loss of memory, but because launching out on my own was a very irrational time for me. I had always known from a child what I ought to believe, even if I wasn't sure that I believed it. Now even this became unclear. Sometimes I thought I knew and sometimes I didn't. One day I would pray to God, telling him I was willing to become a new person and felt that my prayer had been heard. The next day it was as if I was alone in an empty Universe.

Throughout these ups and downs I never had the guts to be honest. I was the founder of the Kedron Park Teachers' College Christian Fellowship and a vocal supporter of the Christian position, arguing from what seemed like a well thought out, conservative evangelical point of view. Yet partly because I couldn't come to terms with my lack of personal belief and partly out of a need to try to justify my behaviour, I became a closet agnostic and even, for a while, an atheist.

Finally, I reached a point where I could no longer believe in anything. I remember vividly one clear night close to Easter, standing on the landing outside my room and looking at the stars. I was struck by the immensity of the Universe and I felt lost.

I said to myself, 'If anyone has tried to find faith, you have. Despite all the responses you've made, you're still defeated. If there's a God out there, then we haven't connected. I've tried to meet him and it hasn't worked. Nothing makes any sense any more.'

That night I made an intellectual and emotional response to my situation which was as clear as any religious conversion. I said out loud, 'When I die, I'll die like a dog. They'll bury me, the worms will eat me and that's it.' It was a cool night, but I sweated.

I didn't feel any sense of release at this decision. But I did understand, probably for the first time, that to discover whether or not God really exists is the most important thing in the world. I was chilled by the knowledge that there were only two possibilities. Either there was a purpose and a reason behind the Universe or else there wasn't. And that resolving the issue one way or the other could make a significant difference to my life. I was not the flippant, superstitious atheist common on campus, but one who like Nietzsche knew there were serious consequences for me and for humanity if life had no ultimate meaning. I felt like a cosmic orphan.

81

The feeling of fear was intensified, I think, by the fact that suddenly there was nothing I could rely on. I'd been brought up with people who had a reason to live, a reason to love, a reason to study and to listen to music. Now it was as if I'd been wrenched from that soil and my roots were shrivelling up in the burning sun. Those roots were useless to me now. I was on my own.

Even then I didn't have the guts to reveal the way I was thinking to anyone else. I kept up the pretence of being a standard-issue Christian. I didn't dare. I didn't want to lose friends, and I was frightened of the disapproval it would bring. But gradually I came to the conclusion that I couldn't live with this farce much longer. I resolved to drop my studies and head off somewhere I wasn't known.

I had been attending night lectures at Brisbane University alongside my college course, but had become completely disillusioned with what I'd found there. I had expected an exploration of truth, time to explore the great themes of the human quest for knowledge about ourselves and our world. Instead I observed a preoccupation with academic trivia, a tired ritual of jumping through hoops in order to complete required course units. I stopped going.

What I discovered then, I have found to be true again and again. I have now visited and spoken at almost every university in Australia. The pattern is the same. There is a blinkered attitude in many of our academic institutions across the Western world, which ultimately destroys learning.

Look at first year undergraduates and you'll see a freshness about them, a spirit of enquiry in their eyes and in their questions. Meet them again in their third year and you find they've become paper collectors, obsessed only with doing what's necessary to get the right grades in order to get the right job. This is a mean and narrow view of education.

With no intellectual challenge in my course and a desire to leave my uncomfortable past behind, I decided to head out to the far west of Queensland. Here there are remote towns that have often acted as a last refuge for people on the run from their past mistakes. I suppose even this was a romantic, immature notion. I thought I could escape into oblivion, to a mythical place where drink was cheap and women were easy. But it was not to be.

It sounds so lame in retrospect, but I was stopped by a combined sense of friendship and obligation. I couldn't tear myself away from the warm friendship and vibrant faith of my Christian mates. On top of that I was one of the organizers of a weekend camp for Christian students which was due to start shortly, and I didn't want to welsh on them. I put off my grand bridge-burning gesture, deciding to get through the camp and then disappear.

We'd invited a speaker to give us a series of Bible teaching sessions. His name was George Francis, a real, fiery fundamentalist. He wouldn't so much preach as put his head down like a bull and charge at his audience. I've seen him preach for an hour and a half and end up covered in sweat, breathing hard as if he'd been in the ring with a world-class matador. And won. But he spoke powerfully against hypocrisy and against moral selfishness. It was our sinful selfishness, not hell, that he warned against.

One night that weekend, he spoke with such power and insight that most of those who were there can point back to it as a significant point in their lives. George certainly hit me where it hurt. He ended his address by saying something like, 'Some of you claim to be Christians but are really hypocrites and humbugs, playing games and full of deception. If you want to meet God, then stand up.' There was an immediate clatter and scraping of chairs as about twenty-seven out of the thirty of us shot from our seats.

I didn't have to stand up. But then I didn't have to respond all those times before either. So what was different this time? Nothing, except that I found myself praying an all-or-nothing prayer which boiled up out of all my internal struggles.

I said to God, 'Secretly I've been an atheist. I'm still not sure if you exist. But if you do, I really, finally and definitely feel this is the last chance. It's got to work this time. If you can enter my life, then I'm a candidate for you.'

I can't find a phrase that really describes what went through me in that moment. It was a completely overwhelming sense of connection with God. The whole direction of my heart and life was swung completely around. I knew, rather than felt that my life was now pointed towards God rather than towards myself. The experience itself doesn't prove anything to anyone except me. To try to convey it is like trying to describe what water tastes like when you're parched. But I knew in my heart that from now on everything was going to be different. Nothing that's happened since has given me any reason to go back on that.

The importance of that moment went much deeper than just a feeling of finally getting through to God. I began to understand something important about him and it was this which made all the difference. What I had not grasped before was that God does not love us when we are good. He loves us. Period.

Almost everything we see and are taught goes against that. Even the best of parents give off the unspoken sense that, 'If you're good, I'll love you more'. We relate our own sense of goodness to the amount of love we receive. The better we are, the more love we can expect. It happens in marriages all the time, too.

I felt as a kid that as soon as I made a mistake, God would stomp out the door. My fifteen previous 'official' attempts at meeting with God (and there were many more private ones in between) were ways of asking him to make me a better person, so that he could accept me.

Only now did I appreciate what the story of the Prodigal Son was about. This parable that Jesus told relates how the son of a well-to-do landowner asks if he can have his inheritance early. The father gives it to him and the young man goes off to the city and spends it all. Broke and humiliated he decides to go back to his dad and ask if he'll give him work as a servant. As he approaches his home, he finds his father is already outside the gate where he has been standing every day, hoping for his son's return. Dad flings his arms around the boy and announces a feast of celebration.

God is just like that. He waits patiently for us, knowing exactly how much we've stuffed up our lives and other people's.

Words I'd heard hundreds of times suddenly made sense to me. The Bible says, 'While we were yet sinners, Christ died for us.' It really meant what it said. As another passage puts it, 'While we were his enemies, Christ died for us.' I recognized that God really loved me. I didn't have to prove myself, I didn't have to bring anything or even deserve anything, I just had to throw myself on his mercy. That made all the difference in the world.

It was no good having a change of heart if I was going simply to forget the past and press on with life. There were things I had to put right. The night after I made that final and lasting decision I sat up until 3 a.m. listing the things I needed to sort out — people I'd hurt, items I'd stolen and so on. Old timers used to call it 'restitution' — putting right what was wrong in relationships.

One of the simplest but also one of the most difficult things I had to do was to write to the school where I had just been given a teaching post. I had done my final high school year there before entering teachers' college and had stolen some beautiful natural history books. Now I wrote to the principal saying, 'I have discovered some books which really belong in your library.'

When I re-read the letter, I could almost imagine God reading it over my shoulder and saying, 'You didn't discover anything. You ripped them off!' I tore up the letter and rewrote it, explaining that I had become a Christian and wanted to admit to the theft, return the books and ask for forgiveness. I don't know precisely what his reaction was. He probably thought I was nuts. But it was all straightened out.

Although I knew that God had forgiven me and that I'd

done as much as I felt possible to clear up the mess I'd made, I still felt uncomfortable. I wanted to be useful, I wanted to be given responsibility, but I wasn't sure that having made so many mistakes in the past, I could ever be trusted again.

I went to see Alan Burgess, a Baptist minister. Without any previous relationship with me, he felt a strange urge to contact me. He said, 'I don't know you, but I believe somehow that you are guilty concerning a secret past. If you want, I'll be glad to counsel you.' He helped me sort out some of these worries. I'm especially grateful to him because he was the first person to whom I was able to spill out everything that had happened in the last few years — my affair, my struggles with belief, everything. That in itself was a liberating experience.

Alan pointed out to me passage after passage in the Bible to show me I was completely restored to usefulness, not only forgiven, and that this was a real fresh start. But somehow I could only accept it in theory; in my heart I could not feel it.

I went back to my residence to be met by a taxi, bringing with it a page that Alan had ripped out of his King James Bible. It was from Paul's first letter to the church in Corinth. He had marked one verse in the sixth chapter, which listed the kind of people who wouldn't 'inherit the kingdom of God'. These included fornicators, adulterers, thieves, drunkards and the like. But Paul went on to say, 'And such were some of you: but ye are washed, but ye are sanctified, but ye are justified in the name of the Lord Jesus, and by the Spirit of our God.' Alan had ringed the words 'were' and 'are' and underlined 'washed'.

The truth of what God was doing finally dawned on me. This is the difference between real Christianity and any other religious teaching. The forgiveness and restoration of God is total and complete, irrespective of what has been done in the past.

The Bible is full of examples. It doesn't hide the warts of its heroes, but shows them up as flawed human beings. Abraham was gutless enough to let another bloke have his wife for the night. David was not only an adulterer, but he had the woman's husband killed to cover up for his actions. Moses and Gideon had moments of cowardice; Paul had men and women executed for their beliefs. Yet God wiped the slate clean for all of them.

Finally understanding these things was a turning point for me. I could look ahead instead of constantly driving with my eye on the rear-view mirror. Forgiveness is the only thing that can bring real healing to a tortured past. It's the only thing that can liberate us. Denying the existence of sin and decrying guilt as a socially-imposed fantasy has in no way reduced the sense of guilt in the modern heart. The real question is not 'What is it?' but rather, 'What are we going to do about it?'

I once knew a guy who was so confused about his sexuality that he sold his $10,000 Harley Davidson motorcycle and spent the proceeds on prostitutes in a desperate bid to stir up his libido and assure him of his gender. Unable to come to terms with his problems, he lost control one day and started firing his shotgun into the walls and ceiling of his home. After he was arrested I visited him in jail, and found a man loaded down with guilt about his past.

He said to me, 'My life's just bullshit, nothing can be done for me.' I recalled then my own feelings of guilt and how I discovered the truth of forgiveness.

I also remembered how, back in Gippsland, my father grew the most amazing vegetables in almost pure cow manure! I said to him, 'Mate, that stuff grows the most incredible cabbages.' That might sound trite, but as I went on to explain to him, God can grow the most extraordinary lives out of the worst excrement of our past. Absolutely nobody is beyond the reach of God's ability to forgive and restore. Believe that and you have a foundation for the reconstruction of lives greater than any social welfare theory.

If people can't discover that forgiveness, they often find it difficult to live with themselves any longer. I spent a long time with one particular bloke, a biker who claimed that one night when he was drunk he had hacked a girl's breast off with a sharpened World War II bayonet. He had then simply dumped her on the steps of a hospital. I can't vouch for the truth of his story, but I can say that he was a man who could find no sense of peace, however much I told him about God's forgiveness. Now you might say he didn't deserve any peace. But this is the real mystery of God, that even given such an act of callous and awful brutality, he is still able to forgive the person who truly regrets and rejects the past and steps by faith into a new life.

Of course, this guy could never undo the damage he'd done, and there's the question of justice for the woman and her family in dealing with a crime this hideous. But this man could not find his way to forgiveness. The last I heard he had joined the mercenaries in Angola.

He said, 'I don't have the guts to kill myself, perhaps someone else will do it for me.'

Perhaps he thought that dying a horrible death would compensate for what he'd done. But there's only one kind of death that can make any recompense, as I tried to tell him again and again. That was the death Jesus died on the cross. He nailed the sins of the world to that piece of wood in an eternal sacrifice, so that even the person who has committed the worst sins in the world can be forgiven.

No wonder Martin Luther King found in Christ inspiration to actively oppose the obscenity of racism while continuing to love his oppressors. 'We will overcome your ability to inflict suffering by our ability to suffer in love', he said. What forgiveness. What inspiration. What transformation.

All in all, going away to college was a real education for me. Now I was headed off to a new teaching post to put my new-found faith into action. But my brief exile as an atheist had not only frightened me. It had given me a real respect for atheists and agnostics — and even for cynics!

As the German theologian, Helmut Thielicke put it, the true believer and the true atheist are very close together.

Suppose you believe there is an ultimate purpose to life. When you see the population of the earth frittering its time away, in a frantic succession of apparently important but ultimately irrelevant activities, you can come close to despair. If you believe there is no purpose to life, you have to face the awful fact that all human activity is irrelevant. The pain that results from these two positions is very similar. 'So,' Thielicke says, 'we see that Nietzsche (father of the "God is Dead" movement) is not the end of the Christian faith, but the beginning of it.'

There is sometimes an intellectual courage in the atheist's position that Christians have been too slow to recognize. Atheists have too often been treated as moral lepers. In fact they are orphans, stranded without roots and without a home. An atheist is a person with no invisible means of support. I've already mentioned the story of the prodigal son. Thielicke says there is a kind of unbelief which is searching for reality and is more real than mindless pew warming or empty religious observance. He sees in the painful pilgrimage of many honest doubters what he calls 'promising atheism'. I have deep affection for my genuine mates who struggle with the church and with phoney religion and mindless belief.

Thielicke talks about repentance (that change of direction required in order to come face to face with God) as a sense of homesickness which causes you to about face and head home.

You can only return home if you had one in the first place. My conversion was a matter of going back home. But if you've never really considered the existence of the God of the Universe as an option, there's nowhere to turn when you're in trouble. No wonder, in our lost and faithless generation, so many people self-destruct.

All these experiences and insights were storing themselves up inside my mind. I can't say I made use of them right away. In fact, I seem to have had a great ability to ignore lessons I've learned until a lot later on. That was certainly true in this case.

CHAPTER SEVEN

Richard Nixon was my hero. He had been for some while. I kept a scrap-book on him for years. I had been interested in him long before he was running for president against Jack Kennedy in 1960. I felt sure he would be president of the United States one day, but when he lost to Kennedy I was heartbroken. I believed this would signal the end of America's greatness.

I'd better fill in the background to this strange notion. I'm not blaming my Dad for my politics, but as in everything else, as a youngster he impressed me with his thinking and I followed his lead in the extreme. From the time we moved from the city to the countryside, he had begun shifting to the right. This, as I've mentioned, was partly due to his disillusionment with the unions and with socialism world-wide. But it was also because of his natural sympathies with his flock.

Farmers the world over tend to be naturally conservative. Aussie farmers are no different. They're likely to say, 'This is my farm, I work flamin' hard to make it pay. I've carved it out of the bush and no wimp of a radical's going to take it away from me.' And they do work hard — up before the crows and often still up in the small hours, going over their books.

Dad was able to see things from their point of view, and his politics shifted over a period of years. As a kid, mine did too. But I went several steps further. My politics came from the kind of things I read as a teenager. The sworn enemy of fundamentalism, you have to remember, is communism. In the simplistic view of the ultra-conservative Christian,

Marxism has two dangerous traits. Firstly, it's atheistic and secondly, its declared aim is to take over the world. This is a caricature, of course, but that's what people felt. They believed that communist agents would infiltrate Western societies with the aim of breaking down the moral fabric of the country. Anarchy would result and the communists could move in.

I used to read avidly a really nasty journal called *The Sword of the Lord*, put out by a man named John Rice. Rice was an earlier and much more abrasive and unreasonable version of the Moral Majority leader in the USA, Jerry Falwell. Rice, I believe, was genuine but dreadfully limited in his understanding of the world, the Bible and the Spirit of Christ. I owned every book and every leaflet he had published and they were too numerous to mention. Some were heart-warming and useful. Others bigoted to the point of brutality.

The Sword of the Lord's line was that the Western world was under threat from a Catholic/communist conspiracy. This was really juicy stuff and right up the fundamentalists' street, however improbable the alliance might seem. They hated Catholicism only a smidgeon less than communism. The Pope, they thought, was the personification of the antichrist, 'the beast' of the Book of Revelation.

It added to this theory the idea which is at the root of South African apartheid — that the black races are descended from Ham (the disgraced son of Noah) who were doomed for ever to be 'hewers of wood and drawers of water'. In other words, black people, they claimed, were inherently inferior to white people.

I find it difficult to believe that I swallowed all this unbiblical and inhumane bigotry at the time, but I did. The fact is that who you listen to determines what you hear. When you choose to listen to voices of a certain point of view, you simply write off those who oppose them. This then reinforces your own prejudices. As a result of reading this drivel (and I used to devour every column inch, even the adverts) I was a walking textbook of prejudices against

92

communists, Catholics and blacks. I must say that in this literature there was also genuinely caring Christian hope and concern. It was a mishmash of the good, the bad and the ugly.

I was a racist in the South African mould. But I thought I was an understanding racist. I would never have joined the Ku-Klux-Klan. In my arrogant, patronizing white way, I simply felt sorry that these people were doomed to inferiority, because of a distant forbear's mistake. I never once doubted that it was appropriate for whites to take charge — so neatly dispensing with the Aboriginal problem in Australia. Genuine concern for a measure of justice certainly remained, but in a paternalistic and superior way.

I am of course ashamed at even entertaining such plainly unbiblical, not to say wicked ideas, but I have to admit to their existence. And as a result I believed Senator Joseph McCarthy, who inspired the communist witch-hunts of the fifties in the States, was a persecuted political hero. In my view, one of the few with the guts to stand up against the communist threat. I not only saw reds under the bed, I believed them to be boldly walking down main street. I even wrote off to the John Birch Society (a far-right organization in America that makes Jerry Falwell look like Fidel Castro), hoping I could join up.

So it was that I cried when Nixon was defeated by Kennedy. Kennedy, you see, was a liberal Catholic. Every fear-mongering word I had read said that should a liberal Catholic become president of the United States, there would be a wholesale persecution of Protestants, resulting in the disintegration of the values of America. This would leave the door wide open for the Catholics' co-conspirators, the commies.

In the same way I feared the rise of Martin Luther King Jr, now one of my great heroes. He, I believed, was a communist riding to power on the back of the civil-rights issue. A dangerous and immoral man, according to John R. Rice.

My obsession with the details of American politics had its

roots not in this dreadful paranoid literature, but back in books like *From Log Cabin to White House* that I'd read as a kid. These books, together with all the frontiersman literature I'd devoured, made me feel much more of an American than an Australian. I even had the voting papers for the 1960 presidential election. My hunger for detail was such that I could probably have told you who was head dog-catcher in New York that election year.

I hated Australian history, even though I taught it. I saw it as boring, lacking any real meaning or sense of destiny. There was a kind of religious feel about the American greats that seemed to be absent in our own cultural background. As a result, I took no interest whatsoever in Australian current affairs. I barely knew the name of our own Prime Minister.

By the time I took up my first teaching appointment in my home town Chinchilla in 1962 at the age of twenty-one, I was a convinced Christian and a rabid right-winger. I was to remain comfortable and relatively unchallenged in these views for the next five or six years.

In the intervening period my personal world was to change a great deal. Firstly, my mother died at the age of forty-two. I'm glad to say that she didn't go before we were properly reconciled. Shortly after my return to faith, I found I was able to talk to her once more. This was one area where the forgiveness I experienced did liberate me. I was able to feel a genuine warmth and love for Mum, and we grew quite close.

She had gone in for routine surgery on varicose veins, but the doctors had great difficulty in pulling her back to consciousness after the operation. Tests showed that she had suffered a cerebral haemorrhage. This they afterwards found was due to an aneurysm (a dilation of the artery) at the base of her brain.

Mum had suffered from high blood pressure for a long while. Bearing children had been difficult and risky as a result. All the same there were six kids now — five which she'd borne herself. She had suffered from headaches, too. It was clear that the aneurysm had been there from birth and that this had been the real cause of the headaches. I realized, with some shame, that there had been good reason for her bad temper; she had been a very sick woman. Pain to the point of distraction was her almost constant companion.

For a number of years she'd received treatment for those pains. But because no one had searched for the real cause, only her symptoms had been dealt with by the use of pain-killers. I don't want to use this tragic situation simply to make a cheap point, but I've thought a great deal about how the treatment of Mum's headaches is mirrored in so much of what goes on around us today.

We live in an analgesic society. A great deal of human activity strives to deal with the pain we feel, without ever trying to get to the root of it. Some people feel under pressure, so they drink heavily. Others can't cope with the reality of their own lives, so they take drugs — anything from dope, through tranquillizers to heroin. Money-making also serves a purpose as a means to divert attention from a hollowness inside. The quest for fame or notoriety can work the same way. Sex is used as an analgesic too — a means of making people feel better, of assuaging immediate appetites without touching the real hunger and loneliness that exists deep inside.

Sexual promiscuity, according to Sexual Addicts Anonymous, is rather like heroin addiction in its pathology. Increased hits to get a feeling of ego pleasure and strength only plunge the victim into increasingly unfulfilled desire.

You can put a junkie through cold turkey or de-toxify an alcoholic, but unless you attack the reason they took to drugs or drink in the first place, then there is a very high risk they'll go back on the stuff. The most basic underlying cause of human pain is, I believe, the fact that people have become alienated from their Creator. They live at odds with the world because they have failed to acknowledge him, and failed to come to terms with his existence, and hence their own meaning and purpose for existence.

Not recognizing God for who he is makes it difficult to make sense of the complexity of the world itself and of our purpose within it. That in turn creates a dissatisfaction which can't easily be explained, and a desire to dull the apparently irrational cosmic ache.

Mum never really recovered. She lingered for a month, and then died. Dad was heart-broken. The moment it was evident she was in danger, he began lacerating himself for not being more thoughtful. He needn't have — to my observation he had been a model husband. He stayed by her bed for long periods holding her hand, reading psalms and praying with her.

Even in that hospital ward, Dad's strength of faith touched those around him. It wasn't unusual when I visited the hospital, to see him surrounded by other people whose own friends or relatives were close to death. They clung vicariously to his belief in God.

Dad insisted on preaching at Mum's funeral. Characteristically he held his grief within himself, in order to speak to his flock. He said, 'If I can't stand up and witness to my people in the hour of my greatest need, I've got nothing to say.' It was the spirit of the old world, the 'whatever tragedy there's been, I'm going to tough it out' approach.

Also characteristically, it was a brilliant message. He talked about the different things people base their lives on and how, when they're gone, their lives disintegrate. He said, 'If my life was built even on the foundation of my love for Nancy, then this day I would be a destroyed man.' He then called people to put their trust in something which transcended the things of this world.

When he returned home, a lonely, rugged man, he went through the house, walking into every room. He would pause for a moment in each and say, 'She won't be here any more.' I guess it was his way of dealing with the loss, steadying himself for the hard road ahead.

And it wasn't easy. I was working and we had small

children to look after. Faye, who was fourteen at the time, had to leave her schooling and help look after the family. She was marvellous. Colin and Joy were still at primary school. Beverley was only a toddler and there was Beth who was still only a baby. It was a tough year.

Just one year later the Smiths were on the move again. This time to Childers on the Queensland coast, not far from Brisbane. Childers is a small sugar-cane township between Bundaberg and Maryborough. My abiding impression of the place was of rich dark red and bright green. The red was the soil against the bright fresh green of the sugar-cane.

Before the cane was cut, the fields were burned to remove thrash and snakes in preparation for the harvesting, which in those days was performed by hand. This was a dramatic sight. Nothing like the stubble burning you see in some wheat-growing areas. The thrash, as Queenslanders call the residual growth, would send flames leaping up a hundred feet or more. The rolling hills of this region would be alive with fire and the air sweet with the smell of burning cane.

There was some semi-tropical vegetation. In areas which had reverted to natural bush, Lantana, a plant grown in Melbourne suburban gardens for its tiny, exquisite flowers, would grow in such profusion in Queensland that you'd need a bush knife to hack your way through it. There were banana plantations and fields of pineapple too.

The most significant feature of the area to me was a vivacious and extremely attractive girl, a local cane farmer's daughter. Her name was Glena Walker.

I actually met her father first. He was a marvellous man and we came to be good friends. He had started with nothing and worked very hard to establish his flourishing farm by the time I met him. He was a Christian of the Brethren persuasion.

Traditionally, the Brethren meet in simple halls with no religious trappings to speak of. The leadership of each church is in the hands of a group of lay elders and each church or assembly runs its own affairs without referring to any other. There is no overall denominational structure. They have a reputation for being extremely strict in their interpretation of the Bible and, on the strength of a number of verses in the New Testament, often insist that women keep their heads covered when in church and forbid them to take any leading role in public worship.

In spite of his strict church background, Ronald Walker was an open-minded and generous man. He was extremely well-liked in the church and in the community; he had the reputation of never having bad-mouthed or short-changed anyone. He impressed me enormously. So did his family. His wife, Sylvia, was and is a wonderful woman and equally I liked their three daughters and two sons.

I was attracted to Glena from the moment we met. Not only was she great to look at, but she seemed extremely happy and free, even though her upbringing was, if anything, even stricter than mine. One thing was immediately obvious, she cared for people. She understood their feelings and could put herself in their position. She lived for others rather than herself.

Despite my interest in her, I made no advances. I had been told she was going with someone else. This put her off-limits, so when we met, we did nothing more than make conversation. The daft thing was that she thought I was dating some girl in Brisbane, which wasn't the case. As a result, we skirted around each other for some while until, during a bit of friendly banter at her home one day, we referred to each others' supposed attachments. Only then did we find we'd been simultaneously misled. The spark of our relationship ignited at that moment — at least from my end of things.

I was teaching at a local primary school at the time and in spare moments would take my reptile collection, now in its prime, around to local shows and rotaries. I became something of a minor local character. In fact, one of the first occasions Glena and I went out together was when I took my collection of snakes to a local fair. I think she thought I was a tiny bit touched in the head.

Nevertheless, our affection quickly turned to a warm love for one another which has never diminished. It wasn't long before we were talking of marriage.

In between time, however, tragedy struck. Glena's father, who had worked so hard all his life, pushed himself a bit too far. The men of the Walker clan have a history of heart disease and Ron had been nursing an impaired heart. He always had tremendous energy and, like me, loved to hunt. The opportunity arose for him to go out to a remote area of western Queensland to hunt wild pig. There are some big, dangerous animals to be found in this rugged part of the country and Ron was out hunting on horseback one frosty morning when a couple of big pigs broke from the bush just in front of him. The excitement of the chase was so great that, at the moment this excellent horseman would have urged his mount into a gallop, his heart protested, went into seizure and he died. He was only fifty-one years old. The whole town mourned for him.

The family was inevitably grief-stricken by his death and I was too. I understood exactly what they were going through, because of my mother's recent death, and it drew me closer to them all. Glena and I, in particular, were brought closer by the loss and we began to make long-term plans for our future together.

Glena had set her heart on becoming a missionary. She had read scores of missionary biographies and was smitten by the romance of the single woman braving it alone in some distant continent. The problem was that she felt that she had no medical or educational skills — although she was a legal secretary, and a very good one — and so she had resolved to go out to Africa to look after the children of European missionaries.

My return to faith had rekindled many of the dreams and ambitions I had nursed throughout my youth of ultimately serving God in some specific way, as a pastor or preacher, missionary or evangelist. I had already set my heart on getting some theological training which would enable me to fulfil those ambitions. The best place for me seemed to be Melbourne Bible Institute.

Knowing my intentions, Glena now thought we might go out to Africa or some other continent together. Since I was a trained teacher, we could become 'proper' missionaries. Her hope was that she could accompany me in some supporting role. At one time she had thought of going to Bible college herself, but in the wake of her father's death she felt she should stay at home and help with the family. She could also save some money for our future life together.

In many ways I am grateful to the academic and theological discipline of the college and also for my studies at Melbourne College of Divinity. Although I went there unsure about what precisely I was going to do when I left, the place gave me a great opportunity to read, often more widely than the course demanded. As you can imagine, I also thrived on the cut and thrust of argument. My father had taught me well, and I became a vigorous, even aggressive debater.

On the other hand, the college had some peculiar rules. Firstly, they advised Glena and I not to get engaged before I joined the course in case I ended up going to Africa and she ended up going to Afghanistan, or something like that. You have to remember that a Bible college is not simply an academic institution, but a preparation for a life's work. The college authorities were concerned about our own welfare and prospects, even if there was a strong paternalistic element in the way we were treated. After a few months at the college, the authorities very generously relented and declared themselves happy that we should become engaged. It was then that Glena felt able to leave home and enter the college herself, the following year.

This was wonderful, since I'd been writing to Glena every day — made possible by a Christian pharmacist we knew who gave me free stamps! Now we were to be together, or almost.

Melbourne Bible Institute, in common with other evangelical

establishments at that time, had a paranoia about sex. They felt that if you had to have young men and women studying together, you needed strict regulations to limit 'fraternization'. In the USA, many fundamentalist institutions still hold to such strict controls. The Bible College of Victoria has developed much freer and broader approaches since its earlier days.

In lectures and at meal times, men and women sat seperately. You could only talk to someone of the opposite sex with the permission of one of the four senior students and only then within view. You had to stand far enough apart so that you couldn't touch. If I wanted to talk to Glena I had to approach one of the male senior students and say, 'I would like to talk to Miss Walker, please.' (I had to refer to her in this formal way even though she was my fiancée.) The senior student would then pass my message on to one of the two women senior students, who would give permission. It was incredibly frustrating.

On one afternoon a week, engaged couples and those whose relationship was approved by the college (you could only establish a relationship with someone if they gave the OK) were given permission to walk around the block outside the college for half an hour. We had to keep together and we weren't allowed to go anywhere else. It all seems unbelievable in hindsight, but the practice was not in the least uncommon for this kind of set-up.

Ironically, Glena was very happy with this situation. She loved rules, and says she liked the teasing of being kept apart. In her final year she became one of the senior students herself. Conservative as I was, I hated this petty-mindedness and did my best to get around the rules. But Glena wouldn't budge an inch on the absolute observation of the letter of the law.

In my final year, while I was working towards my examinations for the Diploma in theology, I became part-time pastor in the Glen Forbes Methodist circuit in a country district not far south-east of Melbourne. Every

101

weekend during my third year at the Melbourne Bible Institute, I spent working with three small rural churches in the area. At the end of the year when Glena and I had completed our studies, they were keen that I continue as their pastor. Being missionaries overseas didn't look like a realistic prospect, so I accepted. There wasn't a full stipend, so I had to teach three days a week.

It was an old mining and farming region near the coast and the largest town was Wonthaggi. But the place was dying. Most of our congregation was old, though there was a scattering of farming families with teenage kids, many of whom I taught during the week. They were a deeply conservative group of church people, but they hung on to the best of the old values, too. It was an integrated community, where young and old could pitch in and do things together — the generation gap was not so visible here. And the people had an old-world sense of warm and practical generosity. So although we earned little in our time there, we never went short, and we felt greatly loved.

Glena and I married straight after graduation. I might have known, had I thought about it, that the Smiths would not get off to a smooth start. In my arrogant and conservative way I had insisted that Glena wear no make-up. I thought this was unseemly for an upstanding Christian girl. But the mother of one of the bridesmaids had encouraged her daughter to wear lipstick and wanted Glena to do so too. There were angry scenes, because I felt our wishes were being interfered with. It was the usual insecurity of someone who wants to run the show, but sees his big day is being hijacked.

Partly because of this debate, Glena was late. It was a scorching Queensland summer day. In those days you stood at the front of the church until your bride arrived. It was a simple Brethren meeting hall, and very hot inside. We stood there, in suit and tie, for what I claim was forty minutes. Glena says it was much less. It certainly *felt* like forty minutes.

It was a close family gathering with plenty of long speeches, so we didn't get away until quite late. We had long distances to drive and we were exhausted and tense. The first couple of days weren't a lot of fun. The fabled honeymoon night was a disaster. Neither of us could manage much except tears of frustration for the first couple of days. I'm glad to say that things sorted themselves out thereafter.

We had a few other problems too. In the confusion and concentrated work of the last few months of college, Glena and I hadn't had much time to make practical arrangements. We had been offered my brother-in-law Bevan's beach house near Rockhampton in Emu Park, Queensland. I had sorted out the money to get us there and back, assuming that Glena would bring enough for us to live on. She thought I was going to sort out all the money for the trip.

Naturally enough, we didn't discover this oversight until we arrived for our month away. But we scraped by. I supplemented our food supply by getting up early in the morning and fishing from the shore. It was a shallow bay and therefore not the best for sizeable eating fish, but we got enough to keep us going.

By the end of the honeymoon, we were pretty broke. We then had to pack up all our belongings, because we were moving down to my first pastorate in Victoria. We had a Holden station wagon, bought on an interest-free loan from the church. Everything we owned was slung on, in or around this vehicle, including a weighty and sizeable library. It was so loaded down that the springs straightened. We set off.

We had three flats on the way down south, each of which had to be mended, costing more money. Foolishly I picked a route which took us down Bulli Pass near the coast of New South Wales. It was so steep it had run-off escape paths for cars and trucks whose brakes couldn't cope. I had to sit on the brakes the whole way down this canyon. The brake linings wore down to the metal and the brake fluid boiled. I didn't realize this until we reached the flat and began sailing through a town. As someone crossed the road in front of us, I jammed on the brakes. Nothing happened. We just kept going, missing the pedestrian by inches.

We could find no one who would fix the brakes on credit, so we limped the last stage into Victoria, rolling up outside our first-ever home, with nothing but a loaf of bread and half a pound of butter. I wasn't due any money for a fortnight and we had no idea how we were going to manage.

Dog tired, hungry and depressed, I walked up the veranda steps. There was a handwritten sign pinned to the screen door. It said, 'Welcome home'.

Neither of us was prepared for the surprise that met us when we opened the door and looked into our new kitchen. These wonderful people had filled the fridge with food and the cupboards with every item we could possibly need. There was milk and bread, meat and vegetables, scouring pads and toilet rolls. They even somehow managed to pick Glena's favourite tea. Our weariness and gloom just disappeared. We felt loved, cared-for and wanted. It was a genuine expression of Jesus' love — a demonstration of his commandment to love your neighbour as yourself. And for us it meant a real homecoming. Just sometimes there are deeper issues than radical or conservative political theories. Sometimes you just want evidence that you are loved.

We only shared the lives of these generous country people for a couple of years, but they have left a deep impression. Their constancy was a background against which my mind began to shift direction in a major reassessment of almost everything I believed. If that shift hadn't taken place, I would have remained a prim bigot in a business suit, inappropriately responding to the troubles of the world.

CHAPTER EIGHT

We had two children at once — and they weren't twins. Within the week after we returned from our honeymoon and settled into Glen Forbes, our family went up by 100 per cent. For their privacy, we'll call them Martin and Greg.

Martin was coming on twelve and his brother Greg was fourteen. They were the sons of Australian missionaries to New Guinea. Their parents were away in the remote, jungle regions of New Guinea and felt the kids should be sent back to Australia as the New Guinea jungle culture was probably inappropriate for their early adolescence. So Martin and Greg needed a home, and we felt able to give them one.

On reflection it probably wasn't the wisest move for a couple of raw newly-weds who'd spent much of the last three years at arm's length and needed time to set their marriage on an even keel. Their arrival placed a few extra pressures on us that we could probably have done without. For example, our house was old and noisy. You didn't have to move much to make the place creak. You can imagine what it must have been like for two shy young lovers in the early days of their marriage, to realize that when they made love, the whole house shouted the story loud and clear. It was pretty inhibiting, I can tell you.

On top of that, I was teaching thirty periods of English and history a week at Wonthaggi High and at the same time pastoring three churches, which could mean delivering up to six messages a week, as well as pastoral visiting.

Still, they were beaut kids and we grew to be good mates. They had their fair share of problems, as any kids that age do. Plus a few more because they were probably feeling a bit unsettled away from Mum and Dad. But they came through it pretty well. We had a few hiccups at school (they went to Wonthaggi too). They took great delight in telling their school pals lurid tales of New Guinea women breastfeeding pigs, together with other bizarre jungle anecdotes. I was once hauled up before the school principal to answer for their behaviour. But what kid in a strange place wouldn't want to find some way of impressing his new circle of friends?

We had some good times together, hunting rabbits for the pot and exploring the local countryside. I was back in Gippsland again, only a few miles east of my old haunts. The house was not only old, it was also on the primitive side. There was no such thing as a flush toilet, only the old chemical dunny out in the yard. Apart from the smell and the flies, the worst thing about these cans was the fact that you had to empty them regularly. This was usually my job, at least in theory.

I can remember one occasion — and I'm sure it wasn't that rare — when Glena got fed up with pestering me to empty the thing and decided to do the job herself. She got on her gumboots, went outside and manhandled the can to a place beyond the yard fence. There she took a shovel and dug a hole to bury the stuff. Glena was always ready to pitch in. She'd have made a great pioneer in the days of the old West.

What I didn't realize was that she had chosen to bury it on the other side of the fence, just at the place where the boys and I would leap over on our way to go rabbiting. Neither did I realize that in her hurry to get rid of the toilet's contents, she had only dug a shallow hole and covered it with turf. A day or so later I spotted some rabbits and legged it after them. I took the fence in one stride and landed — or rather, sank — up to my knees!

Glena has more romantic memories of that house than I have. It was beautifully situated, on top of a hill, overlooking the rolling countryside around. But its age gave us a few problems. The wood had warped so much over the years that the whole place seemed out of true. You could shut and lock all doors and there would still be room for a grown cat to enter. And if a cat could get in, it was no problem for rats.

Our first child, Paul, was born in 1969, the second year we were at Glen Forbes. And his birth coincided with a plague of rats. There had been a story in the newspapers of a child in Tasmania who'd been badly mauled and chewed by a rat. As these things go, the newspapers began a spate of rat-scare stories. They frightened us rigid. Glena went to Cowes, a town on Phillip Island just offshore from where we were living, to have the baby. Knowing he was soon due to come home I had to do something about the vermin.

I think I caught thirteen rats in forty-eight hours. The grandaddy of them all I captured in the bathroom the night before Paul came home. I heard the trap go off at about five in the morning, but that wasn't the end of the noise. The thing went on scrambling around in the bath until I got up around eight. I was horrified to see this monstrous, scungy creature, still able to jump around after three hours in the trap. I put it out of its misery.

We continued to set traps long after we brought Paul home. We put his bassinet next to our bed and every nocturnal creak convinced us that some relation of that animal was coming back to attack our baby.

The church people continued to be as warm and generous as ever, bringing us beans, pumpkins, tomatoes, fruit — most of it home-grown. In our first year they gave us the entire harvest festival display.

It was a bit of a cultural backwater, and the church people were generally even more old-fashioned than the community. They held these wonderful Friday night fellowships when toddlers, teenagers, young singles, parents and grandparents would gather to sing, hear people perform religious songs, recite poems and drink the inevitable cups of tea. It felt like a cosy extended family, wrapped up from the world outside.

This had its good and its bad side. It meant that the bond between these people was strong. They were able to support one another and draw strength from the group. But on the other hand, there was a barrier between themselves and the reality of normal Australian life. The Christians caricatured the 'sinners' as leading lives full of smoking, drinking, gambling and general depravity, while the pagans dismissed the church people as a bunch of self-righteous, killjoy, teetotal, hymn-singers.

The people I pastored, by and large, had no understanding and no real involvement with the day-to-day life of the community — except for those who joined the tennis club, and even that was suspect. They used the church to hold the world at bay. I'm afraid to say I encouraged them to do so.

For instance, I thought pop music was positively anti-Christian and I'd discourage teenagers from listening to it. I felt it was unhealthy and unspiritual. I understood enough to know that it was body music and that it made you want to dance. I wasn't by any means sure that the body was a good thing. I felt it needed to be kept in very firm check.

So when kids decided to become Christians at youth camps or meetings I led, I would get them to burn their record collections as a way of turning their backs on their sinful past. At the time I thought this was the right approach. Christians needed to be holy and separate from the rest of the world. But I was driving a wedge more firmly between them and their schoolmates.

What I didn't realize was that this attitude made it hard for them to keep in touch with what was going on in the world, and therefore all the more difficult to communicate properly with people whose lives were so totally different. Slowly I began to recognize this as a serious problem.

A lot of the kids who came to the church, or who were part of the youth activities I was involved in, also attended Wonthaggi High. My students during the week were sometimes my congregation on Sunday. Some of them would bring me questions and problems which they were struggling with at school. Others were simply confused by what they heard at school but could never articulate what they felt. Yet nothing

I said to them seemed to help resolve their uncertainties. I was out of touch.

Wonthaggi High School wasn't the kind of place for a teacher to build a career in, so it had a high proportion of young staff who'd teach there a while before moving on to more prestigious establishments elsewhere. Most of these young teachers were recent graduates of Melbourne's Monash University.

Monash at the time was a hot-bed of sixties radicalism. They pioneered the introduction of more modern literature to the English syllabus, so that the kids were beginning to deal with the ideas of writers such as the French existentialist Albert Camus. His philosophy caught exactly the spirit of the times. The underlying theme of his work was that questions of right or wrong were irrelevant. What was more important was that each individual should find his own authentic way of acting in the world. What you did was right, if it was right for you.

There were a significant number of the staff who not only held to this point of view but expounded it in the classroom. Their pupils had little defence. This is one of the big questions facing education. Literature isn't simply literature, it is the voice of individuals who have something to say about who we are and where we come from. In this case adolescent boys and girls were reading stuff by men and women who were in anguish in a post-God world. These writers were now looking for some means of finding their way in the world when all the old signposts that once gave guidance to our civilization had gone. Kids need more than academic analysis to make any real sense of such ideas.

Several teachers believed that they had no responsibility whatsoever to provide either moral guidance or example for the children in their care. They had no absolute standards themselves, and saw no reason to pretend otherwise. Such integrity is fine, but they did not remain neutral. If they had any moral duty, they felt, it was to destroy 'outmoded' and 'reactionary' ideas.

109

I saw children put under pressures that they never should have been subjected to, simply out of the intellectual arrogance of young teachers. One senior student in the school, a popular figure and a genuinely nice kid from a fairly conventional background, fled the classroom in tears one day. She had been made to read aloud an obscene poem under the guise of broadening her mind. She protested, but the teacher, who was the one with the power, wouldn't let her off the hook. The poor kid got half-way through the poem before she broke down and ran from the room.

The teacher's comment in the staff-room afterwards on this educational exercise was to say, 'Gee, I really fixed up that prude.'

Incidents like this were fortunately rare. But there was a distinct sense that certain attitudes were OK, and that others were fair game for attack. This caused confusion and perplexity, particularly among youngsters whose parents were Christians or who were Christians themselves. They would come to my church where I would tell them it was ungodly not to believe, and that they must have faith. But that didn't give them any intellectual armoury to fight back with, and before long I began to realize it was because I didn't have any defence myself.

As you can guess, a Methodist minister with strong fundamentalist principles and far-right political views wasn't going to be a popular guy in the staff-room. There were certainly a few exchanges. One woman in particular, Marge, gave me a really hard time. She went out of her way to try and shock this wet-behind-the-ears pastor. She had the habit of letting rip a string of obscenities when I entered the staff-room in order to declare her antagonism to what I stood for.

I can't mention Marge without adding a small footnote. Many years later I was preaching in a Baptist church and was amazed to see her in the congregation. Since leaving the school, life hadn't been easy for her. Marriage break-up and kids on drugs had taken their toll. Eventually, she had been

110

able to see beyond her understandable bitterness and anger, and had found a warm, life-transforming faith.

The Vietnam War was raging all the while I was teaching at Wonthaggi, and it was a central issue of debate in the staff-room. At that stage I was in favour of American involvement in South-East Asia, because I felt it was strategic to stop the 'communist surge'. My hero Richard Nixon was elected president of the United States in 1969 while I was teaching. My support for Nixon wasn't widely shared, to say the least.

The staff-room was a long, narrow affair with small desks where teachers kept books and marked papers. I strolled in one day to find a group of my colleagues clustered together at the far end of the room. They all looked up expectantly when I came in; it was obvious that they'd been waiting for my arrival.

One of the group, a keen intellectual with the mandatory beard and lengthened hair of the counter-culture, had a Bible open in his hand. He turned to me with an expression of mock seriousness and said in a pious, clerical tone, 'Ah, John, we've just been reading the Good Book.' He motioned to the Bible which lay open in his hands.

'And we're just a bit concerned about something it says. Now, obviously, we want to submit to the wisdom of the Word of the Lord.' There was no mistaking his sarcasm.

'We've been reading some of the words of Jesus and I understand he's kind of Top Dog in the Cabinet with you guys. Is that right?'

I tried a wry grin, because I knew I was in for a grilling about my beliefs.

The group's spokesman continued, stabbing his finger at the pages in front of him. 'Jesus says here, "Blessed are the peacemakers".'

He paused significantly and then added, as if musing to himself, 'I wonder where that puts your friend Tricky Dicky in South Vietnam.'

I couldn't find a reply. That's not to say I didn't respond in some way to the jibe. I usually could. What I mean is, I couldn't find a reply that satisfied me. I don't remember what I said. But I do remember the question hitting home and the conviction that I needed to find a real answer.

I began to say to myself, 'If I don't like what they're doing with the verse, "Blessed are the peacemakers", then what do I do with it that's better?' It was a crucial incident; a turning-point. This piece of innocent point-scoring by a colleague made me seriously re-evaluate what I believed. It made me look again at what the Bible said about the things I'd been challenged over by my colleagues: war and peace, wealth and poverty, black and white, men and women.

I turned to the Gospels: Matthew, Mark, Luke and John. I'd always assumed I knew all about Jesus and what he had to say. I'd read it enough. But this time I wanted to get to grips with it. As I read Jesus again, I discovered just how much he referred to the prophets. So I turned to the prophets, those battling, courageous characters of the Old Testament like Amos, Isaiah and Jeremiah, who didn't mind telling the governments of the day what was wrong with them. The whole exercise was a complete revelation to me.

It dawned on me that Jesus had extremely radical things to say to his generation and to ours. He called us to compassion and justice. The prophets said the same thing. The more I read, the more I realized that the tradition I'd steeped myself in, and which prided itself on being biblical, wasn't necessarily biblical at all. This disturbed me deeply.

That particular staff-room conversation wasn't the sole influence which made me rethink so many of my attitudes. Just as my earlier loss of faith developed over a confused period of months, so this time of re-evaluation was stretched over a period of time — in this case, years rather than months. Nevertheless, it was a pivotal point around which many other factors turned.

As a result, what I saw on the TV news and read in the press began to distress me. I watched Mayor Daley's police beat up peaceful protesters at the 1968 Chicago Democratic

Convention. I discovered that the FBI (whom I had thought of as a kind of secular arm of Christianity, the task force whose job was to protect the family of every home-loving American) was busy gathering dirt on private citizens. Next came the CIA, whom I saw as the last bastion against the communist threat. I learned to my horror that they too were less than squeaky clean. The Rockefeller Commission exposed the reality that CIA and KGB played the same game. Any lie, any violation of constitutionally elected government, any murder, any intrigue which would further the ideology of either group was and is legitimized and pursued.

The incident at Mai Lai during the Vietnamese war shook me to the core. This was the case where a marine sergeant gave orders for his men to gun down in cold blood a group of women and children. The sergeant's comment in court when his inhumanity was pointed out to him was, 'It was no big deal, sir.'

Despite my support for the war and my pro-American feelings, I recognized it *was* a big deal. No amount of counter-argument about how the Vietcong had used small children with explosives strapped to their bodies to blow up soldiers could justify this kind of brutality.

I realized that I had been prepared to sanction evil in order to protect what I thought to be good. Then I re-read passages in the Bible like the one in the Book of Romans which asks, 'Shall I do evil that good may abound?' It devastated me. 'God forbid' was St Paul's answer to his question.

The startling pictures in *Life* magazine shook me just as much as they did the rest of the world. The first was of a Vietcong prisoner taken at the moment of his summary execution by a marine with a handgun. The second famous picture of a small naked screaming girl fleeing with her body wrapped in burning napalm was inconsistent with any interpretation of Jesus immortal words: 'Even the heathen love those who love them in return . . . but I say unto you, love your enemies, do good to those who persecute you.'

I began to ask questions I should have asked myself a long while before. How could I give my assent to treating people the Bible teaches us are our neighbours as if they are less than human? And how could I support the pouring of burning tar indiscriminately over women and children?

All this was a million miles from the Spirit of Christ, and it gradually made me shift position. It wasn't so much a change from right to left as a move away from the narrow, closely-defined picture of the world that my beliefs had trapped me in. My left-wing colleagues at school taught me to ask many of the right questions. Despite my argumentativeness, I had been too accepting of the status quo. I could now see that the world needed changing at every level. Personal conversion wasn't enough. The structures and patterns of society needed to be transformed, too.

I drew strength from the account in the Gospels of Jesus charging into the Temple at Jerusalem and turning over the tables of the money-changers and traders. I had never really understood why he did it. I knew there were two ways of looking at the incident. My evangelical tradition said Jesus threw everyone out because the place had become ungodly and they weren't holding enough prayer meetings. People from a more liberal wing of the church would say he did so because they were perpetuating an unjust economic system and the poor people were getting ripped off.

Jesus referred on that occasion to the prophet Jeremiah. The people of the prophet's day were treating the Temple as a symbol of their own glory and power. To them, it was a religious, sanctimonious, safe club. A retreat from the reality of a sinful world — a den for thieves to hide away in. Ali Baba's cave of security. It became clear to me that Jesus cleared the Temple because his contemporaries were using it in the same way. Jesus was declaring, by his actions, that the Temple ought to have been the house of prayer, where people were humble before God. It should be a place where people can begin to understand that God is a God of both love and justice. Far from being a place of security, it should be a place where we are disturbed and challenged by the yawning gap between the nature of God and the nature of society.

Christianity for me had been a cosy escape. I should have realized that something was wrong, not only in Vietnam, but right there in the culture I had been part of for a quarter of a century. But it was as if I and so many other Christians had deliberately chosen not to listen to the people who could tell us what was really going on in our generation. I think we were all a bit frightened of what we might find out.

By now the sixties were coming to an end. It had been a decade when there had been an unparalleled explosion of music, art, literature and protest. It was an age of freedom and questioning like we had never experienced before. Yet it had passed me by. I was going to make sure it wasn't going to get any further past.

Having been challenged by my colleagues and found wanting, I was now determined that if my faith meant anything, then it had to have something to say about now. Jesus had shown me that the gospel was urgent, upsetting stuff, simultaneously political, social and personal. What's more, it was about change. The Bible was no longer a hitching-post, but a signpost directing me on to a compassionate reality.

On Karl Marx's gravestone in London are written these words: 'The philosophers have only interpreted the world in various ways; the point is to change it.' With a growing sense of excitement I was beginning to realize that Marx was right. The world needs transforming. But the desire to change the world existed long before Marx.

CHAPTER NINE

It was 1969, the year of the Woodstock Festival. Several hundred thousand people turned up at a farm in New York State to see some of the biggest names in rock perform in the open air. Woodstock was heralded as three days of love and peace, the great expression of the alternative hippie culture. This festival was going to show America how the world ought to be. If you look at the movie made about the festival, you can see a whole generation of blokes with shoulder-length hair and girls in long, india-print dresses. People had broken out, or so they thought, of the stifling conventions of dress and behaviour adopted by their parents.

Back in Australia, John Smith could be found in his sombre suit, his sober tie and with his carefully trimmed hair slicked down with hair cream.

I had, as I've described, been going through a long re-examination process, during which I even became a closet agnostic for a time. But you'd never have known it. Outwardly I was the archetypal straight and was to remain so for some while. All the changes that went on were happening inside my head.

I taught at Wonthaggi for two years all told, and though I felt under fire from the staff, I liked working with the kids. I was still an inexperienced teacher, though, and I made some classic mistakes. On one occasion I dreamed up what I thought was a stunning idea. I got each student in my three classes to write a novel during the course of one term.

It worked reasonably well, the novels progressed and they produced some pretty original ideas. What I hadn't anticipated was that, with roughly forty kids in each class, I was going to end up with 120 novels to read and mark at the end of term. I spent nights ploughing through the things. What with my already heavy church load, it was a fairly dumb idea. I can thank God for a fortunate capacity to survive for long periods on four hours or so per night!

Because I liked kids, especially teenagers, I had for some while been involved in taking Christian youth meetings and speaking at weekend and summer camps. Mostly I would deliver a fairly uncomplicated, 'you're all sinners and you need to be saved' kind of message. I was able to communicate with kids who had some church background and knew what I was on about. Quite a number of the teenagers I worked with became Christians. I was becoming known, in a small way, as a youth evangelist.

It was probably for that reason that I was asked in 1969 to join the staff of an evangelistic organization called Campaigners for Christ. Campaigners was an organization with similar aims to those of the set-up my Grandfather had worked for. It had been a frontier organization after World War II, providing fellowship, coffee and speak-easy Christian contexts for returned service personnel. It wasn't connected to any particular church and employed a number of evangelists from various Protestant, usually non-conformist, traditions. It acted as a kind of service ministry for local churches who wanted people who were able to present the claims of Christianity clearly, to work for a short period on their behalf in their locality.

It was a change of life and a change of pace for me. For the first time, I was a full-time evangelist, although I had no church to look after. At first, I served a kind of apprenticeship to another Smith, Graham. He was Campaigners' chief evangelist and executive director. Graham was a likeable, friendly bloke. Unlike myself, he was extremely disciplined and knew how to pace himself so that he didn't run himself into the ground. Yet he managed to pack in a tremendous amount of work. I learned a great deal from him both in the techniques of preaching and from his personal commitment in serving God.

I was to work with Campaigners for two and a bit years and in the early days I learned on the job. We used to hold many evangelistic rallies. These were fairly conventional Christian meetings with everyone sat in rows in front of a platform. We would start off by singing hymns or short Christian songs, known in the business as choruses. It was my job to act as compère. I'd get the singing going as enthusiastically as I could, with much vigorous arm waving — a bit like Sir Malcolm Sargent on speed!

Before long I was given my own responsibilities, mostly with youngsters. I'd lead and speak at youth rallies (the same as adult rallies, except the singing was a bit louder) and I'd take lunch-time sessions in high schools, working with the groups of Christian kids already meeting in the schools.

Campaigners HQ was in the centre of Melbourne, so Glena, Paul and I had to move to the city. Our house in Glen Forbes had been church property, so we had to set about buying our own place. It wasn't easy. We had very little money saved up and I wasn't earning enough to support a large mortgage. But Glena's Mum — a widow of course, and hardly flush — sent us some money by post. That was remarkable in itself, because she had no way of knowing how much we needed, or how soon. But something prompted her to send us a cheque which exactly made up the difference needed to meet the deposit.

We bought a house in Boronia, an eastern suburb of Melbourne not far from the Dandenong Hills. It wasn't the country, but it had a hilly view which made the place seem less claustrophobic and there were plenty of trees around. It soon felt like home, even more so when our second child, Kathy, was born in 1971. We've lived there ever since.

I'd been with Campaigners for about a year when I was asked to lead a Crusade in Mount Isa, in the far north of Queensland. It was a big opportunity because I was the last-minute replacement for a well-known evangelist — John

118

Robinson. He was unable to take it on, some other people had declined and they'd worked their way down to me. This was my first crusade. And crusades (as anyone who knows about mass evangelism will tell you) are the business. The evangelist is the person people come to hear and it's dangerously good for the ego. That crusade turned out to be another 'turning point' in my life.

To tell you the truth, if it had been up to me, I wouldn't have picked Mount Isa for my rookie performance in the crusade arena. It was a tough assignment. Mount Isa used to be the Australian equivalent of the Foreign Legion. It was precisely the sort of place I'd dreamed of escaping to when things had gone so wrong for me at teachers' college.

Copper, lead and zinc were mined there and if you were willing to put up with the scorching heat and to work hard, you could make good money. If your marriage had split up and you had heavy alimony payments to make, Mount Isa was the place to make the money fast and live as you liked. That year it was claimed people drank more gallons of beer in this part of Queensland than they put petrol in their cars. The folks of Mount Isa tended to be cynical, hard, often bitter, and not at all interested in religion.

In this respect, they reflected their uncompromising surroundings. It was semi-arid desert country. The dusty soil ranged from a deep red-brown to yellow ochre. The ground was flat and extended for miles, under a great slab of blue sky, to where the horizon was bordered by the dark, sharp serrations of the Razorback mountain ranges.

I've rarely been anywhere hotter. Up in the ranges the large reservoir which supplied the town's water dropped several inches a day simply from evaporation. It was a curious experience on a belting hot day to plunge in for a swim. The water was as cold as ice because of the speed of evaporation.

Because the expiration rate in this part of the country is so great, you could pluck gum leaves from a tree and within a couple of hours crush them to powder in your hands.

Not all the hazards were natural. Sulphur was used extensively in copper production and the fumes of the stuff would rise up from the plants around Mount Isa. In the areas where the prevailing winds blew these gases across the land, it was almost completely barren. The people I was staying with on one occasion were watering their garden with a sprinkler when an unusual gust of wind blew sulphur fumes across the yard. The vapour combined with the water to form a mild, localized acid rain which burnt the leaves of the tomato plants in the garden quite severely. Sensitive plants, like sensitive souls, didn't last long in Mount Isa.

But despite the toughness of the people, the genuine Australian spirit of mateship could be seen at its best here. The individuals were rugged, but they would stick by a mate when times got hard. There's an appealing line in Paul Hogan's film *Crocodile Dundee* when the innocent Okker, straight from the outback, finds himself in New York City and discovers that many people have their own analyst. He reacts in genuine surprise, exclaiming, 'Haven't they got any mates?'

In places like Mount Isa, if you've got a problem, you talk to your mates, or you talk to the barmaid in the pub. You know that over a couple of beers you can usually find a sympathetic ear and it makes all the difference.

There were two other members of the team on this crusade, Richie Gunston and Fred Strong. They gave me a really hard time, for which I'm eternally grateful.

Richie was huge in those days. He had an enormous stomach which made his shirt bulge hammock-like over his low-slung belt buckle. And he'd use his weight like a stand-up comedian. He would hold his stomach in both hands and with some offhand comment, heave it onto the lectern. It was all pretty crude stuff, but out there in northern Queensland he had people roaring. He had a very slang, rootsy style, spiced with a broad, earthy humour which was much appreciated in the outback. And what's more, he yodelled.

Richie would play guitar and sing Country and Western style gospel numbers. He had been a circus manager before he was converted, and to this day has an uncanny rapport with carnies and other travelling entertainers. Country and Western is big news in Australia's rural areas, so Richie went down well in this department. And his yodelling was something to be heard. In the fifties he'd won the 'Australian Amateur Hour', a nationwide radio talent competition.

I thoroughly disapproved of Richie. I found his whole style offensive. I thought he was irreverent and superficial in his approach. And I frankly couldn't see any way that yodelling could be honouring to God. But you had to love his genuine Aussie mateship and incorrigible humour.

Fred Strong wasn't so bad in my eyes, but not by much. He sang classic sacred songs in an almost operatic baritone. I could hardly object to that. It was his shirts that had me worried. I would never preach anywhere without a suit jacket and tie knotted to the neck. I felt I would have been letting God down if I did anything different. I couldn't fault Fred on his suits or ties either, they were admirably dull, as far as I recall. But he had, for my strict tastes, an unbelievably lurid selection of shirts. Red, yellow, bright blue, orange. It was all too immoderate for words. I'd grown up in the belief that people with moustaches were showing off, men with beards were revolutionaries and that anyone with a bright shirt must be an egotist.

In order to get over my discomfort at being on the same platform with this dandy, I used to make jokes about him. I'd say corny things like, 'I've been wondering all my life where the sunset went at night. But I was looking at Fred's shirts in his wardrobe this morning, and now I know.'

Anything to distance myself from them and to make it obvious that I didn't approve. It only made me feel a little bit better.

Here was I, determined to make a good show in my first crusade and I was saddled with these two clowns. Things got quite tense. I, in my usual humble and self-effacing way, told them where they were wrong. This didn't go down well. In retrospect they were kinder than they could have been, considering my self-righteous assumption of moral superiority. All the same, they didn't let me get away with it.

Richie, in particular, pinned me down about how uptight I was. He made me see that here in Mount Isa we weren't talking to the usual crusade-meetings crowd. In most places where a church decides to have some kind of mission, the people who attend come because they've had some previous church contact. Here I was for the first time talking about Christianity to people who'd scarcely ever been in a church in their lives. Their whole attitude to Christianity was different. You couldn't use the same words because they wouldn't understand church jargon. Neither could they be expected to sit down and listen for long periods of time to anything boring; they weren't used to it.

Reluctantly, I had to admit that Richie wasn't doing anything out of self-indulgence or for effect. The plain fact was that he could communicate to this audience better than I ever could. He showed them that Christians needn't be part of some alien species. He was what we Aussies call 'fair dinkum'. Genuine. I realized that I wasn't.

It wasn't that I didn't love people. I did, but I all too easily saw them as lost souls who needed to be saved, rather than hurt and broken people who needed to be made whole. The first approach meant that you were inclined to count up your converts like notches on a gun, on the 'another sinner bites the dust' principle. I needed to see them as real people, to identify with them in their joy and in their pain.

After this, I loosened up a bit. I made a real effort to understand where the people were coming from. By the time we left, quite a large number had shifted significantly from unbelief to belief. In the history of church initiatives in Mount Isa, this was progress. Though I can take little credit for that.

Working with Campaigners was a very fruitful period in my

life. I was learning new lessons all the time. But it was also personally very unsettling. I was still going through the process of looking at everything I believed under my own microscope, measuring it against the Bible and generally subjecting it to rigorous analysis. I felt confused and unsure of myself.

My experience in Wonthaggi had shown me clearly that I was in a cultural backwater which I had cut out for myself. I didn't understand the way most kids felt or why. I was only dimly aware of the music they were listening to, or the stuff they were reading. But I had only picked that up by reading through the pages of magazines like *Newsweek*. I had never gone out of my way to try to understand them for myself.

I was culturally ignorant, too. I don't mean I didn't know who Beethoven was; it was more the case of not knowing why the Beatles were such heroes, why blokes were going around with long hair, why people smoked dope and why so many of them seemed to prefer the East to the West. In short, I didn't understand my own generation. I was, despite the political re-adjustments I'd been making, still operating in a distinctly different culture.

My mates on the Mount Isa crusade had shown me that I'd confused some of the issues. For example, my objection to Fred's shirts was because I had decided that being a Christian meant you had to be a certain kind of person, conforming to certain standards of 'respectable' appearance. I was annoyed at Richie because I had decided that my faith could only be communicated in certain conventionally approved ways. I had confused culture with Christianity. I had made the mistake Christians often do, of turning Christianity into a set of cultural rules.

So, if it was wrong to confuse Christian beliefs with the way I dressed or talked, was there a right way to make them fit? Around this time I came across an American Christian thinker called Francis Schaeffer. His books like *The God who is There* and *The Church at the End of the Twentieth Century* helped me a great deal. He encouraged me as I developed a new way of thinking, by showing clearly how important thinkers from Plato onwards had shaped the way we think, and as a result, the way we act.

I started to see that the actions of people around me (the radical of the new left, the atheist scientist, the peace-loving hippie, the get-rich-quick businessman, and the clock-watching worker) all had their own identifiable reasons behind the way they acted. They weren't simply random, sinful practices by lost souls. Somewhere, even if they couldn't have explained it in words, their way of life was rooted in the way they looked at the world.

For example, if you believe, as a Marxist does, that we are in the grip of destructive historical forces, then you're going to be committed in all you do to affect and change those forces. If you believe, as a lot of hippies did, that people are basically good and that given freedom and a good environment they will inevitably turn the world into a better place, then you work towards individual freedom and peaceful change.

I gradually realized that if I was able to tell where people were coming from, then I could understand them better and therefore I could talk to them more easily.

Even more significantly, I discovered that Christianity itself was more than a set of spiritual beliefs. At the core of the Bible's message is the fact that this is God's world. He conceived and made it, and he continues to be concerned about every single aspect of it.

As God's creatures, we should be deeply concerned with the created world too. Art and literature, politics and economics, science and technology, work and play — even sexuality — are free for us to explore with a Christian mind.

This was an important discovery for me. From that point on, my understanding broadened until I was able to accept that Christianity had a coherent philosophy, a system of thought that made sense. I began to find phrases in my head like, 'reasonable faith'. I could recognize that there was a mystery in life that went beyond mere rationalism, but I could also see that there was a sense and order to the world which suggested the whole thing wasn't an accident.

This thinking was yet another spur to make me look hard at the Bible again. I was constantly reading and re-reading sections of the Bible during this period, because I was keen to discover basic Christian principles that would give a framework for action in all these different areas of life.

The whole process opened my eyes as well as my mind. I had already started reading much more widely. I had confined myself to reading conservative theology and Christian biography for quite some time. But since Wonthaggi I had begun to devour a much more varied diet: philosophy, literature, political theory, science, art history, sociology and biography. Now I was looking at people. Einstein, Sartre, Camus, Hesse, Tolstoy, Gandhi, Martin Luther King, Dostoevsky, Nietzsche, Biko, Bob Dylan, Boesak, Ellul, Germaine Greer, Susan Brownmiller — and a host of others, became of interest to me. But then so did Peter and Tony and Anne and Karen, and a thousand other real human beings with no status or official significance.

Mount Isa had been my first real experience of speaking consistently to people who would normally be beyond the reach of the church. In subsequent missions and meetings I began to notice just how few real outsiders were present. If you looked at the young blokes out in the streets, most of them wore their hair long. Inside the church, or church-run programmes, there was hardly a long hair in sight. I wasn't talking to the right people. That worried me continually.

All my rethinking had begun to make me more and more aware that here was a generation who were searching for something. The children born after World War II had turned their backs on what their parents believed, and they were looking for something to replace it.

But the one place they didn't seem to be looking was the church. Christianity was part of the established order which had to be discarded. I believed passionately that they had never really given it a decent trial. I was excited as never before with the message I had to offer. Here was something that was culturally relevant, that could really tackle the issues they were concerned about. Yet they wouldn't come near the church, so I couldn't tell them. I felt I had to do something about it.

As I wrestled with this, ideas and experiences from my past began to surface. Things began to drop into place. The conviction began to grow that these outsiders were the people I should really be talking and listening to. After all, Jesus didn't say, '*Come*, all you sinners into the church to hear the good news.' Instead, he said, '*Go*, my disciples, into all the world to proclaim the gospel.'

This sense of mission has a history which I should sketch in. It's a bit difficult to explain because it includes a spiritual experience I had when I was in my early twenties. Personal experiences of God aren't easy to describe at the best of times. But it did happen, and it had a direct bearing on what happened next, so I'll give it a try.

Shortly after I returned to my faith, I had been reading through the Acts of the Apostles, the section in the New Testament which deals with the history of the early church. I was struck by the power and conviction with which the early Christians preached their message and how responsive people had been, thousands at a time changing their ways and pledging allegiance to Jesus as the Son of God, despite indescribable oppression and persecution under successive Roman regimes.

My experience of preaching was completely different. I'd gather together a bunch of material that I wanted to talk about, but I always managed to stuff it up. I wasn't clear in what I had to say, and I wasn't convincing either. Yet inside I was so utterly convinced that Jesus could answer people's problems that I wanted more than anything to be able to convey this with conviction. I longed for the Spirit of God to use my words to get through to those who were searching for him. I was so desperate for this to happen that I would sometimes ride my bike out into the countryside in the early morning. There I would throw myself down on a carpet of gum leaves and hammer the ground in urgent prayer to God.

A short while later, I was praying one night when I had an experience of God that amounted to a personal revolution. It was as if I was an empty jug and God poured the essence of his love and character into me, filling me to the brim. I can't prove it, but it was real to me. It was a special encounter with him which many other Christians have experienced, often described as being 'filled with the Holy Spirit'.

Prayer became a completely different phenomenon from that point on; I felt more able to come into God's presence. I found worship more fulfilling and more real.

Some time later, I realized that my preaching had turned a corner, too. Without any particular improvement in technique, people began to respond to what I had to say. I also seemed to be more attuned to the inexplicable nudges that Christians refer to when we say God 'talks' to us or guides us.

It was in answer to one of these divine nudges that, some weeks later, I entered a house I didn't know, only to find a group of Christians praying. As I walked in, one of the group announced that he believed he had a message from God for someone present. Again I can't prove it was a message from God, or that I was the one he was referring to, but I felt as though the man was speaking directly to me. And one of the things he said was that I would become 'an apostle to the Gentiles, not to the Jews'.

What did it mean? Well, St Paul was an apostle to the Gentiles, literally. He believed his responsibility was not to bring the message of Jesus to God's people, the Jews, but to preach to those outside their religious community. The people the Jews referred to as Gentiles. Untouchables, undesirables, even outcasts.

For me, it meant that God was expecting me to take his love and truth not to those already influenced by the church, but to the people outside it.

127

About eight years later, I was praying with a completely different group of people, when another individual repeated the same words.

So, whatever you make of these experiences, you'll understand why, when it came home to me that I was preaching primarily to church kids, I began to make the connections. I felt God was nudging me yet again.

Everything I'd been through seemed to come to a head at this point: all the heartache, the rediscovery of God's forgiveness, the gradual process of radicalization, and my understanding that Christianity could be worked out in the culture as well as the pulpit. Now there were to be some more visible changes. I decided to come out of the closet and start finding out what the 'Gentiles' were all about.

I began listening to the music of my generation. And found I liked it. I didn't find it disgusting, or demonic or any of the half-a-dozen terrible labels rock'n'roll has been stuck with. On the contrary, it was refreshing and gutsy. Not only that, but it was angry, it protested — about injustice, about war and about the rape of the land. I discovered Bob Dylan for the first time. His song 'Masters of War' in which he rages with his cracked, expressive voice against the warmongers who are destroying lives, while sat safe in their offices, affected me deeply. How strange that Graham Nash, rather than the official followers of Jesus, was asking, 'Is the money you make worth the price that you pay when you hang out your soul on the line?'

I found in the music of the late sixties and early seventies a new and exciting world that taught me so much about the feelings of a generation in search of their own identity. I felt suddenly very much on their side. I wanted to identify with the people, many of whom were trying to find answers to the ultimate questions of the Universe and looking quite genuinely for a meaning behind it all.

I began to look for opportunities to talk to street kids. As I grew closer to them and I identified with them more, so I stopped shaving and neglected to go for my regular trim. I became hairier by the day. This was no trendy vicar gimmick. I wasn't trying to be accepted. There no longer seemed any reason to pursue the respectability I once thought was so important. It didn't mean anything any more. A suit was no longer appropriate, so that went as well and I developed a taste for dramatic and rather tasteless floral shirts. The change couldn't have been more shocking.

This obviously had its effect on Glena. She'd married a politically straight and theologically conservative dude who was on his way to being a nice young Methodist minister out in the sticks. This was the man who, at Bible college, had refused to go to one particular meeting because they had a folk group playing. Whose idea of getting through to street kids was to play them Christian choruses on a piano accordion.

Now she was faced with this wild-eyed hairy radical whose sermons were beginning to touch more and more on politics and social issues. He was grooving on Bob Dylan and Crosby Stills Nash & Young, reading Timothy Leary and wearing Levis. It was no wonder she said to me in tears one day, 'I don't even know who you are any more. You're not the same man I married. It's not that I don't believe in you or that I doubt you. I just don't understand the changes.'

In fact, I was the same old John Smith. But I'd been used to sorting out my thinking alone. We had some catching up to do. It turned out that Glena had been heading in the same direction as me but she was just taking a different route. Our marriage has always been like that; we develop separately as people and in our personal relationship with God, and then we have to catch up with one another. It's just as well we did agree with one another over this new approach, because there were many times during what followed, when it felt as though there was only the two of us.

CHAPTER TEN

As I grew hairier, my public statements got a bit wilder. To the church I must have looked like a rebel. And I suppose I was. I began to sound more political, stressing the need for the church to get involved in social issues and to demand justice for those who didn't have the power to demand it for themselves.

Someone once said that where you stand determines what you see. If you stand on a mountain top you get a totally different perspective than you would if you were in the valley below. The kind of place in society that you choose for yourself, or that is chosen for you, colours your view of almost everything. So if you decide to stand alongside those who are poor, who are outcasts, or on the fringes of society, you will read the headlines in the newspapers with different eyes. You will form your opinion of what's going on quite differently from those who have wealth and influence.

I discovered this to be true. Having decided to put myself out to make contact with people who the church didn't traditionally reach, I began to look at the world differently. For example, I had some involvement with a Christian coffee shop in a place called Frankston. Here, in a very short space of time, I met as many weird and wonderful people as I'd come across in my whole life before.

Frankston is a coastal resort, an outer suburb of Melbourne. The venue was called the 'Drift In' Coffee Shop. It was run by a group of local Christians who wanted to provide a place where anyone who had nowhere else to go could hang out. It also gave the people running the place the opportunity of talking to their customers and sharing their faith with them.

Hippies, bikers, street kids and all sorts would descend on the coffee shop, most of them equipped with an honest spirit of enquiry, and a readiness to grapple with the big questions of the Universe. We would often have raging debates about war, peace, life, death, faith and the meaning of everything lasting into the early hours of the morning.

I went to the coffee shop, not only to tell people about the difference believing in Jesus Christ could make to their lives, but also to find out what they had to say. A well-known Australian cynic, a journalist by the name of Max Harris once wrote, 'Christians are a dim, ego-tripping minority which is dead set on telling everybody why they ought to become Christians, instead of finding out why they aren't.' When I read that I thought, with God's help I'm going to meet that challenge. So I started listening to these people, instead of just talking — not always an easy thing for me.

I was constantly refreshed, and sometimes embarrassed by the straightforwardness of their attitudes, especially towards the church. I took one of these guys to church with me one day and I'll never forget it.

Jimmy was a biker who'd strolled into the coffee shop one night. People had got into conversation with him and he kept coming back. He was a pretty wild looking bloke. His jeans were covered in grease and his T-shirt didn't look a lot more savoury. He had a reckless mane of dark hair and a look which spelled aggression.

He didn't seem like a candidate for conversion to Christianity, but one night, after we'd spent some time together, he decided to make a personal commitment to follow Christ. It was an utterly genuine and unforced decision which he took in complete sincerity.

A short while later, he came to me to ask me some questions about things he'd been reading in the Bible. He had looked at the account in the book of Acts where an Ethiopian diplomat, following a conversation with the apostle Philip, asked to be baptized immediately after his conversion. Philip saw no reason against this and baptized him

131

in the nearest water deep enough for the job.

Jimmy faced me with the same question. 'John,' he asked, 'why shouldn't I be baptized?' Baptism, I should point out, has since Bible times been an act in which people have declared their commitment to Jesus Christ. The earliest tradition was to dip people completely under water. This expresses visually the idea of burying your past and being raised up again to new life. It is also a picture of Jesus' own death and resurrection. In many churches it has become an initiation rite into the membership of the congregation.

But Jimmy was not a member of any church and was linked with no denomination. Baptizing him could get me into all sorts of trouble with church authorities. But as he said, 'I've become a Christian. I'm fair dinkum about it. I don't know any churches. You showed me the way to Christ, so I want you to baptize me.'

In the end I couldn't see any biblical or logical reason why I shouldn't. So I baptized him in the ocean. Inevitably, people in more traditional church circles got to hear about it and I was rapped over the knuckles for it. But I still think I did the right thing.

It was after this that I took Jimmy to church. We went to a communion service in a small and very traditional church and his straightforwardness taught me an embarrassing lesson. Jimmy couldn't have looked more out of place among the grey suits and the flowery hats that Sunday morning. He felt uncomfortable too, in what was a totally new environment to him.

The service was long and slow. The hymns were dull and mournful. Jimmy shifted restlessly. The longer the meeting went on, the more his leather jacket creaked. Finally it was time for communion. It was the practice of this church to pass the bread around to each person and to do the same with the wine. Both were deliberately passed to me, ignoring him. I passed it back to him.

All was fine until the silver goblet reached Jimmy. He took a healthy swig and an expression of something close to pain crossed his face. Spluttering and coughing he passed the cup on, rose to his feet and strode out of the small plain room by a side door. Every eye followed him and then turned to fix its gaze on me.

But my mortification wasn't over. Jimmy stuck his head back round the door and started making elaborate gestures for me to join him. It was obvious that he wasn't going to stop, so I rose and joined him, flushed in the face at the spectacle I was making of myself.

I could see that Jimmy was agitated, and he didn't leave me guessing for long as to why. In a fierce whisper he rasped, 'Jesus rose from the dead, right?'

'Yes, that's right.'

'Isn't this the day when you celebrate that?'

'Yes.'

'Ain't that something to be happy about?'

'Yes, it is.'

'Well, I've never watched such a miserable bunch of dudes in my whole life!'

I saw his point. But Jimmy hadn't finished.

'And that wine! I thought I'd drunk everything there was to drink. But that must be the worst stuff ever. If those guys respect Jesus, how come they remember him with cheap junk like that?'

Suddenly I saw this kind of church service with new eyes. It had always been home territory for me, a place of comfort with familiar vocabulary and traditions I had grown up with since a boy. I had been tasting the sweet, non-alcoholic cordial of the Methodists and the cheap port of the Brethren assemblies and Anglicans that passed for communion wine for so long I had never given a thought to how someone else might react to it.

Now I could see that through Jimmy's eyes it looked an eccentric and peculiar gathering of people muttering to themselves in a private gloom, before chewing bread and sipping juice.

It was a valuable lesson. It taught me that if I am ever to

133

invite people without a church background into a place of worship I am responsible for, I must make sure they're not alienated by obscure words or practices. It is so easy for people to feel unwanted or the odd one out.

As my paths led me more and more to meeting people outside the confines of normal church activities and buildings, I began to meet people who didn't feel simply rejected by the church (in fact, the church has a better record than most in taking on people who no one else will give time to). They just felt rejected, period. I began to see how the people at the bottom of the pile found it tough going in a world where you are nothing unless you are successful.

I grew up with the idea that in the West, everyone had the chance to make something of their lives. That if you ended up poor, it was your own fault. Poverty was the result of either extravagance or laziness. I had no notion of just how difficult it could be for someone without educational or family background to know how to make our society's system work for them. The more I met people who felt voiceless and powerless, the more I began to see life from their point of view. In the words of the old song, I look at life from both sides now. As I began to identify with their problems and needs, I began to make connections with my own past that I had never made before.

The themes of Victor Hugo's book *Les Miserables*, which I had read as a kid, came alive to me once more. I realized that this was more than a book which tugged the heart-strings, it was about what can happen if you give hope to someone whom the world has consigned to the rubbish heap. Jean Valjean in that story was sent to prison because he stole a loaf of bread to feed his starving family. At the root of his crime was a poverty he couldn't be blamed for.

I also recalled an incident which happened to me while I was at Bible college. I used to play the piano accordion. I had a beautiful Scandelli accordion, with mother of pearl inlays and it was my pride and joy. I left it one day on the seat of a borrowed car and a thief managed to get the door open and steal it. I was furious and was keen that justice should be done.

Within twenty-four hours the police caught the thief, a young Greek boy. When the case came to court, the boy's social worker was called as a witness in his defence. I was disturbed and moved by what he had to say.

The boy lived in a poor district which adjoined the wealthy suburb where the college was situated and where the car was parked. His family were recent immigrants and neither the boy nor his parents could speak English. They still owed a great deal of money on their air tickets from Greece, but had been unable to find work. The whole family lived in one barely-furnished room in a block of shabby flats, where they slept on the floor.

Here was a kid whose family had no money at all, a stranger in a strange land who found that only streets from his squalid home lived people whose affluence he could only dream about. Seeing an expensive and highly saleable musical instrument in a car that was easy to get into must have posed an irresistible temptation.

I was stunned by this tale and felt deeply sorry for the kid but didn't know what to do about it. I'd like to say that I rushed around, helped the family sort out their problems and put them on their feet. But I didn't. I just felt bad.

Just after I graduated from teachers' college, I came across a situation that was positively Dickensian in its injustice. Even then, in the midst of my most right-wing period, it enraged me.

I was living in Chinchilla, Queensland at the time, and since I had a few months to spare between graduation and starting to teach, I took a job as a jackaroo on a large sheep station not far away. A jackaroo is simply a hired hand employed to play a part in the normal sheep-herding, sheep-dipping, fence-mending exercises of these sometimes vast acreages.

This sheep station was owned by the Scottish Australian

135

Company, a large company run by a manager who lived on the property with his family. When I first started work there, I ate, as was normal, in the mess with the rest of the guys. But when the manager found out I was a minister's son, I was invited to eat with the family up at the station, with all the silverware and the bone china. They thought it was improper for someone whose father had status to eat with the men. I stuck it for a couple of days, but in all conscience I couldn't accept this false division of status and asked if I could eat with the rest of the blokes.

In any case I could see that the other guys would give me a hard time of it, if I hob-nobbed with the boss instead of mucking in with everyone else. They took the mickey out of me enough as it was. I was twenty-one, but a pretty raw recruit in some ways. I admitted I'd never ridden before, so, of course, they put me on a horse with a mouth like iron. They told me it liked to chase kangaroos, and sure enough it did. We surprised a roo in the bush one day and with just a nudge, my mount set off after it at a terrific gallop. I lost a stirrup immediately and was carried, wobbling all over the place, way off into the bush. The horse was totally out of control. We went for miles, with me clinging on for dear life, completely lost.

I looked around to check my bearings, when I suddenly saw this old gum tree rushing towards us with a low branch hanging down just ready to sweep me off the horse's back. I lay down flat with my head in its mane and narrowly avoided decapitation. The animal kept pounding along, dodging between the trees until it slowed to a halt, exhausted.

A few of the guys had witnessed the start of this terrifying ride and I was the butt of a few jokes that evening. But it was good experience; and I came through it all right. Aussie blokes give the green-horn a rough time, but if you tough it out with good humour, the mateship that develops is deep and lasting.

There was another young jackaroo, a kind of junior, living and working on the station. He was an orphan, a lonely kind

136

of bloke. Someone had befriended him before he'd come to work at the place, and that Christmas they sent him a puppy. He loved that dog, it was just the kind of loyal companion he needed.

But the well-fed station manager would hear nothing of it. 'You'll have to get rid of that mongrel,' he told the youngster. 'We've got enough mouths to feed around this place without worrying about an extra dog.'

The station manager lived extremely well, with a house and furniture provided by the station. The addition of one small dog that would have meant so much to this lonely individual would have made no significant difference at all. It was a cruel and unthinking decision and the kid was heart-broken.

I was enraged at the injustice of this. It was the first time I had experienced someone with power using their authority with what appeared to me to be complete indifference over someone who was in no position to defend himself. Once again, I kept my feelings to myself. I didn't think it appropriate to express them. It wouldn't be the same now.

Incidents like these, and my early reading, all started to connect and add up. I began to observe how our society, like most affluent societies in the West, stacks the odds in favour of those who already have, so that they can get even more: 'The rich get richer and the poor get poorer'. Later, after much work in prisons across the land, I came to an even more tragic conclusion: that the rich get richer, but the poor get prison. At first it was just a feeling, a gut anger at what was going on. My message only started to develop an edge when I began to make the links between my feeling that such inequality was wrong and biblical evidence that God said it was wrong.

It would be inaccurate to say that all the things the Bible says about rich and poor and their response to one another became clear to me at that time. But I did discover many of the principles of God's teaching about poverty and justice in those years of the late sixties and early seventies.

I found in the prophets of the Old Testament — those often cantankerous men who went roaring about Palestine giving 'what for' to whoever deserved it — a rich vein of social justice. Isaiah was just such a man. In the fifty-eighth chapter of his prophecy he says that God wants the people of Israel to know that they're the worst kind of religious hypocrites. It's all very well them worshipping like crazy, doing every kind of ritual imaginable, but God says, 'At the same time as you fast, you pursue your own interests and oppress your workers. Your fasting makes you violent, and you quarrel and fight. Do you think this kind of fasting will make me listen to your prayers? When you fast, you make yourself suffer; you bow your heads like a blade of grass, and spread out sackcloth and ashes to lie on. Is that what you call fasting? Do you think I will be pleased with that?

'The kind of fasting I want is this: Remove the chains of oppression and the yoke of injustice, and let the oppressed go free. Share your food with the hungry and open your homes to the homeless poor.'

These words cut close to the bone in all sorts of ways. They speak to our world just as much as to the Israelites, especially when Isaiah starts to talk about the homeless. He doesn't say build special housing projects or hostels. He says, 'open your homes.' That means give the poor what you would expect for yourself and don't treat your home as your castle.

Isaiah continues to quote God's words, 'If you put an end to oppression, to every gesture of contempt, and to every evil word; if you give food to the hungry and satisfy those who are in need, then the darkness around you will turn to the brightness of noon.' In a world where the flaunting of material prosperity is itself 'a gesture of contempt', the Bible has a relevance to the way we live which is hard to deny.

I saw in passages like these — and there are many — a kind of charter for a real concern for and commitment to those people who are pushed to the fringes of society, those who sociologists called the marginalized — those who are pushed out into the margins. From that period on I became concerned not only to speak to the educated, but also to those who felt that they had been left behind and had nothing to hope for. I believe that it is to people like these, the unemployed, the unglamorous and the unacceptable, that the gospel of Jesus Christ has the most to offer.

In the evangelical tradition of the twentieth century from which I come, and to which I remain loyal because of its commitment to the essential truths of biblical faith, such notions of social justice have often been treated with suspicion. It smacks too much of politics and of a preoccupation with this world rather than the next, a diversion from the real business of getting people saved.

It is obvious that I don't agree. I certainly believe people are separated from God, that we need to come to terms with him and that means facing up to the fact that we have done wrong. I recognize that this involves coming to God, acknowledging our own wrongdoings and accepting that, through his life and death, Jesus Christ has offered us a way to get back in touch. Our ultimate personal hope is to humbly place ourselves at God's disposal.

But this is not just some spiritual experience or exercise. We must return to God because in that is the only route to a genuine wholeness, the unity of mind, body and spirit that God intended us to enjoy when he made us. But that encompasses a wholeness in social terms too. Genuine salvation (being saved) results in people working to make the world whole too — 'Thy will be done on Earth as it is in Heaven'. It means a mending of our personal relationships and a resolve to fight against all the forces which would pull us apart.

There's a remark that Jesus made which has been used as an excuse for doing nothing about the injustices in societies. He was eating a meal in a friend's house shortly before he was to die, when a woman broke open an extremely expensive bottle of perfume and anointed Jesus' feet and wiped them with her hair. Some of his disciples (especially Judas, the group's treasurer, who was later to betray him for thirty pieces of silver) were annoyed at this extravagance. They said, 'This perfume could have been sold for a large amount and the money given to the poor.'

Jesus replied, 'You will always have poor people with you, but you will not always have me with you.'

This remark sounds callous on the surface, but Jesus was not talking about social justice. He was making a quite different point. He was saying, there's nothing wrong with being extravagant, or going to great personal cost in an act of love and worship to God. In fact, Jesus was quoting from the Old Testament book of Deuteronomy, in a section on the social and economic laws to be observed by the people of Israel. The passage Jesus referred to starts by saying, 'Not one of your people will be poor if you obey (God) and carefully observe everything that I command you today.' Among the laws he alluded to was one which instructed, 'Do not charge interest on a loan to a poor person.' But later, in a very human understanding of the way things work out in reality, the Old Testament writer continued, 'There will always be some Israelites who are poor and in need, and so I command you to be generous to them'.

In other words, if they obeyed God's commands, which demanded fairness and generosity, it was possible to eliminate poverty. The passage implies that poverty in Israel was a direct result of their failure to live by those principles. This puts what Jesus had to say in a new light and makes sense of Jesus' own total commitment to the sick, poor and rejected people of his own day. It warns that poverty is not simply personal in its cause. It is structural. Unjust social structures institutionalize poverty and powerlessness. Many people fear words like these, seeing them as communist beliefs. In fact, whether they were believed by Marx or not, they certainly were believed by Moses, Jeremiah, Amos and James.

In the context of our own day, this means that we don't have to accept poverty and injustice as inevitable. It is, at least in part, a result of the break-down in society and our own abandonment of the biblical principles of justice, truth and mercy.

I've always liked the way William Temple, Archbishop of Canterbury before World War II, brought this home. He said, 'Jesus didn't die in a cathedral between two candles, but on a cross between two thieves, on a town garbage heap, in a place so cosmopolitan they had to write his title in several languages.'

This is where the church needs to be, too. If, as Jesus claimed in the Sermon on the Mount, his followers were to be 'light for the whole world', then it makes sense for that light to be spread where there is 'darkness'. Light drives away darkness. You don't invite the darkness to the light, you invade the darkness with the light.

Coffee shops were only one way of talking to people who wouldn't normally come to church. I started to explore other possibilities. In doing so I found myself in the vanguard of something called the 'Jesus movement'.

The Jesus movement first emerged in America during the late sixties and early seventies. It grew not so much out of, but as a response to, the developing alternative lifestyle which characterized that period. There was a new spirit abroad among this generation of young people. They wanted to kick out the values of materialism and competition which they felt were fostered by the establishment. They rejected what they thought were sour and repressive moral codes and opted instead for freedom of thought, sex, creativity and experience.

It was the age of 'sex, drugs and rock'n'roll'. While this is a glib description, all three played an important part in the proceedings. Free love was a key phrase. Marijuana and LSD were the two drugs most frequently used; they were given almost mystical status at the time because of their supposed ability to 'expand the mind' and 'heighten awareness'. Rock music acted as both background atmosphere and as a voice for that whole generation, providing anthems and poetry which encapsulated the vision.

The church, alongside the state, technology and industry, were part of the package which was discarded by the counter-culture. It wasn't that the youth of this era had rejected religious experience. It was desperately searching for some authentic meaning behind the Universe, unpolluted by association with the unfashionable past. This pilgrimage was to lead many to explore the religions of the Far East and the magic of the ancient world. The church was not an option. It was generally felt to have sold its birthright to the established order and lost its right to speak.

Despite this understandable rejection of the traditional church, there were still hippies, freaks and people with counter-culture connections who became Christians. Naturally, they wanted to share their new-found faith with their own generation, so they began to explore different means of communication that would convey what they believed, without the stigma of old-style church.

This was how the Jesus movement was born. In the image of the long-haired Jesus, scourge of the establishment, they found a perfect and appropriate hero. Preaching Jesus, rather than the church, led to the setting up of all sorts of alternative church structures, many of them communally based. Jesus rock music developed to express their feeling.

It wasn't difficult as even the Doobie Brothers were singing, 'Jesus is just all right with me'. A number of significant performers were converted at that time, in contrast to the growing number of suicides and drug-related deaths of such rock geniuses as Janis Joplin and Jimi Hendrix and far too many others. Barry McGuire, angry counter-culture protester of 'Eve of Destruction' fame, became and remains to this day a stunning convert to hope and Christian love. Leon Patillo, lead singer of Santana, Chuck Girard and the very fine guitarist, Phil Keaggy, and later on Little Richard and Bob Dylan, became enamoured by the vision of Jesus, though the status of belief of the latter

142

two has been less clear than the others. The Jesus movement also used the hip jargon of the streets and produced hundreds of Jesus papers, modelled on the many underground papers which were such a feature of the times.

I was slow to understand all this. But once I woke up, things started moving fast. As I started meeting more and more hippie kids, I discovered also that they were very responsive to Jesus, his life and what he had to say if this could be demonstrated in a contemporary way. I discovered that when they were shown clearly what Christianity really was, shaken loose of the culture that surrounded church, they found it a genuinely alternative and attractive lifestyle. They had a real hunger for spiritual answers to their many questions. Many of these people became Christians.

I began to correspond with communities and groups of Jesus people in the States. I made particular links with a group in Spokane, Washington and another, known as the Christian World Liberation Front, working in the radical university suburb of Berkeley, California. They produced a sharp, culturally relevant magazine called *Right On*. I learned a lot from their various approaches and also gathered together scores of Jesus papers to see how they communicated their ideas in this form.

I wasn't alone in Australia, either. Not only did I find many like-minded people in my locality with whom I could work, I discovered others who were coming to the same conclusion about how to communicate the message of Jesus to the hippie culture. John Hirt, a radically-minded Baptist minister in the city of Sydney, had started up a place called the House of the New World which was attracting a host of street people.

Nearer home, Kevin Smith and John U'ren were working with a traditional evangelical organization called Scripture Union in Melbourne. They were revolutionizing its approach to meet the needs of this new generation, launching a series of coffee shops called 'Theos', that were very successful in putting Christianity back on the streets. They also established

143

an excellent underground-type Jesus paper called *Theos Son*.

About the same time I decided, with a bunch of mates, that it was time to start our own paper. In 1971, in co-operation with the group in Washington, we produced our first edition under the modest title, *Truth*.

It was self-consciously hard-hitting and alternative. We published issue one in time for Christmas. The front cover featured an image of the crucified Christ, with the headline, 'Happy Birthday, Jesus'. It caused quite a stir in the Christian community. But more importantly, it made people look hard at what the birth of Jesus really heralded. We printed something like 5,000 copies and gave them away free in the streets. The paper included interviews with people who had become Christians, analysis of the world situation from a Christian point of view, and a clear statement of the claims of Christianity in street language.

All this was done while I was still employed as a youth evangelist by Campaigners for Christ. Our relationship became a little strained. I no longer looked or sounded like the person they had taken on two years before. I don't think I made it easy for them either, because in my new-found radicalism I tended to be very blunt in putting across my opinions. And that included my communication with my bosses. I wasn't always as gracious as I could have been.

Things came to a head in the early months of 1972. It was a hot summer and we had just discovered that Glena was pregnant with our third child, Lyndal. The news media were full of the Sunbury pop festival, to be held just north of Melbourne in January. It was being described as Australia's Woodstock and thousands were expected to attend.

I was due some leave and decided to go, with Glena and some others, and check out the festival. We intended to give out copies of *Truth* and talk to people about what we believed. There was some resistance to this idea by some of the executive of the organization, who understood there would be nudity and drugs at the festival and questioned whether it was appropriate for a Christian minister to be seen there. We argued the point. I was convinced it was exactly where I should be. And anyway, I pointed out, I was taking my own holiday time to do it. We went. Why was it legitimate, I asked, to show slides in church of naked black folk in foreign mission situations, yet forbid mission among hip naked kids. Were they racists (black breasts are safe, but white ones are salacious)?

Glena was feeling lousy from a bad bout of morning sickness, but she gamely struggled into her first pair of jeans (we were still in the process of catching up with one another) and set off for Sunbury.

It was an extraordinary experience. There must have been in excess of 40,000 people there for that sun-baked weekend. It started out, as Woodstock had just over two years earlier, with a great sense of optimism and destiny. There was a feeling that this generation could change the world for the better. We sang in those days, 'We can change the world, rearrange the world'. By the end of the weekend, there was just a collection of tired, grubby people; some hungover or coming down off trips, some feeling sexually used; others wondering if they were pregnant. And all of them sitting in a garbage heap of empty beer cans and discarded food wrappers. The dawning of a new age didn't seem quite so imminent in that context.

It was a memorable weekend for both Glena and I. There are all sorts of cameos that still stick in my memory. I was queuing up at one of the public phone booths and the girl in front of me was speaking to her mother. She couldn't have been any more than fourteen and she was being constantly pawed by a lecherous, older guy. She was calmly telling her mum that she was down at the coast, staying over with her friend's auntie, reassuring her that she was safe and all was OK.

I also vividly remember a young girl dancing wildly in solo oblivion, drugged out of her skull. She was watched closely by two predatory males who, when she finally fell to the ground, leaped on her and used her up. They were like dogs.

There was a memorable set from the main stage by the Australian singer, Billy Thorpe. During one of his songs he let rip a great string of obscenities in a scream of rage which seemed to last a good five minutes. He successfully invited the mostly tripping crowd to shout the obscenities with him in a kind of communal rebellion against the old world and its values. A few minutes later, in his gravelly voice, he launched into 'Somewhere Over the Rainbow'. The childish song of sweet romance seemed to touch a naïve chord in this hopeful, but in so many ways hopeless, audience. Strangely, this sweet song seemed to extract the most enthusiastic response of all.

We got into hundreds of conversations during the weekend, many of them open and searching. One I particularly remember took place in the early hours of one morning. A group of newly-liberated young men and women were discussing the issue of abortion. They were arguing that abortions should be made legal as it was an issue of personal freedom. Suddenly one girl in the group burst out, 'It's all right for you bastards to talk like that. I've had three abortions and I know what a mess it's made of me!'

There was a river running through the Sunbury site and once again there were people who wanted to be baptized. They felt that this was the place where they could best serve notice to their contemporaries that a change had taken place in their lives.

I didn't do the baptizing myself this time, but I was in the thick of things and spoke to the crowd. It was a remarkable scene. These people were standing up to their knees in the muddy, slow-moving river, while naked and semi-naked people who had earlier been skinny-dipping, lounged around on the banks and made off-the-cuff remarks at us all.

One of those being baptized was a guy who had been part of an outlaw biker group. He had been a hard-drinking, hard-fighting reprobate, but had been personally transformed through his encounter with Jesus Christ. After he had been pulled out of the water, he stood in mid-stream and

146

told, in a simple and direct way, exactly what the gospel of Jesus meant. The audience was silenced by his sincerity and passion. And by the fact that he didn't use religious words but language they understood. This was real communication.

For Glena, this was her first proper introduction to what had, for the last year or so, been my world. On the one hand she was shocked at the amount of drink and drugs consumed and by the completely casual attitude towards sex. But on the other hand she warmed immediately to the honesty of these people. She spent hours in conversation with different groups and individuals. She was struck, too, by the sheer numbers of kids who had only the vaguest sense of direction in their lives and no real belief or framework to live by. She sat on the side of the hill reading her Bible and came across some words in the book of the prophet Joel which seemed to sum up everything we had experienced that weekend.

Tears streaming down her face, she showed me what she had been reading. It said, 'Multitudes, multitudes in the valley of decision'.

She looked across this sea of people and said, 'John, here they are. But where is the church?' Glena, by her own route, had come to the same conclusion as me. We both understood why we were there. Because the church plainly wasn't. True, the good old Salvation Army were dispensing free cool drinks with their customary gift of showing love in a practical way. And John U'ren and Kevin Smith were there with a group helping them. But that was it. The Christian representation among this vast crowd was minimal. Glena and I both knew we were in the right place.

I returned from Sunbury, stunned by the experience, but excited at the same time. Sunbury had shown me that there were people who were prepared to listen to what Christians had to say, if only we were prepared to go and meet them on their turf. There was a lot that could and should be done.

When I arrived back at work at Campaigners after my holiday break, I was called into the office. I was told that, after an executive meeting, it was decided there wasn't any future in our relationship. I had to go. There is really no point in rehashing the rights and wrongs of what went on between us. Simply to say that it was agreed that I should leave Campaigners that day, but that I would be given three months pay and the loan of a car for that period.

As always in these situations there are different ways of looking at it, depending on which side you are on. My father, for instance, thinks I pushed them into it and that they were generous in their settlement. I admit that I had been abrasive and that I was pushing my ministry in a new direction. Certainly they needn't have given me more than a month's pay, and the use of a car was a magnanimous gesture. Nevertheless, I was sacked. The church's responses are often remarkably like corporation responses.

I returned home knowing that Glena and I were on our own. It was a lonely feeling. What would happen after the money ran out? I have never felt so vulnerable and unsure of myself. I had come back with such high hopes of making a real impact on the people the church wasn't reaching. And now it looked as though the whole dream was about to be shattered.

Who ever heard of a sacked evangelist? With arms around each other, we wept by the kitchen sink, acutely aware of two little children and a third newly formed within Glena. In a sense, more than one pregnancy and future birth had occurred. A whole new ministry was being born.

CHAPTER ELEVEN

I needn't have worried. I should, I suppose, have had more confidence that if God had set me off on this track he would give me the opportunity and resources to follow it through. He did, but we had a few dodgy moments on the way.

We had some immediate difficulties to face. We already had the second edition of the paper pasted up and ready to go, but no money to get it printed. I could have used some of the three months' salary from Campaigners, but I'd given an undertaking that I would only use the money for myself and my family. We needed $450.

Glena said, 'I believe God's with us in this, go ahead and publish it. You won't have to pay the bill for a month.' But I wasn't so sure. I had absolutely no support from any outside source which could finance either the paper or anything else. And in 1972, $450 was a lot of money. But Glena was firm. She made me send it to the printers.

Later that same day, two cheques arrived in the post. They exactly covered the amount we needed. They came from two anonymous Adelaide University students who knew nothing of our circumstances, but just felt they ought to send us some money. It was stunning.

The paper duly came out, but under a different title. A lawyer friend had warned us that we ought to change because there was an existing Melbourne tabloid daily paper of the same name. It could lead to litigation if we weren't careful. We were reluctant to change the name because even though there'd been just the one edition, we'd had hundreds of letters and many requests to republish. To change the title could be confusing at the very least.

Then one day, Glena and I were reading the Bible when we came across that simple but beautiful statement by Jesus, 'You will know the truth and the truth will liberate you (set you free).' Now, the word 'liberation' was very big at the time, both in revolutionary and Christian movements. Since liberation meant freedom, we decided to change the paper's name to *Truth and Liberation*. We needed a name to call the trust we had to set up to receive any funds we were sent for my ministry. And so struck were we by the concept, that we decided to call ourselves Truth and Liberation Concern, or TLC, 'Tender, Loving Care'. It might sound a bit dated by now, but it meant a great deal to us at the time. (We now work separately under the name Care and Communication Concern. The original organization has continued with a more local suburban ministry. None of the current leadership there were with us at the founding of the paper or the name.)

I wasn't left idle either. I received a lot of invitations to visit high schools, to speak at universities and other Christian gatherings. But once the three months' pay had run out we had no regular income. I was given some welcome help from a man called David Cummings who was Director of Wycliffe Bible Translators, in sorting out my finances and setting up the trust. But it took a while before funds came in.

There was one fortnight when we received just one dollar. We started eating our way through the contents of our cupboards. It was getting scary. On the way to speak at a high school, I stopped by the side of the road and prayed, 'God, I don't care if I have to eat grass, but I can't expect my family to do that. Please do something. Show me this isn't some mad venture of my own, but that you're with me — that this is right.'

When I got home, Glena met me at the door with a big smile. She was holding a fat envelope in her hand. It had been dropped in earlier that day by a group of Christian students from Monash University. Knowing how little students had to spare, Glena said, 'I'm not going to open it,

I'm scared it will be single dollar bills'. It wasn't. They'd collected $120. It covered the month's mortgage repayment and food. It was quite amazing in its timeliness.

Although they were difficult days, I have to say they were exciting too. Glena and I found our faith and our beliefs tested almost every day in some way. But God kept smiling on us and providing for us in many remarkable ways.

Everything was done from home. Glena not only looked after the two children but acted as a super-efficient secretary and book-keeper. Her days as a legal secretary were not wasted. She enjoyed the involvement, but it took its toll.

For quite understandable reasons, the children began to object to the amount of time their Mum had to spend on the phone. At one stage we were receiving more than thirty calls a day on our home phone — some of them complicated, desperate and lengthy. If the phone rang, the kids would create merry hell, getting into cupboards and generally creating mayhem. It was bedlam. But we survived.

Things must have begun to look up after a while, because I was able to buy my first motorcycle, a Honda 500cc four cylinder. I can tell you, it wasn't a decision I came to lightly.

I can date my interest in the bike scene back to the time when I was working for Campaigners. I was driving on the main route that takes you north-west out of Melbourne towards my old childhood haunt of Bendigo. I was mid-way through my shift from straight to radical at the time — orthodox on the outside but beginning to get concerned about the people on the fringe.

As I drove along, I passed a sizeable bunch of rough-looking bikers parked by the side of the road. They all wore the same emblem, a kind of coat of arms, on the backs of their jackets. They were obviously one of Melbourne's outlaw bike clubs. They weren't doing any harm to anyone, a few of them were tinkering about with their machines and the rest were lounging around sinking a few tinnies, but they looked pretty menacing even so.

151

Oddly I felt a surge of compassion for them. I thought to myself, here's a bunch of guys that no one will really want to know. I can't see the local vicar making much headway with people like that. I began to pray from that time that God would raise up someone who would be able to get alongside bikers and be able to show them something of the love of Christ. I never for a moment measured myself up for the job. I felt I was too straight altogether. I just hoped there would be someone around who could.

Only a short while later, I went to a Christian youth camp and met a couple involved with youth work for the Baptist church, called Eddie and Elma Pye. Eddie was British and had made something of a name for himself as a stunt motorcyclist, a sort of English Evel Knievel. He liked the way I approached kids and told me that if I really wanted to grab the attention of teenagers, then I should get myself a motorbike. In response I said, 'Eddie, if you knew anything about my accident record you'd never even think of such a thing!' But he kept up the pressure, convinced I should do something about it. He was later a valued member of God's Squad Motorcycle Club.

As time progressed I began to meet a few bikers — people like Jimmy and others. And I was able to lead a few of them to the point where they decided to become Christians. I began to get a feeling for what some of these guys were like. Despite their hard words and their hard living, they were often as vulnerable and as lost as anyone else. On top of this, the more I dug into Jesus' life, the more I was challenged by his policy of reaching out to the people no one else would talk to. He was prepared to meet with the despised tax gatherers, the inferior Samaritans and of course the ostracized lepers.

I began to ask myself who the Australian equivalent of a leper was. I reckoned it probably had to be the outlaw biker. The Hells Angel's and the many other bike clubs also formed, were both feared and loathed by conventional people. They kept the bikers at arm's length and the feeling was mutual.

All these thoughts sat at the back of my mind during 1970 and 1971. In the meantime Eddie pursuaded me to join forces with him, to make some inroads into the motorcycle subculture. Together we formed something called the Christian Motorcycle Association. A seed farmer named Norm de Vaux had a bit of spare land and offered us a paddock that we could use for dirt-track riding. So we'd hold these dirt-track meetings where kids with bikes could come and race around the track. Then we'd finish up with a barbecue under the stars. Eddie and I used these opportunities to talk to them about our faith and about their problems. These weren't outlaws by any means, but through them I began to find out just a little bit more about the bike scene.

In 1971 I was invited to speak at a large annual Christian youth event on the Gold Coast in Queensland. The Gold Coast is just outside Brisbane and is a sort of Australian equivalent to Miami Beach. When I got there I was surprised to see among the 1,000 youth delegates a bunch of guys on big motorcycles, mostly Harley Davidsons. It turned out they came from Sydney. Their leader was Paul Eddison, a really beaut guy, who had formed the club in order to get to talk to bikers. Motorcycle clubs have names, so they had to think what to call themselves. Because they are outlaws and take pride in being renegades, bike clubs have tended to choose names which stand as a challenge and an affront to more conventional thinking. The last thing they want to appear is nice. That's how the Hell's Angels chose their name. And there are many others who've carried on the tradition. In Australia, for example, there are the Devil's Henchmen, the Undertakers, Satan's Cavalry, Fuehrer's Curse, Black Uhlans, Iron Horsemen, Filthy Few, Coffin Cheaters, Immortals, Vigilantes, Outcasts, and so on.

This bunch of Christians were operating from a different point of view entirely. They wanted to meet outlaw bikers on their own terms, but they needed a name which reflected what they believed. At the time, a popular American 'hip' detective TV series called *Mod Squad* was in vogue in

Australia. A girl suggested that in line with this, *God's* Squad might be a sharp name. So the club became 'God's Squad'.

We got on famously. They sat me on the back of their big Harleys (not the front, yet) and I began to get a taste for the joys of motorcycle riding. I was impressed by their courage and their convictions and we kept in fairly close touch when I returned to Melbourne. I helped them as a pastor and they helped me understand the ins and outs of the bike scene.

Slowly the idea took shape that forming a Christian-based motorcycle club was the best possible means of making contact with the biker fraternity. The more I thought about it, the more God seemed to be saying to me that I was the one who ought to be talking to bikers. It was as if all the changes he'd been developing in me over the last few years had this purpose in mind. This was something I was destined to do.

It was, too, a question of putting my money where my mouth was. If I was convinced that Jesus' example led me to show his love to those people no one else wanted to know, and if I had identified the outlaw bike scene as just such a community, then what alternative was there? But it wasn't logic which drove me to get involved with the bike scene. It was an increasing sense of God's call which I could no longer ignore.

If you get the impression I was reluctant, then you'd be right. I wasn't drawn to bikers in the same way I was drawn to the hip and rock culture. My own spiritual pilgrimage had led me to identify strongly with the anger, confusion and aspirations of that generation. Despite their waywardness, they were often protesting against the same things I wanted to change.

Like them I had learned to hate violence, to love peace, to admire the beauty of the countryside and also the beauty of people. The counter-culture was a creative movement. It spawned music, poetry, literature and art — all of which I loved. And it had its intellectual side. Wherever you went, especially in universities, you met polemic and argument, wit and good conversation.

It had also made a dent in the myth of the macho Australian male, though looking around today, not much of one. I think masculinity has a place, but so does gentleness and sensuality. One of the gentlest and most sensual pieces of literature in the world is the Song of Solomon in the Bible. It's a beautiful piece of erotic love poetry. God isn't simply portrayed in the Bible as a figure of strength and judgment. The prophet Hosea describes him as picking his people up in his arms and holding them to his cheek like children. And of course Jesus comes off the pages of the New Testament as both strong and eternally gentle.

Personally I have always loved things which are soft to the touch: the delicacy of a baby's skin, the warm fur of animals, the quality of silk and satin. And while I enjoy the driving rhythms of rock'n'roll, I also respond to lyrical, melodic music, and even classical music. There is a quality of what might be described as femininity which men can and should discover in themselves. The traditional gruff quality of maleness often disguises an inability to deal with those entirely legitimate feelings.

The values of the bikers cut across those ideas. There were many of their attitudes I found, and still find, offensive. I wasn't attracted to their chauvinism or their tendency to violence, their devotion to a limited range of music or their philistine approach to the finer things in life. But in following the historic Jesus I felt a call to be their friend.

That might sound patronizing. It isn't. I have never seen people who wear colours and ride motorcycles as in any way inferior. I didn't get involved in the bike scene out of any Victorian sense of pity. It was really a case of them being there, and of God saying to me, 'They're people as much as anyone else. Go out there and show them you think so.'

And, as I will explain, I found among bike riders other qualities which would put many Christians to shame, especially in their loyalty and deep friendship. There is also among them a brutal honesty which demands nothing less than respect in return.

155

I should state clearly for the record that although, from this point in the story, I became involved in the outlaw biker scene, it has never been my whole life. Throughout this period I continued to work in churches, high schools, universities, colleges, at public events and on the streets with a complete spectrum of people. I still do. I have been described as a 'biker priest' and I love my brothers and sisters in the bike scene, but I don't want to misrepresent myself in any way.

Chronologically, the formation of Truth and Liberation Concern came first and my work as an evangelist and Bible teacher continued throughout this period. While I was engaged in my internal tussle about reaching people on the bike scene, I was still working from home, rushing around with prodigious energy, speaking here, there and everywhere. I was also editing *Truth and Liberation*, whose second edition had run to 10,000 copies. Things were moving at a hectic pace which has hardly diminished since.

As I travelled around speaking, I began to share my developing vision for some kind of ministry in the bike scene. Eddie Pye, who had sown that seed thought, was still right there with me, and one by one other Christians with an enthusiasm for life on two wheels introduced themselves to me. It became clear that there was in and around Melbourne a group of people who felt the same way I did and they were committed enough to do something about it. What's more, they knew a whole lot more about bikes than I did. It became clear that we had the makings of a motorcycle club of our very own. It gave me a tremendous buzz to know that I wasn't on my own in what a lot of people must have thought was a crazy scheme.

With the agreement of the Sydney God's Squad, we decided to form a Melbourne chapter of the club on somewhat expanded and reviewed lines. We could, if we'd wanted, have started an entirely separate operation. But this seemed both pointless and egotistical. The guys in Sydney had come up with the idea and name, and as far as we were

156

concerned, they were both sound. They were more than happy for us to get going, so we followed accepted motorcycle club practice and travelled to Sydney to receive from them, as the original members, the right to wear colours.

There were weaknesses in thinking and practice in the Sydney club, which eventually led to their dismantling. I gave all the support I could pastorally, but Sydney was a long way off. In many ways, our own shape was quite unique and vastly different in the way it worked.

Every bike club has its own colours or patch, sewn usually on to a denim or leather sleeveless jerkin or waistcoat, called a 'cutoff', which is worn over your leathers. The Sydney God's Squad had designed an emblem which featured a scarlet celtic cross with another, smaller black cross in the centre and the legend 'God's Squad' in gothic script around it. It was very much in keeping with bike club chic.

There were seven of us who made the trip to Sydney, and this small band of original Melbourne Squad members became known as 'the Secret Seven'. There was myself, Eddie Pye, schoolteacher Rod Hodgson, Bill Patterson, Ken Pell, Peter Kirby, and Roly Smith. Each were remarkable characters in their way, with an incredible amount of commitment to the work and a genuine love for bikers.

Roly deserves a special mention because of the toughness he showed in coming to terms with a genetic malformation which left him with only one workable foot and a withered arm, to which is attached an artificial forearm and metal claw. He still rides his eighty cubic inch Harley, adapted so that the controls are all on one side. On his left arm the metal claw grips the nearside handlebar. With the bike circuit's penchant for nicknames, Roly inevitably became known as 'Claw'.

We picked up our colours on 13 May 1972 and entered a three-month probationary period before the official launch of the Melbourne God's Squad in August of that year. We were then a club in our own right, able to add other members and award them colours without reference to Sydney. John

Smith, son of a Methodist minister, one time right-wing hardliner, was now President of God's Squad, a motorcycle outfit. It was hard to believe, especially for me.

I had bought my first bike shortly before the official launch date. A Honda 500cc four cylinder bike seems a bit tame these days when there are so many 1,000cc machines around, but in 1972 it was really quite respectable. None of us could afford a Harley and there was not then the stigma attached to Japanese bikes that there is now.

The bike was delivered to my door. I thanked the delivery man, put on my crisp new leather jacket and decided to try it out, wisely in the company of my mate, Rod Hodgson. In those days in the state of Victoria, as long as you had a provisional licence, you could hop straight on a bike as big as you liked, without any experience whatsoever. I sat astride this powerful machine at the top of the hill outside my house, feeling very ill-at-ease, only too conscious of my accident-littered past.

I gripped the handlebars, examined the bike closely and then, with a lost expression, turned to Rod in acute embarrassment.

'I know this sounds silly, mate, but where's the gear shift on this thing?' I asked. That was how much I knew about bikes. Having received my first lesson, I set off gingerly down the hill. Within twenty minutes, Rod had run into the back of me. He had been looking over his shoulder and quite unlike his usual careful style, looked forward just too late to avoid collision with my almost stationary bike.

Come to think of it, my second bike which I bought a few years later was smashed up almost before I'd gone anywhere on it. I'd ridden to Gippsland with the Squad and was sitting on my brand new Kawasaki 900, when this loony outlaw biker came roaring across the field, doing donuts. A 'donut' is when you hit the front brake and allow the back wheel to arc around in a circle, leaving a circular scar in the grass. This drongo came screaming across the paddock and did his last donut, straight into me.

I had to learn to ride quickly. A group of guys gathered around me, most of whom were experienced riders, some of them with ten or more years in the saddle. I was almost thirty years old and, while I wasn't exactly beginning to feel my age, I wasn't the young daredevil I might once have been. I didn't quite have the bravery that comes with reckless youth. But nevertheless I had enough of a sense of call to make me put up a good front for the guys I was riding with. After all, I was the President and founder of the club, and that was something to live up to.

In the bike scene, if you're the leader, then you have to lead the pack. So with gritted teeth I'd lead off, pushing myself to keep a decent pace, riding harder than I really felt was safe. In these early days, I would lean into the curves but my spirit would sit bolt upright, rigid with fear in some tight curves — especially on wet nights looking into oncoming headlights on high beam! My stomach would churn and I suffered with acid heartburn out of sheer anxiety. It was some months before I felt confident enough to take to these trips with any kind of ease.

As you can imagine, I had my fair share of falls. In biker parlance it's called dropping your bike. Well, I dropped mine a good few times, which caused a great deal of hilarity and mickey-taking from the rest of the guys. I found out later they used to call me 'Autumn Leaves', because I was always falling off. I naturally defend myself from such gross exaggerations.

But it wasn't all due to my habit of attracting disaster. The Honda Four was a real mongrel of a bike, and from the start we knew something was not right with it. The problem took a long time to diagnose, but in the end we reckoned that salt water must have got into the petrol tank forming rust residue while it was being shipped from Japan. The needles and seats in the carburettor would clog up so that fuel would spurt out of the overflow tubes, where the wind carried it onto the back wheel. As a result, if you were driving in damp conditions, the tyre would turn slick and slippery, especially treacherous

159

when you were going round curves.

Two accidents and a couple of close calls have been the result of deliberate attacks by car drivers. Wearing a back patch on a big bike certainly invites trouble from some drivers. It's a lonely trip to be run off the road, injured and bemoaning an injured bike at 2 a.m. It was a healthy experience to ride a mile, so to speak, in somebody else's boots.

I remember one particular occasion, some time later on, when we were going over the Black Spur out of Melbourne. It has some steep curves and I was riding with some of our most experienced riders, who were right up my exhaust pipe. I was not feeling too happy and, as usual, pushing myself just beyond my limits. I was aware of the bunch behind me, but was just beginning to pick up confidence, when — whooosh! — she went from under me. The back wheel lost grip and down I went. Fortunately, there was no oncoming traffic and the guys following me took evasive action.

There were a few moments like that. The worst in the early stages was on an occasion when I was due, oddly enough, to speak at a businessmen's breakfast. Although I didn't quite look the part, I was still ready to speak to anyone who wanted to hear more about what difference Jesus Christ could make to their lives. The roads were very wet and as I braked for some traffic lights, the back wheel, sprayed with petrol, slid out and failed to hold its own on the surface, and down I went in a heap. I hit the ground thumb first and drove the first joint out of its socket and back so that it stood poking out at right angles to the back of my hand.

I was taken straight to a public hospital where they stated that it needed an X-ray. I then had to wait until 2p.m. to be attended to. To me, this was another example of how people on the fringe without power and status are treated. On a later occasion when we took Lyndal to a public hospital to have her bandages removed, some time after intricate plastic surgery to her face, we had to wait from 10a.m. until 5p.m. Handcuffed criminals and ethnic migrants shared our fate also that day.

160

When the Honda Four's end came, in fairly spectacular circumstances later on, I wasn't sorry to see it go.

All this sounds as if riding a bike is purely a hazardous and hard occupation. Certainly you're vulnerable on two wheels, and wet or cold can make life pretty unpleasant. But in the warm weather, with a gentle breeze in your face, it's a fantastic way to travel.

I first sat astride a motorcycle with great fear, but despite the hazards I quickly became a convert. Nothing beats a bike for getting through traffic, and the powerful growl of my Harley is still music to my ears. Since the beginning, I graduated from Honda Four to Kawasaki 900cc Z1, to Harley Davidson 1000cc Sportster — then from a second Sportster to my current 1340cc 80 cubic inch Harley Limited Edition Heritage Softail.

But it's one thing to master the rudiments of a powerful machine, to overcome fear and learn to enjoy the experience. It's quite another to get out and earn the respect of outlaw bikers — some of the most hard-bitten men you're likely to meet in the country of Australia — or any other country, for that matter.

CHAPTER TWELVE

The news media love a novelty. And I suppose a group of mean-looking Christian bikers was kind of novel. We did appear pretty dangerous with our long hair, beards and scuffed leathers. They look striking even in blurred press photos. So we received a lot of coverage from the moment we got going — much of it good, but some of it positively dangerous.

In that first year I could probably have papered our lounge room with press cuttings. Journalists wrote stories about us in newspapers across the country. Whenever we hit town for any organized event, there'd be the obligatory interview and photo call. Everything from Australian *Vogue* magazine to major European tabloids have since then written up the story in one form or another.

Mostly this was good for us, because it put us on the map from the very beginning. This meant that people who wanted to meet us would seek us out so that we didn't always have to make the running. And by and large we've had a fair press.

But we were sometimes written up in ways that were less than helpful. The *Herald*, one of Melbourne's newspapers, did an unfortunately sensationalized piece entitled, 'God's Squad Rides to Gangland', with sub-heads like 'tough bikies get into gear with the gospel'. The journalist ended the feature by saying that although we were prepared to show love to everybody, 'This will be tested when the God's Squad meet the Hell's Angels'.

The writer probably had no idea what danger he could have been putting us into. Clubs like the Angels are very jealous of their reputation. If they think someone's trampling on their turf, or if they smell even the merest whiff of a challenge, then they take action. We weren't about to barge in on the Hell's Angels, or anyone else for that matter. We wanted to establish relationships.

Our policy first off was to establish ourselves as any bike club would. We held regular club meetings on a Monday night at our house, elected officers, rode together and tried to make ourselves generally known.

We ran into the outlaw bikers fairly early on. Elizabeth Street in Melbourne on a Saturday morning was a big scene in those days. It was the motorcycle centre for the whole of the state of Victoria. It was wall-to-wall motorcycle and spares shops. Everyone would come into town, park their bikes, buy the odd nut or bolt, hang around looking at the bikes that were for sale and generally talk motorcycle talk. Now and then someone would roar down the street between the tram tracks, doing a mono for the sheer hell of it — lifting the front of his machine off the ground and powering it along on the back wheel alone. By and large, the length of two city blocks belonged to the bikers for three hours on Saturday morning, and the cops left us alone.

There weren't just a few bikers either, there would be several hundred bikes parked around the place. Walk down Elizabeth Street on a spring day and you would see almost every kind of bike in the book, lined up diagonally to the pavement, front wheel pointing out.

Outlaw bikers have always revered the Harley Davidson, and they really caught the eye with their massive bulk and tear-drop fuel tanks. I have to agree it's the boss machine of all. Below the Harley in the pantheon of machines come the British bikes such as Triumphs, Nortons, BSAs or the rarer AJS. It's all right to be seen on them. There was a degree of tolerance for European bikes like Moto Guzzis and Ducatis, and a certain respect for the German BMW. Certain kinds of Jap bikes were reckoned to be within the pale, but this was limited to the most powerful models only.

Of late, Japanese super bikes are the vehicle for straight highway racers and tourers. Animosity towards 'jap crap' is such amongst most outlaws these days that a Japanese bike rider may be ordered to park it around the corner away from the preferred Harleys. One favourite T-Shirt caption reads — 'Japanese Motorcycle Repair Kit'. The words surround an ominous green hand grenade.

It really was the place to go if you were the least bit interested in bikes. And of course for us it was the ideal opportunity. We played it pretty cool. We're not the kind of people who'd go wandering round pestering people, handing out religious leaflets or asking them to come to church. Not that we were afraid of being beaten up, rather it would have destroyed any credibility we might have had. No one would have bothered to listen to us. I understood from the very beginning that this was one place where I had to keep my lip buttoned. We had to earn the right to speak through relationships.

So while I wasn't too afraid of taking a punch or two, I was worried we'd be ignored. And to begin with, we were held at arm's length, but that did not mean we went unnoticed. We'd walk around and mingle with the crowds, but you could see guys fix their eyes on your colours and you knew you'd been registered. Often they'd give you a look of dismissal before turning their backs. We did get laughed at and people would crack jokes at our expense, but we didn't react aggressively. We didn't wimp out either. We looked OK, which was important, and we had a couple of big, solid guys who gave us a bit of presence.

After a while, we became as much fixtures on the scene as anyone else and we found ourselves dropping into and being included in conversations, recognized as a legitimate part of the scene. It was important for those first few months just to be seen around. So we went to the places where bikers would meet, like the annual Bathurst races, rock festivals and swap meets (meetings organized to swap spare motorcycle parts). It was here that we began to meet and strike up friendships

164

with some of the characters of the bike scene. Their names were often as colourful as their personalities: Ball Bearing, Buzzard, Animal, Gorilla Snot, Bingo, Ferret and many more.

We were accepted up to a point, because we went to the places bikers were, rather than expecting them to come to us. We had good bikes and good riders. We talked a language they could understand, and while we made no secret of the fact that our values and attitudes were different, we didn't set ourselves up in order to attack them for who they were or the way they behaved. All the same, we were essentially outsiders trying to get in. We could talk to people, and earn credibility on an individual level, but as a club we weren't yet able to command real respect. We were still the new boys on the block. Then we gained a couple of important new recruits who made a big difference. The first one was Spiv.

Spiv's real name was Howard Ham, and he was a member of the Huns. If I had any preconceptions or stereotypes about the bike scene before I got involved, the Huns effectively destroyed them. These weren't a bunch of cretinous meatheads who beat up old ladies because they hadn't the brains to do anything constructive. The Huns had started life as the Melbourne University Motorcycle Club. In their early days they were simply a group of students who liked big machines and who gravitated towards one another for that reason.

But over the years — the return of a number of embittered Vietnam war vets had something to do with it — they had evolved from undergraduates looking for a few laughs, into a very hard crew indeed. In short, they turned outlaw. But they were a particularly fascinating group to talk with because they combined intelligence with an embittered, nihilistic outlook on life. One of the club members, known as Heretic, was really smart. You really had to have your shoes on to run with him in a debate. He wasn't too hot at proposing ideas, but he had a savage and incisive intelligence which could butcher your argument into small pieces and make you look an idiot.

Spiv came from a middle-class family and joined the Huns originally because of a passion for motorcycles. By the time I met him, he had long black hair, a bush of beard and constantly wore dark glasses. He was an experienced and highly-skilled rider. But with the Huns, he says, the values he'd learned from his Protestant family gradually became warped. He remembers one occasion when he ran down and seriously injured an old man, but was much more concerned about the possible damage to his beloved machine than he was about his victim.

After five years in the club, one of his closest friends lost control of his bike in a ninety-mile-an-hour run from the police, and was killed. Grieving for his friend, Howard was struck by the emptiness and futility of his own life and over a period of time found his way back to the truths of Christianity he'd learned as a child.

Having become a Christian, he started looking for a way of serving God that would enable him to share his beliefs with his old bikie mates. When he discovered us, he knew that this was what he'd been looking for. He joined the team and eventually became, for many years, Vice-President of the club.

This was a real breakthrough for us. Howard knew a lot more people on the scene than we did, and it meant that we now had a real, personal link with the outlaws. Howard had a mate in the Huns who was known as Quince. He was baptized a Roman Catholic with the name Peter O'Neill. He had joined the Huns when training to be a physical education teacher at Melbourne University. Half-way through his second year, this tall, fit young guy had a bike accident and broke his leg so badly it finished his phys.ed.prospects. When we first met him, he was limping around in callipers. After an interval studying for an arts degree at another university, he joined the civil service and became more involved with the bike scene.

The bar-hopping, party-going camaraderie of the early

days of the Huns soon degenerated into a hatred of anyone outside the circle. At the time the Huns were reputedly second only to the Hell's Angels as the hard men in the district. Peter, who was a tough, aggressive individual with a lot of presence, got sucked into the downward spiral of dehumanizing behaviour.

Howard and a number of other Squad members had conversations with him and initially found him very resistant to the idea of Christianity. Although his brother was a priest, he had reacted against the church and thought Christians were idiots. But slowly he began to realize he was dissatisfied with himself and the mask he had to wear to keep up with the Huns' group image. One night, after an argument and a few punches at the clubhouse, the hot-headed Irishman ripped off his colours and walked away from the Huns for good. He had decided he wanted to become a Christian and he joined God's Squad.

It is worth saying at this point that it is a whole lot more difficult for blokes like Howard and Peter to leave their club than it is to write down. Loyalty and brotherhood are iron principles in the bike club. To leave under any circumstances isn't easy, but to leave because you've become a follower of Jesus can earn you a lot of abuse at the very least. It took them both a great deal of courage.

Peter had class. His strength and his short temper had made him a well-known and well-respected figure among the outlaws. The fact that he, of all people, chose to throw in his lot with the Squad did us a power of good. And again, because he knew the bike scene inside out, he was to open many avenues for us to explore among the people who were his friends.

The more I met bikers and talked to people like Howard and Peter, the more I understood about outlaws and the workings of their clubs. I also began to think hard about why they choose this particular lifestyle.

I came to the conclusion that the bike scene has much

167

more to do with style and a sense of belonging, than with the simple desire to be as wicked and anti-social as possible. It is a strange mixture of 1850s wild-west gunslinging bravado and the heraldic tradition of the Middle Ages.

There's the romance of being a freewheeling pack of tough dudes, answerable to nobody but themselves, who can cause panic and disruption wherever and whenever they turn up in some strange town. Their powerful motorcycles add to this hard-riding cowboy image, as they go in search of adventure across the plains.

The heraldry of club colours gives bikers the appearance of medieval knights, mounted on their steely chargers. Ever-loyal to their coat of arms, they are prepared, at the drop of a helmet, to fight in its defence against the merest slight. The most hideous insult any biker can undergo is to have his patch ripped off, either by a rival club or in disgrace by members of his own brotherhood.

It really began in the fifties, in the post-World War II disorientation expressed in the famous movie *The Wild One* with Marlon Brando. The best-known brotherhood is the US-founded Hell's Angels, now spread around the world from Melbourne to London to Amsterdam to Auckland to San Francisco.

Motorcycle gangs began to organize themselves in much the same way as the rival street gangs had in New York and other large cities. The motorcycle gangs or clubs in Europe and in Australia picked up on the idea, and before long the familiar death's head emblem could be seen on the leathers of bikers all over the world. It must be said, however, that you or I couldn't simply start up a chapter of the Hell's Angels. Permission for the right to wear colours is jealously guarded by its sentinels in the States and is only granted by application in person. So the original members of Melbourne Hell's Angels had to travel to America before they could be established with a charter in their own right.

Similarly, dozens of other bike clubs were formed. The

Angels are a select group, because they are highly selective about their membership. They don't make it easy to join and they don't want just anybody. There are thousands of motorcycle enthusiasts with a taste for a bit of rabble-rousing, far more than could ever hope to gain entry into this most senior of bike clubs. This is not in any way to say that the other outlaw bike clubs are significantly inferior, but it must be admitted that they are almost all modelled, in some way, on the Angels.

One club in our country claims both a longer history and a bigger membership, but others would claim quality is superior to numbers. In actual fact, God's Squad, with the Sydney chapter forming in the late 1960s, may well be the longest continuous club in this country.

The clubs are known as outlaws to distinguish them from the more respectable motorcycle associations, which exist purely to act as a social focus for people who like bikes. These groups neither wear colours nor expect the same kind of priority in terms of allegiance and time.

Outlaw clubs are both tribal and military in their regime. The hierarchy is rigid and authoritarian. It is usual to have a President, a Vice-President, a Secretary and a Sergeant at Arms. These officers may occasionally be challenged, but their power within the club is not in the least nominal. They have real clout and they're quite prepared to use it.

No one who happens to ride a Yamaha 125 can expect to walk off the street and join up; there are a number of conditions and tests to be passed before they can be awarded their colours. For a start, if you want to be an outlaw biker, it stands to reason you've got to have a decent bike. If you want to join the Angels, then it has to be a Harley. Nothing less will do. The Angels are fiercely loyal to this make of superb American machinery. And when you think that a new one will set you back at least $14,000 (or £7,000), that's a fair obstacle to begin with.

The Angels also expect their recruits to have a certain kind of style. They don't look for violence or gross behaviour.

They look for a particular carriage, a massive self-assurance which commands respect and the ability to demand it if necessary.

Most clubs expect candidates for membership to serve a period of probation as a 'prospect'. This is no Sunday School picnic, either. A prospect is obliged to do whatever rotten jobs are demanded of him by any of the members — a bit like a 'fag' in the old British public school system (though suggest to anyone in an outlaw bike club that he's a fag and you probably won't live to tell the tale). Once his loyalty and readiness to submit to authority has been proven, then the prospect is initiated into full membership.

Once a member of the club, he can be sure of the undying loyalty and back-up of his brothers, for this above all is a brotherhood. His fellow members will stick up for him under any circumstances, in whatever trouble, for whatever reason. The code of 'my brother, right or wrong' is unbreakable. In return he must never allow the name of his club to be besmirched and must be prepared to return the unquestioning loyalty he has been given.

It is this bond of brotherhood, because it cuts across all other relationships, that is usually the cause of whatever inter-club trouble there is. It isn't surprising to observe that the great majority of violence on the bike scene takes place between rival groups of bikers; outsiders are seldom involved. But mostly one club will rub along pretty well with another, because they are part of the same outsider mentality and they share a great deal, both in their love of bikes and in their like-mindedness.

Firm friendships often develop between members of different clubs. But if a member of one club does something that can be regarded as offensive to a member (or even the name) of another club, then all other loyalties cease to have any significance. And if a member betrays his club or even leaves it for benign reasons, he may well be violently attacked by the very mates who yesterday promised undying mateship.

170

It's easier to put it this way. One guy in club A fancies a girl who's associated with club B and makes advances. Someone in club B finds out. That means trouble. It may be sorted out between individuals, but if it isn't, then the two tribes could go to war. For full-scale hostilities to break out, there usually has to be a more important reason than this, though people have been very seriously injured simply because there was a suspicion that one guy was involved with another club's woman. It becomes a question of honour, just as it would have in the Middle Ages.

This sense of brotherhood and belonging is absolutely central to biker philosophy, and is therefore one of the main reasons people join. What Freemasonry does for the small-town businessman, motorcycle clubs do for predominantly working class guys with a rebellious streak. I've already talked, in an earlier chapter, about the degree of loneliness and isolation there is in our society. People can't exist alone; families don't provide the bond they once did and in our fragmenting culture it is difficult for individuals to find the dependable relationships and loyalty they genuinely need.

You can work for a company for thirty years and then find you've been given the kiss-off virtually overnight. You can reveal your innermost feelings in confidence to a valued friend only to find it has been spread vindictively around your circle of acquaintances. But once you're a member of a bike club, then you've got mates who, though they may be dangerous or foolish, unthinking or cruel, are nevertheless there. You can be sure they'll watch your back.

I'm convinced that many blokes get involved in the bike scene because they need some kind of identity or self-image they can't find elsewhere. It acts both as a refuge and as a means of letting the world know you're somebody. If you feel discarded or unwanted, perhaps because you're ugly, inarticulate or just plain bad company, wearing leathers and roaring around the locality with tough mates on a big bike can do wonders for your confidence.

It can work the same way if you're weak and indecisive,

incapable of running your own life. You may have been put down and discouraged from an early age and want people to sit up and notice you for a change. If you're an outlaw biker, you certainly aren't a nobody, and if you know you're somebody special, it doesn't matter if people think you're scum or are frightened of you. Making waves gives you a much better feeling than being ignored.

By analyzing these motives, I'm certainly not trying to say that the guys who join the bike scene are a load of inadequates who couldn't cut it anywhere else. I discovered very early on that if you start generalizing or stereotyping bikers, you can go badly wrong. When we first started getting involved with outlaws, we found that one club had a young intern doctor from a local hospital in its ranks and another counted among its members the headmaster of a primary school. One of the Sydney Hell's Angels at the time was a lecturer in education at a tertiary college. Although these were exceptions to the rule, quite a number of the wild-looking guys we met were holding down perfectly respectable day jobs. People join outlaw bike clubs for a variety of personal reasons.

Neither am I trying to excuse the way outlaws live or treat one another. There have been, and continue to be, some fairly gross goings-on. The fact is, bikers tend to be an angry and anti-social bunch. They are outlaws precisely because they can't accept the shape society wants them to fit into. Their whole existence, everything they stand for, becomes an angry gesture at everyone else. As a result they have developed a way of life designed to distance themselves from polite society which they feel wants to emasculate them.

Many bikers, usually the more hard-line, anarchistic characters, who adopt an aggressively anti-social image, refer to themselves as the 'one percenters'. By this they claim they are the one in every hundred who refuse to lie down beneath the weight of pressure to be like everyone else. The attraction of the Angels, and other groups like them, is sometimes the appeal of anarchy and lawlessness. Freedom

172

is an almost religious word to them.

But free they certainly aren't. As in most all-male set-ups, there is a considerable group pressure to conform. A club member has only to step out of line and he'll get hammered. The clubs demand that the interest of the club comes before wives, children, parents or any external interests. They demand absolute commitment. And yet at the same time I have seen compassion and a commitment to their wives and kids which is stronger in evidence than in many a middle class executive's family.

When a group of red-blooded blokes get together and sink a few pints, then the temptation to act the goat becomes less easy to resist. A group mentality takes over and people attempt actions they would probably never dream of doing by themselves. That's how people get beaten up, women get raped and members of the public menaced. But this 'let's have some fun' syndrome, which nobody can back off from for fear of appearing chicken, is not peculiar to bikers. It is common in most male groups, including rugby players, soccer fans, policemen, soldiers and high-school students.

And the bike scene is essentially male and masculine. Women are treated as possessions, who come a poor second to the bikes. No woman can join an outlaw club. If she has a long-standing relationship with a member, she can wear colours which state that she is the 'property' of the club in question. Women are essentially sex objects, expected to answer to the call of their particular master whenever he wishes. There are even women known as 'onions', whose role within the club is to service any member who feels so inclined.

It is not that uncommon for a biker to have a wife and family in his 'normal' life and also to have a girlfriend who'll share his bed as part of his club lifestyle. Although there are, of course, many men who are happily and faithfully married to one wife. But the outlaw life is generally speaking a young man's game and sex tends to be treated a bit like fast food. You eat when you're hungry at the first and nearest opportunity.

Knowing this to be the case, I was surprised when I first started meeting with bikers, to see the number of women — some of them extremely good looking — who were prepared to accept this kind of treatment. It seems that despite the progress feminism has made in the last twenty years or more, there are still some women who prefer to take a submissive role and who like their men to be a bit more exciting and dangerous than the average pen-pusher.

However, it is both interesting and saddening to note that, at many biker gatherings these days, most of the women are very young. They attach themselves to the bike clubs for excitement, or maybe a sense of security or identity, and often out of rebellion against their parents. But the dismissive and often inhuman treatment they are subjected to means that they soon see the writing on the wall. They realize they are being used and that there's no future in it, so they get out.

I could probably list a catalogue of horrors and misdeeds that I've witnessed among the motorcycle clubs in Victoria. People love horror stories, especially if it reinforces their prejudices against minority communities they love to hate, and I might even sell a few more copies of this book. But I refuse to exploit my position among these people, many of whom I count as friends. I don't share their values or their view of life. But I respect them as people who are not prepared to take the easy way out.

Much of what they say and do is as inexcusable as the actions I have observed in big business, politics and in the arena of internal relations. No one who can put a man or woman into a psychiatric ward simply because they believe in Jesus, as the Soviets do, can claim any more or less sympathy from me than a biker who beats up a member who wants to leave the club because he has become a Christian. No one who drops bombs on Libya and calls the civilian deaths they cause 'collateral damage', can expect any more respect from me than a drunken outlaw who knifes an innocent member of the public because he stepped into a brawl. Bikers wear different suits, that's all.

During this whole period, I kept changing my own suits, or rather swapping hats. One minute I would be organizing a bike run to the Calder raceway, and the next I might be sorting out somewhere to stay for some itinerant hippie who'd turned up on my doorstep. Then I might be off to speak to a businessmen's lunch or to debate the meaning of life with a learned professor at some university or other. Life couldn't have been less dull for me or Glena, especially as it all centred around our own home, where we were trying to bring up our kids and maintain some sort of family life.

CHAPTER THIRTEEN

At one stage more than 35,000 people had our home address. We were printing that many copies of our paper, *Truth and Liberation*, and it was going to acid heads, freak communities, motorcycle gangs and prisons, as well as to anyone walking the street who was prepared to accept a copy. And the only address on it was our own home. So anyone who felt like looking us up knew where we were.

The people who tended to get hold of the paper were often very mobile and therefore news of what we were doing spread throughout the underground network. We had all sorts of desperate men and women turn up on our doorstep.

One guy decided he wanted to come to see us, so he rode his Harley (which had no proper saddle) all the way down from northern Queensland. He made the journey of 1,500 miles sitting on the frame. Of course you make someone like that welcome, organize a place they can stay and spend time finding out what their needs are and why they've come all this way. This is an extravagant example, but multiply these chance visitors by hundreds and you'll get a picture of our life.

At least twice a week, usually on Mondays and Wednesdays, we'd hold Bible studies in the place. One was a regular God's Squad meeting, the other was open to anyone. Our small lounge room was packed to overflowing, with people hanging out of the windows. It was a revelation to the neighbours, particularly on Squad nights, to see thirty or more guys on big bikes roar up the drive.

Not all our visitors were exactly welcome. One night, Glena was alone with the children because I was away for a fortnight, taking a series of meetings somewhere. She went to bed, fell asleep and had a strange dream — so she thought. It involved motorcycles crunching on the gravel path, knockings at the bedroom window (which was on the ground floor at the front of the house), obscene comments in the dark and talk of breaking into the house.

In the morning, she tried to convince herself it had been a nightmare, but it had all been so vivid that she couldn't be sure. When I heard about this on my return, I checked with the neighbours. Sure enough, a motorcycle gang had driven up the street in the early hours of the morning and turned into our drive. They had obviously got our address, possibly from the magazine and decided to pay a visit. From the admittedly scant information available, it seemed they hadn't intended it to be a friendly visit.

Potentially, this was a dangerous situation. I feared for what might happen to my family if there were more such visits. I was shaken too by my own anger at the possible threat to my family and began to wonder, as many people do, what my reaction would have been. I lean towards pacifism, but in defending my own family, I'm not at all sure those principles would hold. I was only too aware that my hunting rifles were in my study and that in a situation like that, I would be tempted to use them.

I hoped and prayed, as I have ever since, that I am never placed in that situation. There's a verse in the Old Book which I am fond of and which our family finds great reassurance in. It says, 'When a man's ways please the Lord, he makes even his enemies to be at peace with him.' Now I know that doesn't apply universally. There are people who have been murdered while in the middle of doing amazing work for God and humanity — Martin Luther King, for instance. But we know he can protect us, and we feel that particular incident was an example.

But even with that faith in God, there were still times of fear. Years after that we began receiving regular obscene phone calls. The caller on some evenings re-dialled until he filled our thirty-call answering machine. The most extravagant stream of obscenities were mixed with death threats to myself and assurances that the caller knew exactly where we lived. These calls continued almost daily for months.

There was enormous pressure on us as a family, and particularly on Glena, whose pregnancy was advancing. I was away a lot and when I wasn't there, she'd be anxious for my safety on the bike. However, she enjoyed the fact that we were for the first time really working as a partnership. It was the closest we'd come to fulfilling her earlier dream of being together in some overseas mission. She proved to be an excellent organizer with a sharp eye for detail.

People would call at the house or phone all day; the place became a tramping ground for a motley collection of individuals, many of whom needed counselling or simply friendship. Glena was always prepared to give good advice, provide a shoulder to cry on and dispense an endless stream of coffee, tea, biscuits and home-made cakes.

Because of my escalating involvement with the bike scene, we had a lot to do with young blokes, many of whom came from deprived or broken family situations. Interestingly, there have always been a larger than normal proportion of single men among the people we have worked with. Most churches and church organizations find that they are dealing with an abundance of women. This has always been a mark of our success. That's not a chauvinistic statement, it means we were reaching people the church wasn't getting near. Glena's warmth and openness gave her a vital mother-cum-older-sister role with a lot of the guys who became connected with us.

Of course, we had two very small children at home and when you have people in and out of your house whose history you know nothing about, you worry sometimes. After Lyndal was born later that year, we made contact with a really derelict biker; an enormous, lanky guy with jeans so filthy they could probably have been registered as a germ warfare factory. I can still see Glena's face frozen with alarm as he swooped down and picked up our new baby, enfolding her in his massive arms. But his battered, hardened face softened and melted as he looked at Lyndal, and Glena breathed an inward sigh of relief. Guys like these gave us a lot of surprises. Their appearance was so often deceptive. And children can be an amazing communication bridge between hostile adults.

Things came to a head about a month before Lyndal was born. We couldn't cope at home much longer. We desperately needed premises we could work from. Glena phoned our good friend John Blacker, a Methodist minister who ran a set-up called the Sunshine Community Centre, which was doing a great work with deprived families in Melbourne's western suburbs. He had good contacts with the hierarchy of the Methodist church (soon to join with the Presbyterian and Congregational denominations to form the Uniting Church of Australia). When Glena asked if he could see whether the Methodists had any property free, he set to work with a will. It wasn't a moment too soon.

Glena was finding the work and the stress too much. She began to vomit and went to see the doctor. She told Glena in no uncertain terms that she was doing too much. She was also putting the baby at risk. The doctor declared that if she didn't slow down drastically, she would put her in hospital.

Glena returned from the surgery distressed and weepy to find John Blacker on the doorstep with another friend of ours, Ross Rogers. Glena invited them inside and promptly burst into tears, telling them what the doctor had just told her.

'Don't worry,' they said, 'we've got something to show you.'

They put her in the car and drove to our neighbouring suburb of Bayswater. There they showed her 265 Canterbury Road, an old, grubby, white-weatherboarded, single-storey house with broken window panes. It was surrounded by overgrown grass.

Glena was not immediately impressed. The local Methodists

had been using the place as a drop-in centre for local kids, but they had been unable to cope with these tough teenagers, who had knocked the place around a bit. The house had then been left vacant and vandals had broken in and wreaked even more havoc. One of the rooms had been painted black, which did nothing to lift the sense of gloom. All Glena could see was a broken-down shell of a building with a rickety veranda, apparently sinking in an acre or so of boggy ground. But Ross used his imagination and expertise to enthuse her about the potential of the place, given a little repair, paint and carpet.

It was at least premises and it definitely had possibilities, which was much more than we had before. We prepared to move in. Eventually, through the generous gift of a local doctor who supported the work of God's Squad, we were able to buy the premises and surrounding land.

With Glena's prodigious organizational abilities, teams were organized to paint the place (it became orange, which was a trendy colour at the time) and to knock down as many walls as we could without the house caving in. Glena also sought out old theatre seats from a cinema that was closing down. In quite a short time we had a habitable centre.

In middle of all this Lyndal was born. It was September 1972, and I was booked to lead a series of Bible studies at a youth camp in New South Wales, carefully scheduled so that I would be back home by the time Glena was due. But the day after I left she went into early labour and was taken into hospital. It was really tough on poor Glena to have the baby alone after all she'd been through in the past nine months. Her family were well over a thousand miles away in Queensland and so there was no one close to be with her. I was dreadfully disappointed not to have been there. I was present when both Paul and Kathy were born and count those experiences as some of the most moving events in my life.

However, I did get to see her for a while the next day. Hearing of the problem, a Sydney businessman, at great personal expense and in a remarkable demonstration of thoughtful concern, flew me back to Melbourne for the night. I rushed to see Glena and Lyndal, flowers and cake in hand, and spent the day with them before flying back the next day to finish my series of studies.

The move out of our home marked an explosion in our activities. It was an intense but extremely exciting period. We found this generation was unusually responsive to the idea of Christianity. People with no real background in the church and no previous understanding of the Bible hungrily devoured the information they were given. They said, often in as many words. 'This is exactly what I've been searching for.' I couldn't count the number of people who said, in genuine surprise when they truly understood the Christian message, 'Why didn't anyone tell me this before?' We felt we had tapped a genuine need.

The house was used twenty-four hours a day. This was the great period of the drop-out. In the warmer months of the year, young, disaffected Australians would drift round the country, carrying with them the barest minimum required for survival. Word got around, both through our paper and the formidable underground network, that 'Truth and Lib', or 'TLC', as we came to be known, was a place where you could usually crash out for the night.

From the moment we opened in Canterbury Road, the place became alive. Officially it was God's Squad property, but in reality it was a great deal more than that. It was the Squad's official club-house and meeting place, and there was much biker activity for that very reason. But we had all sorts and kinds of people arriving all the time. There'd be acid heads and homeless young alcoholics, university students who'd thrown in the towel, and people who were just passing through and simply wanted a place to lay their head.

The house served several functions. It was our administration centre, it was a place for meetings, a drop-in centre in the daytime and during the evening, and then a hostel at night.

People just descended on the place. We soon had to organize a roster among Squad members and others so that there was someone around at night to supervise things. People would turn up at odd hours of the night. Groups of bikers might arrive and want to talk. Other people who were feeling bad or lonely and knew they'd get a hearing would also drop by.

It wasn't easy using such a small space for all these different purposes. And having people sleep on the premises was always a hassle. But we felt we were offering a useful service, so we kept going.

We had a rule that anyone staying overnight had to be up by 8.30 the next morning because we needed the space for daytime activities, but they seldom were. The people who came to sleep weren't the easiest people to organize, and they often resented any attempt to interfere with their own freedom of action. You'd get guys who were dope heads who'd spend half the night on the streets trying to score, then arrive at three or four in the morning, and not want to be disturbed until 2 p.m. the next day.

They weren't the most hygienic bunch you'd want to meet either. We had a supply of blankets for those that needed them, but often these characters were attached to the same flea-ridden piece of rag that had accompanied them faithfully around the country for months. You would arrive in the morning to start work, open the front door and literally stagger back as a wall of fetid air from the unwashed bodies assaulted your nostrils.

We'd walk in and the place would look like a First World War dressing station, with groaning bodies lying all over the floor. Then, of course, we'd have to rouse them out of their blankets and clean the place up for the day's activities. It often took some time, because not only did they inch their way out of their slumbers at a snail's pace, but they had usually left all the dirty crocks and cutlery from the previous night.

I arrived later than usual one morning to find the guys had struggled up but had left a great heap of rumpled blankets in the middle of the floor.

'Now c'mon fellers,' I said in the most encouraging tone I could manage. 'Who's left all these blankets here? It doesn't take a lot just to tidy them away does it?' I lifted up the edge of the first blanket to show willing, only to find the grubby form of one of our regular customers curled up like a possum underneath.

On another morning I turned up at Canterbury Road and came face to face with a government health inspector. My mind went into panic mode. I knew what he'd find the moment he walked in the door. I'd noticed the previous night that there was a pile of coffee cups in the sink, with green-grey mould growing all over the dregs in the bottom. People always left the mugs until we ran out and then washed each one before using it. My heart sank. If he saw the place like this, we'd be closed down for sure.

I got someone to keep him talking, raced inside and started shaking the dead-looking lumps on the floor. I turfed their complaining bodies out and started stuffing their sleeping bags into cupboards. It must have looked hilarious with me charging around ordering these half-wiped-out freaks into a frenzy of cleaning. We filled the atmosphere with enough air freshener to destroy the ozone layer and scrubbed the coffee mugs clean.

Exhausted but relieved, I strolled out to the veranda as nonchalantly as I could, to invite the inspector in. It was only then that he told me he hadn't really come to inspect the premises. He'd heard that the place had been turned into some kind of drug rehabilitation centre and wanted to check it out. After a cursory glance around, he expressed himself satisfied and left.

We had some strange characters coming in and out of the place. I particularly remember Smelly John. He was the lanky biker who had swept baby Lyndal into his arms. He was one of those bikers who took immense pride in wearing his 'originals'. It used to be common practice in the bike world never to wash your Levis. You bought one pair of jeans and wore them constantly, unwashed, until they rotted. In some clubs it was the custom to urinate on another's Levis as part of some peculiar initiation rite, or even to rub blood into the denim. Add to that liberal doses of oil, grease and other nameless substances, and before long these originals got to be pretty gross.

John's were in a fairly advanced state of disrepair and they made their own distinctive contribution towards supplying his nickname. While we're on the subject of originals, I can recall another guy, 'Chopper', who used to hang around the place and whose jeans were so far gone he had to staple them together every time he put them on. He had no zipper at the front and held himself together with a giant safety pin. He would sit in the front row during our Bible study sucking noisily on a huge, filthy, slimy dummy.

Some of the people we had to deal with were in various states of psychological and emotional disrepair. Acid took a disastrous toll of burned-out minds in those years. We had more than one university psychology major who'd dropped out of their studies after overdoing psychedelics. People like this used to turn up because we were the only church organization they knew who would understand what they'd gone through and were prepared to give the time to help. I remember one acid head in particular who swore, whether he was tripping or not, that he had an eight-foot hairy spider with salivating fangs next to his bed. Some of these guys had no real means of discerning fantasy from reality.

When you're dealing with people like this, there can sometimes be moments of real tension. We were a young movement and the volunteers we had helping were young too. They did a great job, but sometimes their inexperience meant that they couldn't handle these crises and one or other of us would be called out of our beds to deal with the situation.

One of the members of the Resources Group, and Secretary of God's Squad, was a real winner of a bloke, Norm Briddock. He's an ambulance officer and therefore a trained paramedic.

He was especially handy to have around in these situations. One night he was called out to deal with a ruckus between Jimmy and Byron. Byron had an alcohol problem but was pretty inoffensive most of the time. One day he really got on the wrong side of Jimmy, whose habit was to sniff petrol fumes. He was slowly going off his head with it. He threatened Byron with a knife, so Norm calmly stepped in, removed the weapon and restored things to as near normality as things ever got.

On another occasion, one of the people we were working with who had a drinking problem as well as smoking a lot of dope, threatened to take his own life. He was swallowing pills from a bottle in one hand and waving a hatchet in the other. He claimed he would cut anyone down who tried to stop him. It was all very melodramatic but ultimately futile, since once the pills had taken effect he would have passed out and we would have sent him straight to hospital to be pumped out. But our alarmed volunteers hadn't the experience to realize this.

We really threw people in at the deep end and asked them to deal with situations that would perplex professionals. They did brilliantly, considering the circumstances.

Just as a footnote to this story, the guy in question came up to me one evening after hearing me preach and handed me a semi-automatic rifle and 500 rounds of ammunition. He told me he had found a first-floor room in Collins Street which faced on to a busy thoroughfare in the heart of Melbourne. From there he had planned to fire into the crowds and see how many people he could get before the police got him. I can't tell whether he meant to do it or not; perhaps this was another of his grand gestures. But the rifle was real enough to send a shiver through me and to make me thank God that his work in that man's life had prevented the possibility of a number of deaths. This gentleman went on to establish a drug rehabilitation centre.

This wasn't the only time I had to deal with weapons either. We're moving a bit ahead in the chronology now, but after one sermon I gave at the centre, I found I had inherited a small armoury. A medieval-type mace, a hatchet, and five switchblades had all been handed in by people who professed to have been converted that night.

God's Squad was active on all sorts of fronts during that first year. We began to make very good contacts with outlaws, and became progressively more recognized and respected as time went on. But the Squad didn't limit its activities to bikers. I'd often take a group with me to high schools or church missions and coffee shops where the arrival of a group of motorcyclists inevitably caused a stir. Eddie Pye, it turned out, had been absolutely right when he'd suggested that motorcycles would help pave the way in talking to kids. We were careful not to use them as gimmicks, but they did break down barriers between us and the youngsters who would normally run a mile rather than talk seriously to someone who described himself as a Christian.

It was at one of these out-of-town events that we had a run-in with the Count. While we had a good relationship with a lot of bikers, I can't pretend we were universally popular. The Count, whose real name was Chris Matthews, didn't have any time for us at all. He was riding with an outlaw group in La Trobe Valley called Satan's Cavalry, and he'd set his heart on breaking us up. He was a big, imposing, dark, wild guy with a flaming temper. And when he'd got a few drinks under his belt he could easily lose control. When drunk, he seemed to have the strength of ten men.

A few of the Squad guys and I were talking to a bunch of rather nicer than usual kids, mostly from church backgrounds, at a coffee shop out in Gippsland. Suddenly the Count, drunk as a skunk, lurched in the door. We ignored him for a bit, but he started acting up, hurling creative obscenities at me as I tried to hold the attention of our audience. The Count soon got fed up with the merely verbal and decided to break the show up good and proper. He strode, or rather lunged for the microphone and tried to wrest it away from me. A couple of the guys tried to grab him, at which point chairs began to fly and the whole coffee shop dissolved into a shambles. After a fairly fierce struggle, Norm Briddock and Howard Ham were able to grab him and bring him temporarily under control.

In the meantime, one of the organizers of this event was so incensed at the Count's behaviour that he went off and called the police. This wasn't at all what we wanted. We knew that the Count had already had a few unfortunate brushes with the law and realized that if he was arrested, he could be in serious trouble. The police don't like bikers and they take any opportunity they can to get one in their clutches. We also knew that once the drink wore off and his temper had burned itself out, things would look a bit different.

But the cops had been called and there was no way we could stop them coming, so two or three of the biggest and most expert Squad members on hand, who were also trained in the martial arts, bundled him under a table in the corner of the room, held him and sat on him to keep him still. Another put a large hairy paw over the Count's mouth to make sure he didn't contribute anything further to the proceedings. The police duly arrived, looked around and said, 'We hear there's trouble here.'

'No trouble here,' we replied, looking around innocently at the room which we'd put back together, and trying not to let our eyes wander to where a red-faced Count was writhing under a table beneath the combined weight of some heavy motorcyclists.

'But we heard there was a fight,' persisted one of the officers.

'Oh yes, well there was a bit of a scuffle earlier on, but it's all sorted out now, thanks.'

They shrugged and left.

The alcohol took a while to work through the Count's system and it wasn't until the early hours of the morning that he calmed down. But when the storm was over he was happy to discuss things. We talked and prayed together and that night he decided that Jesus Christ was the person he was looking for. Eventually he and his wife came and lived in a caravan at the back of the centre in Canterbury Road, and were responsible for supervising the people who were sleeping on the floor overnight. He also became a God's Squad member and was a tremendous asset in sharing his own faith with his mates among the outlaws.

For us, these were heady days. People would come to us from nowhere and get converted on the spot. It wasn't that I had a great sales technique or that we brow-beat these people into submission. They just turned up at the centre, where we welcomed them and made them feel they were someone worth knowing. They'd get fed and looked after and they'd ask why. If they wanted to know badly enough, we'd tell them what Jesus Christ meant to us and what he could mean to them. But we wouldn't use a million Bible verses, we'd talk to them in words and cultural images they could understand. It was all so simple we couldn't understand why so few other church people seemed to be doing it.

And there were more amazing events to come in the following years, although I very nearly missed it all by frying my brains on the Nullarbor Plain.

CHAPTER FOURTEEN

There wasn't any real need to take my bike on a 6,000-mile round trip across the Nullarbor Plain, one of the bleakest semi-desert regions in Australia. Most people agreed it was a crazy thing to do in mid-summer. My family and friends told me I wanted my head read and tried to dissuade me. In the light of what happened they had good reason for saying, 'I told you so'. But I went anyway. I must hasten to say that I did have a sense of calling and destiny about the journey.

There were three reasons for riding to Perth, in the far corner of Western Australia, and back again. Firstly, I was keen to see how the Jesus movement was operating in this prosperous city. I was only too aware that back in Melbourne, we'd been thrown into a situation where we were suddenly dealing with a whole range of social problems like homelessness and drugs. I wanted to see how they dealt with these things on the other side of Australia. Particularly, I was anxious to meet a man called Geoff Hopp, who ran an organization called Jesus People Incorporated, which I'd heard was doing really excellent work with street kids.

Secondly, I was excited at the possibility of exploring this part of Australian terrain. I had by now started my collection of gum nuts, wattles and acacia pods. I wanted to gather an example of seed from every one of the 600 different varieties of eucalypt. I also wanted to collect and catalogue every one of the thousand species of wattle. Here was a chance to get a few I'd never been near before.

My third reason was related to my own identity and calling. Despite being such a forthright and outspoken man, the challenges of breaking into an alien culture sometimes caused insecurity — a need to prove my fitness for the task. This is less true now than it used to be, but I've always felt the need to prove to myself the validity of the calling I felt. In this particular case I was still very much aware that I was President of a motorcycle club, yet I was probably the least experienced rider in the group. I wanted, I suppose, to undertake some heroic trial of strength to show that I was one of the boys. No one could doubt your biking credentials if you could casually drop into a conversation, 'Of course, when I rode across the Nullarbor Plain . . .' It was a bit foolish, but I felt I had to do it.

There were about fifteen of us altogether, mostly from the Sydney Squad. Among the Melbourne contingent were Howard Ham and the Count. There was also a group in a back-up car who were going to meet us at various stops on the way. It all went fairly smoothly on the 500-mile trip from Melbourne to Adelaide and on the next leg of the journey from Adelaide to the edge of the Nullarbor.

Things began to go wrong from there on. Everyone slept on the beach before setting out across the Nullarbor — well almost everyone. Despite knowing that we had to set off at daybreak the next morning, I stayed up talking until the wee small hours. After a couple of hours snooze I woke in the grey dawn and felt dog-tired. I didn't relish the prospect of the journey ahead. Even that early in the morning, you could feel the gathering warmth of the sun. We were at the start of a heat wave and we had no salt tablets.

You just don't embark on such epic journeys without proper preparations, but we did. The Nullarbor is no friend to travellers. Its aboriginal name means literally 'no trees'. All you'll see is a lot of low, scruffy, scrub — the typically Australian twisted and tortured desert vegetation that survives precariously in the hot, sandy soil. To the untrained eye it looks a flat expanse of monotonous grey-green, broken only by the occasional ridge. But for the naturalist, there are a thousand fascinating creatures living in this area: spiders, lizards, snakes, and larger mammals such as kangaroos,

190

wombats and lesser-known smaller marsupials. In the early 1970s, this section of the highway was a dirt road in an awful state of disrepair. The huge transport trucks would wreak havoc on such surfaces.

The road was covered by a layer of what we call bull dust — very fine particles the consistency of talcum powder. It's treacherous stuff to drive through, and when a road train goes past (large articulated trucks with up to three enormous trailers linked behind) it will kick up a cloud of bull dust which can hang in the air, like a thick mist, for hours. The dust also settles in the many pot-holes in the road, so that you don't know they're there until you're on top of them. That can be particularly dangerous on two wheels. On occasions a stake was driven into the road with several old tyres thrown over it to warn motorists of huge, axle-breaking holes in the highway.

We embarked on our journey. The Count, a go-for-it-merchant if ever there was one, took off at about seventy miles an hour on his Honda 750 Four with its high-rise bars. And the rest of us followed on behind. Soon our convoy was stretched across the bleak landscape.

We weren't long into the journey before my back tyre went. The sun was well and truly up now and the temperature over the century Fahrenheit. Howard, always concerned for my well-being, stayed behind with me to fix the puncture as the others went on ahead. Getting the back wheel off a Honda Four is no easy business. Howard and I sweated for an hour or so before the repair job was complete and we could carry on.

But with the heat, no salt tablets and the lack of sleep, I was beginning to lose it. Heat exhaustion was taking its toll. I could scarcely stand. It would have been asking for trouble to stay out where we were. We had to make for shelter.

The nearest habitation was a place called Ivy Tanks which was still a good stretch ahead. I draped myself wearily over the bike and set off as fast as I could. I was in such a daze that I couldn't even keep the throttle open properly, so I adjusted the screw on the accelerator at about 60 mph and let the bike drive itself. I lay across the fuel tank, my chin on the instrument panel and my feet hooked back on the rear light and let the thing run, hoping I didn't meet any pot-holes on the way.

I was in a semi-comatose state for most of the journey, hallucinating, seeing mirages of petrol bowsers which would tell me I'd reached Ivy Tanks, only to see them disappear. I went over one dent in the road and heard a clatter behind me. My tape recorder and a couple of other pieces of gear had come adrift from their moorings, but I didn't care. I rode on, fearing that my failing mental grip would leave me wandering into the desert scrub should I dismount to recover the gear. Finally, the so-called motel and solitary petrol pump that make up Ivy Tanks hove in sight.

I braked to a halt, virtually fell off the bike and staggered inside the truck stop. The owners took pity on me and let me stay there for a few hours, but we had no money for a bed so I lay sprawled out on the relative cool of the concrete floor. Howard, who I'd left behind in my urge to seek refuge, caught up with me here and with great kindness nursed me, mopping my brow with lukewarm water. Howard remained my constant companion and guardian angel throughout this trip, for which I'll always be grateful.

The temperature at Ivy Tanks was a hundred and thirty-five degrees Fahrenheit in the shade. And all we could get to drink from the truck stop were soft drinks. Water is in short supply in such places. I was so dehydrated I had to drink a great deal to replace my fluid levels and the sweetness of this liquid felt like salt water to my tongue.

We waited until nightfall, by which time I was a little recovered, though not completely. The temperature was down to the low hundreds, but mine was still up. It had never been our plan to travel by night, because the nocturnal animals, roos and wombats, make a surprising mess of vehicles on impact. Motorcycles are not fitted with the mandatory bull-bars seen on almost all trucks and cars out west. It's only too easy to collide with them as they stand startled, frozen in the glare of the headlights. Nevertheless, we decided to press on to the township of Nullarbor. There we knew we could get cold bore water and I would be able to take a shower and bring my temperature down.

We reached Nullarbor without further mishap and I sat for an hour or so under a cold shower of artesian water. It's no good for drinking — the minerals make it taste bitter. But it felt wonderful. My temperature went down temporarily, just enough to allow us to press on.

We caught up with the rest of the crowd in Eucla, which is on the border between the states of South and Western Australia, just over half way between Melbourne and Perth. Eucla was our nirvana because there was a reasonable motel there. We soaked in the luxury of the motel swimming pool for a long time and spent the best part of a day recovering as best we could. Probably several of us should have been hospitalized.

The rest of the journey to Perth remains somewhat vague to me. I remember we failed to meet up with the car at the twin mining towns of Kalgoorlie and Coolgardie. There was a mighty confusion, with the people in the car thinking we were behind, which we were, and then deciding that we must have gone ahead, which we hadn't! Somehow it ended up with them missing us completely and driving back to Sydney. It was vaguely reminiscent of some of the Australian explorer disasters.

They took with them one small but vital piece of information. The list of addresses of the people we had come to Perth to meet. But we did have the address of the Christian camp where we had arranged to stay. So when we arrived in Perth, dusty and exhausted after our trip which had taken us six days of hard riding, we turned up only to be told, second hand, that we wouldn't be welcome at the camp. The people who ran the place were worried about our appearance. They thought our dirty, scruffy long hair was dishonouring to God and not a good example. It's hard to recall these experiences without a bitter, righteous anger. After all, it was the Christians' own founder and leader, Jesus himself, who said, 'Man looks on the outward appearance, but God looks on the heart.'

We were shaken and angry at this snub. We were also adrift in a strange city without the phone numbers or addresses of our contacts. We ended up under the main freeway which crosses the Swan River and decided to make our way down the river bank and spend the night there.

Feeling dejected and rejected we huddled into our cheap sleeping bags among the rats and rabbits and passed a poor night. Early the next morning two policemen spied us on our illegal camping ground. We saw them drive off, presumably to get back-up, so we broke camp as quickly as possible and made for the city centre.

In retrospect, it was all useful experience for me because I began to realize what it feels like to be an outlaw, regarded everywhere with suspicion and discouraged from staying in any one place for too long. We were even turfed out of a pub although all we asked for were non-alcoholic lemon drinks. We were at the time desperately thirsty. 'We don't serve bikers,' was the explanation. We got the distinct impression Perth was not too keen on God's Squad.

That evening we were wandering aimlessly around Perth's tourist centre among the window-shoppers, when a utility truck crowded with drunken yobbos screeched to a halt and chucked a young man out into the middle of the crowded shopping street. He was bound hand and foot and stark naked. In a futile effort to make for cover this poor guy, totally humiliated, began hopping along the sidewalk like a kangaroo. It turned out that the poor coot was getting married the next day and this was his mates' idea of a stag party lark.

Their victim wasn't finding this a bit funny. His mates were coasting up and down the street in the ute, laughing uproariously at the misfortune of their pal. But he was visibly upset at the spectacle he was causing.

I felt for him and couldn't let this cruelty go any further. So without thinking about it, I went over and began to untie his hands and feet. This didn't please his mates in the least and they jumped out of the truck and tried to stop me.

I grew angry and said, 'Listen, the joke's gone far enough. You're acting like a bunch of idiots. If you were really his mates, you'd give the poor bloke a break.' There was a scuffle and someone punched me in the face. They grabbed the guy, bundled him back in the truck and shot off, leaving me with a rapidly-closing right eye.

The final disaster in Perth was an interview I gave to one of the local newspapers, who had heard there was a bunch of long-haired Christian bikers in town. With the interview over, the journalist asked me off the record how we were enjoying Perth. In my tiredness and depression, I told her how rejected we felt.

A story subsequently appeared on the front page of the *Westralian* in which I was seen, after only twenty-four hours in Perth, to be attacking the church in Western Australia. I was hurt and enraged by this shabby journalistic breach of confidence, and it did a lot of damage to my relationship with Christians in that part of the country. It was never my intention to set the church up as a target.

Shaking the dust of Perth from our feet, we headed south-east to Albany on the first leg of our return journey. Albany is on the stretch of coast in the far south-western corner of Australia and a former whaling station. Here disaster struck again. Twice.

First my battery went. We had little spare cash and had to chase around the town to get a second-hand one. The others went on ahead, all except Howard who, in his quiet, unobtrusive way, sorted me out again and tried to keep me out of even deeper trouble.

We found a battery, eventually, but in trying to repack the gear on the back of the bike I let one of the octopus straps go. These elasticated thongs are great for fixing luggage on a bike or the roof of a car but if you let one go when they're under tension, they have a habit of flicking back at you. They have large hooks on each end so that they can be fixed on, and if these catch you, you know all about it. This one hit me in the corner of the left eye — the one that wasn't black! Instinctively, I rubbed my eye with my gloved hand. The bike was leaking brake fluid from the master cylinder and I had some on my gloves. Now I had some in my eye and it stung like crazy.

We were several hours behind the others as we set off east along the coast road to Esperance at the western end of the Great Australian Bight. Howard was riding some way behind me to make sure nothing else untoward happened, or to pick up the pieces if it did. Every now and then, he would come around a bend and find my riderless bike parked by the side of the road. Smith was off in the bush, collecting gum nuts again.

We were OK riding in daylight, but as dusk fell I began to have difficulty seeing things. My right eye was still puffed up and my left eye wasn't functioning properly. I had never fully recovered from the heat exhaustion on the outward journey and I hadn't slept properly in Perth. I mentioned none of this to Howard; I thought we'd just push on.

The road gently winds a bit between Albany and Esperance and there are signs to indicate each bend ahead. It was dark by now, but my headlights picked them out. I registered them automatically in my befuddled state and rode the curves fairly well at about sixty or seventy miles an hour.

After a few more hours driving, I glimpsed what I thought was another curve sign. But this time, something didn't seem quite right. The road didn't curve. Suddenly I found myself across the middle of a T-intersection, running rapidly out of road. I jammed on the anchors and looked ahead in horror. What could I do? I could see only long grass and a few lower bushes. It looked as though I could ride it out. I'd go off the road and into the bush.

Thump! I hit the embankment that had been hidden by the tall grass and the bike flipped head over turkey. Howard, riding behind, saw my tail light arc against the night sky. I was still holding on to the bike for the first two somersaults and then we parted. But not for long. I had only just hit the dirt when several hundred pounds of Honda hit me in the back. I was laying there, pinned to the deck with the hot exhaust pipes burning a hole in my leg, when Howard squealed to a halt and sprinted towards me.

He pulled my mangled machine off me and bent down to see how I was. I told him through gritted teeth that I was fine. Seeing I was not seriously injured, he checked the bike. It was in pretty poor shape but still rideable. I tried to move my right arm. A shaft of pain and the scraping of bone ends told me I'd broken my right collar-bone. My heart plummeted. What was I going to do now? Obviously I needed hospital treatment, but the last thing I wanted to do was sit around for hours until a country ambulance arrived to take me into Esperance ten miles away.

And I didn't want to make a fuss. This was Smithy, President of God's Squad. So when Howard came over, looked at me anxiously and said, 'You OK, John?', I acted macho.

'Yeah. I'm alright. I've just hurt myself a bit here.' I indicated my shoulder, 'I'll be OK.' Howard looked at me suspiciously.

'You sure?'

'No worries. I'll manage.'

Reluctantly he brought the bike over and I struggled on. It was then that I found I had no strength at all in my left arm. I persuaded Howard to lift it up so I could rest my hand on the throttle and insisted on riding into Esperance. I felt every single bump in every metre of that ten-mile stretch of road.

The hospital discovered I'd broken my collar-bone in three places. They also found I had a temperature of 103. They kept me in for a week. I was so desperate to complete the journey and I'd had to give up, a quarter of the way back. I felt like a boy with mumps missing his birthday party.

The Honda was trucked back to Melbourne and a group of

mates passed the hat around for my airfare back home. I wasn't exactly welcomed as a conquering hero, and a good few heads shook wisely when they saw me again, arm in sling. But I'm unrepentant. It was a hard experience and good education. I'm glad I went.

If asked to do it again, I'm not sure what I'd reply. My feelings say, 'Once is enough'. But I still felt a sense of assurance that it was meant to be. I think I'd do it again, albeit with better preparation.

Norm Briddock, ambulance man, friend and resident scourge, tells me I should have stayed in bed for a further two weeks after I got home. But Sunbury Festival, which had become an annual event, was looming again. Many people had been praying for my injury to heal and, though my shoulder was still painful, I felt I was recovering fast. Sleeping on the rocky ground wasn't going to be easy, but I had to go. The previous Sunbury had marked a kind of baptism into the counter-culture for Glena and I, and I was very keen, after a year's experience, to return and work once again alongside John Hirt, Kevin Smith, John U'ren and their teams.

We'd all gained much experience and confidence in the intervening year. I think we were each of us bolder and more at home. I certainly felt that way. I really enjoyed talking to the idealistic, optimistic kids who came to Sunbury. I felt close to them. I was, despite my leathers, basically a Christian hippie who happened to ride a bike. I used to wear a sticker on my helmet that came from John Hirt's House of the New World in Sydney. It ran, 'Brake the hate habit, love your neighbour'. It wasn't exactly bike-scene creed.

So, collar-bone or no collar-bone, I simply couldn't miss Sunbury and I didn't. I didn't miss the next one either, which was to be the last. And ironically, that year we almost got caught up in a battle between the Angels and a new group on the waterfront. Skinheads.

CHAPTER FIFTEEN

The skinhead cult had grown very big in Melbourne by the summer of '74. The idea was a British import, a style of dress and aggression adopted by the football hooligans and tough street kids of UK cities.

You saw them everywhere, their hair shaved to a stubble, giving them the appearance of a race of hardened convicts on the loose. Skinhead gangs were outlaws too. But they were generally younger and less organized. They didn't have an equivalent to the motorcycle on which to focus — they were loose liaisons of bored mates whose only excitement came in causing a bit of a ruckus. From the earliest days of their appearance on the streets, they declared themselves the sworn enemies of bikers. There were a number of scuffles and full-size fights in the Melbourne area during that period.

As is often the case, other kids would imitate the style without taking on board the behaviour patterns. So if you saw a skinhead walking down the street, you often couldn't tell from looking at him whether he was the genuine article or not. Short hair was in, just as long hair had been in '69.

This very problem gave the police at the Sunbury Pop Festival that year some pause for thought. The peace, love and freedom of the late sixties had dissipated substantially by 1974. The steam, or rather the optimism, had gone out of the movement. This year, Sunbury was more of a regular open-air rock concert. And it attracted a wider range of people.

The skinheads were there and so were the bikers. There were a few skirmishes between the two early on and the police wanted to stamp out the problem before any major confrontation took place. What were they to do? It wasn't easy to identify the skinhead gangs from skinhead fashion followers. So they took the easy option. They booted out the bikers.

The outlaw bike clubs were obvious; they wore black leather jackets with big patches saying exactly who they were. The police cleared them off the site, in one case by removing the club's gear — tents and all — while the guys were having a swim. They dumped it unceremoniously beyond the perimeter fence.

But they left God's Squad and they left the Hell's Angels. We weren't included because it was understood we were a Christian group, there to talk to people and not to make trouble. Why they decided to make an exception of the Angels I don't know. It could be because the Angels were older, more stable, more self-assured and therefore less likely to go looking for trouble. That was certainly true. If trouble came looking for them they dealt with it ruthlessly. But these weren't excitable youngsters on the warpath, they were grown men who generally kept themselves to themselves.

They had set themselves up like warlords at Sunbury. They found a comfortable spot down by the river, with a refrigerator full of beer, run off their own petrol generator. They had armchairs, beach umbrellas, the lot. They didn't look as if they had the least inclination to move and that may have been an additional reason why the police left them alone.

We had only recently begun to make contact with the Angels. A number of Squad guys had struck up a good relationship with one of their better-known members, a man whose black hat gave him the mystique of a western gun-slinger. His name was Buzzard, a very likeable man. We were all greatly saddened when he died in a car crash some while later. Through Buzzard, I came to meet the President of the Melbourne Angels, Doug Scott, known to his members as the 'Father'.

At Sunbury, Doug asked me and a couple of Squad guys if

we'd mind looking after the Angels' camp while they went for a swim. We were happy to do this, feeling that this was a gesture of both confidence and a measure of respect on their part.

Later on during the weekend, the word came through that a large group of skinheads were massing for an attack on the bikers. They could see that the odds had shortened considerably in their favour now that the other outlaws had been ejected. Two or three hundred skinheads against around sixty bikers made things look a little easier for them. And this was no idle rumour. They had baseball bats, metal bars and chains, and they were ready for action.

One of the Angels approached me as President of God's Squad and asked, 'Are you guys going to stand up and fight with us? This lot don't give a stuff whether you're Christians or not. You're still bikers and you're going to get it as well. So are you joining forces with us or not?'

We talked and prayed among ourselves and resolved what we'd do. I took a message back. I said, 'We want to make it very clear that we're not gutless wonders. We're not going to run away from confrontation. When the skinheads turn up, we're going to walk up the hill as a club and confront them.'

I explained, 'Our egos are not in this world, they rest in the fact that we believe the God of the Universe loves us and therefore we don't have anything to prove by winning a fight. So we're going to go up to them and ask them to lay down their weapons.'

The Angels looked at us as if to say, 'You've got to be joking'. Darkness was falling and I noticed one of the Angels, Affy — a massive Torres Strait Islander, unusual in that most of the Angels are white — standing there shaking his head in disbelief at this madness. His dark face grew darker still in the twilight and he had a chain in one hand and an iron bar in the other.

They told us that if we went up that hill to meet the skinheads, we'd be mocked and then beaten to a pulp. I replied, 'I don't think it's going to work out that way. We believe God's with us and that somehow he's going to sort this out.'

It all had the ring of Old Testament times when the Israelites asked to be delivered from their enemies. I continued, 'We won't lose any honour or dignity by confronting them. We don't find our dignity by beating someone over the head. You can teach a cockatoo to scratch someone's eyes out, you can put boxing-gloves on a kangaroo, and set two dogs to fight each other, so fighting doesn't prove humanity or maleness or anything else.'

We agreed to wait with the Angels until the skinheads arrived at the brow of the hill. They had to come. They had said they would and the bikers had refused to back off. Everyone's dignity was on the line. Every rule in the book said that there would be a battle. But there wasn't. We sat together for hours, but the skinheads never showed. To this day I have no idea what stopped them. But something did. I can't prove it, but it is still my belief that God heard our prayer and stepped in in some miraculous way.

It might seem an anticlimax that the skinheads didn't make their promised appearance. But a lot of bloodshed was saved, because the Hell's Angels, though outnumbered, would have taken the bulk of skinheads with them. And it was an excellent opportunity for God's Squad to show that we weren't wimps, yet neither were we prepared to compromise our beliefs, even in the face of physical risk. I think our stand made a real difference to the way we were viewed on the bike scene generally — and among the Hell's Angels in particular — after that night.

And we've had some good and generous responses to our policy of making sure we're seen around and being available to talk — simply being ourselves. A member of the Angels at one of the Hell's Angels' annual festivals looked around at the collection of outlaw groups camped around the site and said, 'All these guys try to outdo us, but you just do your thing, and we respect you for it.'

Another put it this way. 'Look, we don't buy what you're

selling but we respect you. You come to where we are. You're not like all those self-righteous bastards in the church. You blokes are fair dinkum. You're genuine motorcycle riders and you've got guts.'

It's not my intention to ride on the backs of the Angels, or anyone else we've met on the bike scene, in order to sound good. I hope my reference to conversations we've had isn't misconstrued as a betrayal of confidence. I'm simply trying to point up what kind of people we were and how people reacted to us.

The irrepressible Norm Briddock thought he'd met his match one year at the annual Bathurst races. He was walking down the main thoroughfare when a huge gorilla of a biker, with a large tyre iron sticking out of his back pocket, stepped out and barred his path. He said something like, 'I could rip the colours off your back and stomp you into the ground.' He then proceeded to outline a comprehensive list of gruesome tortures he was capable of inflicting on the luckless Briddock, who by now was sure his number must be up.

Then he paused for effect and said, 'But I'm not going to. D'you know why?' Barely waiting for Norm's strangled reply, he continued, ''Cos you guys are fair dinkum.' Then turning to address everyone and no one in particular he declared, 'If any of you blokes touch these fellers, I'm going to fix you up for good.' As generous a testimonial as you could ask for.

I've already told something of the story of Spiv and Quince and their influence in giving God's Squad this kind of credibility on the bike scene. We were then given additional clout by the addition of two more senior outlaws, known as Mongrel and Ferret.

This sounds a bit as if we were collecting recruits to make the Squad look more authentic. That has never been our intention. My aim from the very beginning was, as St Paul put it, to 'by all means save some.' I wanted the bikers I met to know that someone cared enough about them to say, 'I'm a Christian. I'm around and available if you want to talk about it. I'm not going to stuff the gospel past your back teeth, but I'll try and make myself as visible as possible so you'll know where to find me.'

That's always been the way the Squad's operated. The fact that we have members who used to be outlaws, simply shows that what Christ has to offer is important enough for these guys to change direction in their lives. In turn that suggests to more bikers that we might just have something worth talking about.

Mongrel was Vice-President of the Coffin Cheaters, a particularly hard-nosed outlaw band. Christened Colin McKenzie, we first met at a biker funeral, of which sadly there are many, often as a result of bike accidents, but occasionally by more violent means. Mongrel was often called upon to play 'The Last Post' on his bugle, a skill he'd picked up in the navy.

He came from a poverty-stricken background. His father was an alcoholic and his mother showed little interest in him for the first few years of his life. He was brought up in an orphanage. He left at the age of fourteen, only too glad to put the cold institutional life of the orphanage behind him. He trained as a naval rating but didn't like the military life much better. He resisted the discipline imposed on him, but still had to serve for six years.

After his discharge he drifted fairly naturally into the bike scene, because it was both anarchistic and yet regimented at the same time. He worked his way through the ranks of the Coffin Cheaters until he became Vice-President and one of the chief stirrers. He's not a big bloke, but as hard as nails and afraid of nothing. He hadn't known a lot of love in his life and that affected him deeply.

From the earliest days, it's been Squad policy to go to funerals. It's a way of showing solidarity and concern to these guys at their moment of deepest need. The loyalty and bond between bikers goes so deep that these hard men, who normally despise open displays of emotion, are not ashamed

204

to weep publicly on the death of one of their mates. So we're always ready to go to funerals, and in our occasional role as unofficial chaplains to the outlaws, we are sometimes asked to conduct them.

This was how we met up with Mongrel. After the funeral, he introduced me to some of his mates: 'This is Gorilla Snot, this is Animal . . .'

I looked at these tough blokes and I couldn't think of anything worth saying. All my rounded preachers words and Christian phrases seemed out of place. So I looked into his eyes and prayed inwardly, 'Lord please show this man that I care about him.' I had no way of knowing how much Colin was torn apart by the absence of real love in his life.

Many months later he said that when we were introduced he saw a sense of genuine concern in my eyes that he'd never experienced before and that made him want to know what was behind it. We met again several times after that and subsequently he turned up at the centre on Canterbury Road.

In between time he'd met and talked to a number of the other Squad guys. We spent some time together that evening and he talked about the number of women he'd slept with and said with great feeling, 'But I've got no idea what love is. Do you think God could change me so that I'll know what love means?' His cry was so like the words of the song by The Foreigners: 'I want to know what love is'.

We prayed together and, though I couldn't tell at precisely what moment he settled it, he very shortly surrendered his life to God for the first time.

We've never believed in delivering immediate directives as to how people should behave when they become Christians. The leaves on the trees don't fall off in the autumn, they're actually pushed off by the beginnings of the budding of the new shoot. There's no point in running around trying to pull the old leaves off trees so they'll look better. If the tree's alive it will happen. In the same way, we accept people and expect that principle to work in their lives in due course.

Colin had an immaculate paint job on the tank of his

chopper, 'Easy Rider' style Harley. Technically speaking, that is. It was a picture of a leering demon whose tail curled round and ended in a deliberately phallic shape. In the corner he had a running streaker with an enormous erect penis. It was very much the old-style Mongrel and it must have cost many dollars to have done. Nobody mentioned it. No one took him on one side and suggested it might be inappropriate. Then after a day or two he appeared and the image had been scraped off. He had looked at it and decided it wasn't right any more.

Colin didn't find things easy in the early stages of his Christian life. He went back to his old mates one evening and, realizing perhaps for the first time how much he genuinely cared for them all, he told them so in as many words. And he told them about his new-found faith. But they threw it back in his face and said they preferred him the way he had been. It wasn't easy for someone like Colin to demonstrate the love he'd struggled so hard to find, only to have it rejected out of hand.

Like most people who become Christians out of a difficult past, he had struggles and sometimes fell on his face. But the transformation was remarkable. He was still a terrifically gutsy, earthy individual, and that's good news. God never expects us to become someone we aren't. But he received a real sense of direction in his life and a real warmth. The obvious change in his life, combined with the fact that he was known everywhere on the scene as a classy biker, gave even more notice that the Squad wasn't an outfit for polite people with simpering smiles.

If statistics are anything to go by, he did well to get out when the going was good. Of the four Vice-Presidents of the Coffin Cheaters in that decade, Colin is the only one left alive. The others all met untimely and nasty deaths. One died of a heroin overdose, the second wiped out his bike in an angry chase after a motorist and the third was shot by a former club member, after a violent gang rape.

Some while later we were joined by Ferret, a lean guy who

was as tough and uncompromising as they come. His given name is John Conrau and he was one of the founding members of the Hell's Angels in Melbourne. Ferret is fairly tight-lipped about his outlaw exploits. Some of our guys have painful memories of violence and perversion they would rather forget. Ferret became a gentle, caring man, whose favourite piece of literature is St Paul's first letter to the Corinthians, chapter thirteen: possibly the greatest passage on the meaning of love written in any language.

It has been fascinating to see how many Squad members and their spouses have gone on to become social workers, youth welfare officers, youth detention centre workers and so on. Ferret and his wife, Sue, went on to run a home for teenage kids from deprived backgrounds in the city. Close on thirty or more have discovered some kind of calling to work full time with people in need in the city of Melbourne and elsewhere.

In some ways it would have been easier for guys like Spiv, Quince, Mongrel and Ferret, once they'd experienced this revolution in their lives, to turn their backs on the scene and start all over again. And in one sense they have. Yet having aligned themselves with the God's Squad, they've continued to be part of the biking world. That's been essential, in showing their mates that they're still around and haven't rejected them, even though they've changed their values. If Christianity means anything, then it has to be seen to stand up among the people who know what you were like before.

On the downside, you have to return to many of the old haunts where the same people and the same pressures still exist. You can be very vulnerable and unsure of yourself when faced with a way of life you may once have found so agreeable. So people who were outlaws sometimes find themselves stretched agonizingly between two worlds. Even though one life has proved itself to be a fraud, the new life of following Jesus Christ is a hard one, and it's tempting to go easy on yourself.

Some of the guys in the Squad dislike going back to events like the Hell's Angels annual rock festival held each year outside Melbourne. This raging weekend of day and night drinking and carousing, with strippers and big boobs competitions on stage and pounding heavy rock and blues music, can put a lot of pressure on someone who's not really secure in their faith. It can be tough even for those who are. But it says a lot for their courage and for their desire to show they care, that they're prepared to go. Some have been so fully healed of their past that there is no particular pressure — they are just sad to see old mates deteriorate early through drugs and grog in excess.

Sometimes they have to make a public stand to show that they can't accept some of the excesses of the biker lifestyle. We have some Squad rules which cover this. For instance, we have a no-drinking regulation. This only applies when we're on official God's Squad business. Some of the guys enjoy an occasional beer, as I do. In Australia we produce wine, the best of which is the equal of anything you'll find in the world. I have a small cellar which I delight in sampling. I consider good wine to be one of God's gifts, but I would never belittle anyone who was convinced, like my father and many of my friends, that they should abstain.

I hasten to say we are totally committed to the Bible's command not to be drunk. We also recognize that the greatest drug problem in Western culture is excessive alcohol consumption. Frankly, this issue is a hot potato with many Christians and I hesitate to talk about it, since there is a vast difference between Christian attitudes in my own country and in Europe. I am not a traditional man, but a biblical man. The abuse and lack of self-control in our culture has tragic consequences. John the Baptist was a tee-totaller. Jesus drank wine, but he was controlled and disciplined. I think one of the most stunning evidences I've seen of the power of a real Christian conversion is in this realm. When a seriously-addicted alcoholic finds faith and is so changed that he or she can have wine with a meal with no destructive consequences, and no return to alcohol dependency — you have a powerful change.

For some of our guys it's been a major problem and they just have to totally quit. If it's a problem, there is no doubt — give it a total miss. I believe our call to sensible and godly control has bred a maturity that is not produced by putting a total embargo on drink.

Despite working among extreme drug and alcohol cultures we have had an excellent record in the field and do not find drunkenness a problem among our young converts. Some of our folk obviously have histories which demand total abstinence until real long-term healing is clearly evident. For others, weaknesses seem too ingrained and a life of total removal is necessary. I guess this applies to many situations. I would never encourage a mate with an alcohol problem to be involved in spreading the Christian message in pubs. Yet I personally, having no alcohol problem, delight in doing that. I'm virtually as much at home chatting in a pub as in a chapel.

Over-consumption of drink is a particular characteristic of the bike scene. Many of the worst sides of outlaw behaviour arise because people get off their faces on booze. So at Squad functions we have a no-drink rule. We still go to pubs, as a club, to meet other bikers. We have no objection, as some Christians do, to being seen in such 'dens of iniquity', but we'll keep to soft drinks there. When you're riding bikes, which can be lethal machines at the best of times, it would be dangerous and irresponsible to drink. I have no statistics, but it is common knowledge that many of the accidents in which bikers are killed or maimed would not have happened if they were sober.

Sometimes Squad members have to react to things which happen around them and which call for some kind of public response. I have seen a group of the guys who've been invited to an outlaw-club party, turn their backs as one man when a stripper took the stage. This wasn't out of prudishness or embarrassment so much as a statement about the way women are treated as objects for sexual kicks.

On another occasion there was a thoroughly inhuman incident where a group of bikers were humiliating a young teenage kid. Young blokes, especially those who find it difficult to fit in, hang around the fringes of the bike scene; they get a vicarious thrill from being among 'real men'.

In this instance there was a poor, socially inadequate kid, with thick spectacles, who was trying to find some sense of identity by trying to be a friend of bikers. The guys he was with were getting bored with this twerp and decided to show him just how insignificant he was. These drunken bullies first smashed his glasses to make him even more vulnerable and then degraded him totally by encircling him, forcing him to his knees involving him in obscenities with one after the other.

Colin McKenzie came upon this horrifying scene. With the decisive instincts he had developed as an outlaw, he summed things up and with typical guts stepped straight into the circle of bikers saying, 'Right, that's enough.' Helping their trembling victim to his feet, he walked the kid off and looked after him.

I'm not pretending that this kind of intervention happens often, nor that it is typical of the bike scene, though it isn't the worst thing of its kind to take place. But it demonstrates an aspect of our presence among this fraternity.

I am constantly surprised by the contrasts I find as I meet with my mates in this scene. The human ability to perform the most astonishing acts of love and self-sacrifice on the one hand and yet equally to be able to destroy each other and themselves.

Human beings are remarkable. Someone once said they are the only creatures on the planet with the ability both to laugh and cry. It's true. We laugh because of the glorious possibilities of life. We cry because of the gap between our dreams and what we achieve. We are capable of experiencing and fostering overwhelming joy and also unspeakable horror.

There are two examples I often quote when talking to high

school students. They both happened around the same time and they sum up these two extremes of human behaviour. Some years ago an airliner crashed into the Potomac River in the United States. It was mid-winter and the survivors were plunged into the icy waters. A helicopter rescue team spotted a survivor who was holding another out of the water. They lowered a ladder. He made sure the person he was holding was winched up, but refused to climb to safety himself. Repeatedly he swam to other, weaker passengers keeping them above water until they were rescued. When the helicopter returned to the scene to pick him up, he was nowhere to be seen. Exhaustion and cold had taken its toll and he'd drowned.

The news teams interviewed his friends and family. Everyone agreed that this was no isolated act of selflessness. His whole life had been characterized by his care for other people. This is the kind of Christ-like action humans are capable of. There are a million examples of this kind of sacrificial love.

While this was happening in one corner of the globe, Pol Pot, the Kampuchean tyrant, was executing young men who wore glasses, in case they might just be intellectuals and therefore a theoretical threat to his regime. Under his brutal destruction of the country, young men were lined up by the side of the road. They were then castrated and forced to eat their own genitals. It is horrific to relate, but this is the world we live in and these are the depths to which our fellow humans are prepared to stoop. And the Australian and American governments, who among others, gave tacit support to Pol Pot at the time, cannot consider their hands clean of such brutality. We are at odds with a club called Russia, and so is Pol Pot. So we were allied on the basis of mutual hate with an Asian version of Hitler.

Bikers are human and so they also are capable of good and bad. This was sharply pointed up at a funeral I attended in Western Victoria some years ago. It was a large funeral for a particularly popular biker, killed in a road accident. This was no typical working-class kid. He was the son of a state senator. As a result, there was a visible division between the mourners. There were the lad's family and friends, very straight and highly respectable, together with his bike-club mates.

One drunken biker decided to terrorize a car-full of funeral guests, by climbing on the hood and urinating on the windscreen. At the graveside a couple of his mates, who'd probably been drinking beer since the early morning, came over to the graveside after the formalities were over and relieved the pressure on their bladders as if this was normal procedure.

Yet among the many middle-class, tight-lipped, frozen-faced mourners, were a couple of guys in leather, with tears streaming down their faces, making genuine efforts to comfort their dead friend's grieving mother. So grateful was the senator for the contrasting kindness of the bikers, that he provided a keg and barbecue for them to come back to after the funeral.

When you witness such events, you realize that stereotyping anyone is both impossible and unjust. I'm involved in the bike scene to try to get past those public prejudices. And because of that, the Squad sometimes has to defend the cause of the bikers against the public forces of law and order.

I believe in law enforcement. It is absolutely essential. I don't have a rosy attitude towards humanity. Its excesses must be kept in check. But I also believe in justice. The law must be enforced and dispensed with justice, otherwise it loses its value and integrity.

I think police officers in most Western countries have an extremely difficult job. Often they know what's happening and who's to blame, but either the cumbersome nature of the law or the quick footwork of lawyers and villains mean that they can't be brought to book. This is a frustration and leads some officers to dispense their own rough justice. I can understand that, even if I can't condone it.

God's Squad have usually had very good relations with the police. Melbourne's Chief Superintendent Wookie, until he retired, made sure his officers knew the nature of our work. This gave us no immunity from the law, but it freed us from suspicion and the kind of close attention bikers invite. But almost all of us, at one time or another, have had unpleasant exchanges with policemen. This has been due to the kind of stereotyping I described earlier.

Bikers have a bad name and, being so visible, present an easy target. It has to be said that many bikers live close to the edge of the law and often stray over it. But this is no excuse for the systematic harassment and abuse which has sometimes gone on under the guise of police work. Too often policemen will take one look at a leather jacket and reach for their notebook.

I even discovered that one police department had an extensive file on me. Inside contacts made it possible for me to read my file, only to find that it contained information that was both unsubstantiated and plain wrong. It suggested that I was only masquerading as a minister of religion and that I had once been involved in a ruckus at a hospital at a time when I was taking a youth camp on the other side of Melbourne. Official approaches to have these internal lies rectified provoked only scorn and refusal from the superintendent at the time.

Police officers, especially young men who feel they've still got something to prove, see the bikers as a type rather than as individual people. When this happens, it's easy to justify injustice and inhumanity. Without wishing to over-exaggerate, it is the same principle which was behind the extermination of the Jews in Nazi Germany.

I wouldn't suggest that anything like such injustices have been meted out on outlaw bikers, who can't always be described as the pure and innocent. But there have been too many occasions when the police have overstepped the mark. I know of one instance when police with a warrant to search for stolen Harley Davidsons, raided a Hell's Angel's flat and

213

turned the place upside down. As part of their search for these huge American motorcycles, they tipped the occupier's records out of their sleeves and left them scattered on the floor. I've heard of the Devil lurking in the grooves of rock'n'roll records, but never a Harley!

In the West, we pride ourselves on living in tolerant and civilized conditions. It is often said that a society is measured by the treatment of its weakest citizens. The Hell's Angels, the Coffin Cheaters, the Huns and the rest, scarcely come into that category. To reinterpret the phrase, I would say that a culture can also be measured by the way it treats those who deliberately flout the consensus and refuse to toe the line. When they are treated with justice and humanity, we can genuinely be proud of ourselves.

CHAPTER SIXTEEN

God's Squad played, as it does today, only a certain (if occasionally dramatic) part in my life. The centre on Canterbury Road was more than thriving — it was bursting at the seams. By early 1973 we had knocked down every available wall and within a few years we still couldn't fit everyone in.

This was all right in the summer, because then we would set up speakers on the veranda and people could sit under the trees on the patch of ground between the house and the main road and still hear what was being said. In the end I had to abandon speaking in the central room and come out onto the veranda and preach from there.

The Monday night Bible studies, originally started in our home for God's Squad, now drew hundreds each time. We attracted people from all over the city, often people who had found faith and meaning through the work of the centre, but found it difficult to fit in with the traditional church patterns where they lived. And together with them came a lot of people who were hearing the Christian gospel for the first time in languages and images they could understand.

The mix of people changed. We had many coming early on, because of our work with bikers, but what with the mission work we were doing on all sorts of other fronts, we gathered a wider bunch of disaffected people and in this group, many more girls — quite a few of them in their late teens.

We were pleased the numbers were increasing, but because of its speed it was very difficult to keep pace with events. Besides all this, we were travelling Australia: speaking in schools, universities, service clubs, rock concerts and at many different events. There were some excellent people around who were gifted in dealing with individuals or small groups but there was no one who could take on an overall leadership role when I wasn't there. This was becoming an urgent problem, not only because I was often away taking missions and camps, but because I was due to go to the US for six weeks.

One of the members of our resources group was Rob Hopkins. He was a pilot for Ansett, Australia's largest internal airline. He approached me with the idea of going overseas. He thought it would do me good to travel and gain some insights from others who were dealing with the same sort of people we were. He had some concessionary tickets which would give me a free flight to America and cover any internal flights I might need.

I jumped at the chance. Here was a long dreamed-of opportunity to visit some of the Christian initiatives in a number of US cities I'd heard so much about. I had never in my life been out of Australia before and I was very excited at the prospect. It was arranged that I should go in August. But the problem of who should take charge of the place in my absence still remained.

That was when I met Mike Peele. Mike was teaching at the time, but before he had become a Christian he had been both a legitimate businessman and had done some drug dealing on the side. A Canadian by birth, he had spent some years in the States, and knew the counter-culture inside out.

I was introduced to Mike through his son who had heard me preach at a youth convention and had subsequently become a Christian. Mike and I met and I took to him immediately. He had qualities that are rare in Australia, particularly among our hippie-type circle. He had a great deal of self-assurance, and the knack of putting people instantly at their ease. He was a strong character, but didn't need to rant and rave to show it. Despite my strong sense of calling, I often struggled with my own feelings of insecurity,

216

in those early days, so he was a tower of strength.

Shortly after we met, I asked him if he would consider minding the shop while I was in the States. He agreed, and joined us unofficially about six weeks before I flew out.

In retrospect, it was one of the weaknesses of the growing Jesus Movement all over the world, that major leadership appointments were frequently made under phenomenal pressure, and at ill-advised speed. Crisis decision-making led to many disasters, not only for us, but in some of the leading similar movements in the US and Europe.

But with massive human tragedy and demand, we grabbed any resource in personnel or property we could lay our hands on. Some 5,000 young people claimed to find meaningful faith through the first two and a half years of our work. Many of these felt alienated from the church and from the state. Responsibility for housing, rehabilitation, counselling, friendship and fellowship fell on our shoulders — ill-equipped and short-staffed as we were.

Mike's arrival seemed timely. While I was in California I wrote and asked him formally to join the staff. And when he finished his teaching job, he joined Truth and Liberation Concern at the beginning of 1974, our third year in operation.

So, feeling nervous and rather alone I set off for America. It was a dramatic change of life and pace for me. I had been standing on my hind legs, preaching, teaching and counselling people practically non-stop for the last seven years. Now the boot was on the other foot. I think I spoke in public only once in forty-odd days. It felt very strange.

I went to Berkeley in California. This was the place where so much of the student radicalism of the late sixties had sprung from, most of it centred around the university. By 1973 the energy and idealism that had marked this movement had largely dissipated. I walked down Telegraph Avenue, once one of the great centres of the counter-culture, only to find it populated by the sad victims of a dream gone sour. I was propositioned sixteen times to buy drugs by an assortment of vacant-eyed people.

Every telegraph pole down the street was plastered with a hundred competing posters for rock concerts, health food co-ops, readings of poetry and Eastern meditation. There were also messages to missing children from their parents. One simple notice caught my eye. It read, 'Dear Suzy, your mummy and daddy still love you. We are searching everywhere for you. If you come home, we will give you a Lincoln and buy you anything you want.' It was all so tragic. Everywhere I looked I saw kids of fourteen and fifteen, looking jaded and lost. Terrifying.

I'd come to Berkeley to meet up with Professor Jack Sparkes, the leader of the Christian World Liberation Front. Jack would stand at the university steps on Sproul Plaza, the site of many large political demonstrations in the sixties. Wearing his army green overalls, he would preach with passion and intellect from an open Bible to the students who passed. He had been converted as an atheist professor, simply by reading the Old Testament and the Gospels. He had been overwhelmed by the life and teachings of Christ.

I was impressed not only with Jack, who was addressing the major issues of the day with real Christian insight and vigour, but also with his church. The church was devolved into a number of community houses, each of which was a household church in its own right. I saw how community gave a real strength and unity to the lives of the people there. I began to think of our centre back home and the many homeless and churchless people whom we were attracting. Realization dawned over just how important to the growth of these people a loving, caring and worshipping community could be.

Towards the end of my time in America I stopped off in Houston. I'd seen a film back in Oz about a place called the Church of the Redeemer, an Episcopalian (Anglican) church whose minister was Graham Pulkingham. With my Free Church background I'd always thought Anglicans a bit stiff and formal. But here in Houston another prejudice bit the dust. The people here held in beautiful balance the richness of a structured liturgy with the freedom of the Holy Spirit. There was a definite pattern to their services, yet there was always space for people in the congregation to make their own spontaneous contribution to worship. I felt enriched as a result.

A remarkable event took place on my first evening here, and it concerned my son, Paul. Paul had begun to suffer badly from asthma from the age of three. He had a number of allergies to which the asthma was connected. He would often contract bronchitis at the same time, and had been hospitalized on eight occasions already. And we didn't know how to handle it. He had been through a number of close calls before in oxygen tents.

That evening, I went to one of their church services. I was quietly soaking up the gentle atmosphere when I was stricken by total panic. What if Paul had a bad asthma attack? My itinerary had been vague and Glena had no phone number for me. What if he died? It was something I had feared several times before. Now for some reason I felt a chill of dread creep over me.

In the midst of this fog, I heard one of the church's elders speaking. She said, 'There is someone here tonight from the other side of the world. He is from thousands of miles away and his son has asthma.'

I can't remember her precise words, but she mentioned his age which was correct and said that he was undergoing an attack at that moment. 'Your heart is filled with fear and God has told me to ask you to come up for prayer,' she continued. I was completely stunned. No one in this church knew me. And yet what she had said was so specific, she had to be talking about me. Still dazed I made my way to the front of the church.

The woman welcomed me, prayed for me and then for Paul. I returned to my seat. And then she added, 'I don't have a verse of scripture for you, but I believe God wants me to give you this verse of a hymn. "Peace, perfect peace, with loved

219

ones far away. In Jesus' keeping we are safe, and they".'

I am sometimes sceptical about 'revelations' which are made in meetings like this. Often they are very general and could apply to a number of people or situations. But I believe that God spoke to that woman. I found when I phoned home that Glena was staying with her family in Queensland at that time and Paul did have a serious asthma attack. But because she was home, Glena's brother-in-law was nearby. A sufferer from asthma himself, he was able to pass on techniques that could control Paul's attacks. Paul has never needed to go back to hospital with his problem since. He appears now to be asthma-free.

Direct revelations from God can easily be passed off, but they do occur. He has many ways of communicating with us, some more obvious than others. One morning I woke up, absolutely clearly awake, almost with a start. An agnostic might say I was struck with the immediacy of an idea. But to me, with my firm belief in the supernatural, I was sure I was receiving an instruction from God. The idea was very direct and unambiguous.

'When you go back to Australia, begin teaching straight from the Bible.'

I was perplexed by this notion. I rather prided myself on my communication style. It was contemporary, a mixture of current issues, Bible references, and contemporary quotations. It had earned me something of a reputation in my field. I thought, if I go back, open the Bible and start teaching, then I might start losing people.

The answer came back, 'I will worry about that. You just do your job. Start with the book of Acts.'

That's just what I did. I returned home from America with this thought uppermost in my mind. I told the team what had happened and began studying the book. At the first opportunity, I started teaching from verse one. I still find it hard to believe the results. On those Monday nights I opened up the book of Acts, which is the story of the early church community from the moment Jesus left the scene. I wasn't to reach the end of the book until seventy or more weeks later, by which time the whole place had changed.

I began to explore it in a very down-to-earth way since most of those listening to me were biblically illiterate. The Bible was completely new territory for them. We took it like a pilgrimage, because the early church was just like us, starting out on a life with God.

How it happened I can't say, but people started coming in their hundreds. I'd started the studies to give some strength and biblical education to the staff and to God's Squad. In the end we peaked at 500 people sitting outside with their pillows and blankets, hungry to hear what God was saying. And though this was straight Bible teaching, every night more people would ask how they could become believers. We would end up talking to them until one and two in the morning.

This gave us an extra problem. What were we going to do with all these new Christians? We tried to feed them into churches around the city, but a lot of the kids felt alienated and uncomfortable because they were unused to church and in some cases they were made to feel unwelcome. Many of them didn't bother. Monday night was their church and they didn't want to go anywhere else. I was concerned about this, because my US trip had shown clearly the need for real church community.

I discussed this question with local churchmen, a number of whom admitted that if we started sending all these people their way, they wouldn't be able to cope with the influx. So we agreed that to meet the needs of these people, we had better form ourselves into a church, with all the proper sacraments of communion, baptism and marriage. My days of more formal pastoral experience in the Methodist circuit were now to become very useful.

I had been wondering whether we should start a church even before leaving for the States, but had been reluctant to do so. We'd had some offers of help from established churches, which we took seriously, but with the kind of people who were coming our way, none of the solutions seemed to work. Reluctantly, we felt we had to go it alone.

You may wonder why we couldn't just carry on the way we were. After all, we had a building and a congregation. Weren't we a church anyway? In my view we weren't. We were just a loose association of people, many of whom drifted in and out of the place. We needed to become a family. That meant we had to become an identifiable, answerable fellowship of human beings. Like any family we needed traditions, agreements, accountability and expectations from each other. We needed a certain amount of order and discipline.

We began to meet on Sunday afternoons. The Monday Bible studies continued, attracting large numbers. Over the next few years we covered an immense amount of ground. We explored Paul's two letters to the Thessalonians. That was a young church too, facing similar problems to us. They, like us, had young guys who wouldn't work, because they thought it was OK to bludge off the state and people in the church in order to go round talking to people about Jesus. It was all very practical. These letters also applied directly to our own dying, self-destructive, disintegrating society, just as they had done in the dying stages of Roman civilization, when the letters were first written.

We moved on to the Book of James, a book that drives you to prove your Christianity by the way you live. Then we went on to Ephesians, which brings in the family. But there's some tough stuff there on relationships between husband and wife. All this was new to our congregation, which must have had more divorcees per square inch than any church in the city. In fact, this teaching was so new that we broke off so that I could give some lectures on the male and female in Australia, to see the weaknesses in our relationships within our culture. And so it carried on. And these weren't twenty minute sermonettes. It was an hour and a half of solid teaching. Yet people came back for more. I was glad I'd woken up that morning in California to hear God telling me to teach straight from the Bible.

Our church family had grown so large we needed a bigger house once again. Glena had a genius for making places homely and welcoming, and her flair had made our scruffy little building into a real home. Knowing that we now had to enlarge our premises, she was determined that it shouldn't become institutional.

The father of Roger Falconer, one of our Squad members who died tragically in a road accident in 1980, was an architect. Colin Falconer kindly offered to draw up the plans for a long building that could be sited behind the house. And in the meantime I met a wonderful, eccentric man called Alistair Knox, who had pioneered his own brand of environmental architecture using mud bricks and second-hand beams. He was something of an Australian legend in architectural circles. I met him when I preached at the church where he was a member, and he offered to help.

We had seen the mud-brick idea in practice and knew that it was possible for a committed group of people to construct a building by making their own basic building materials. We needed a project that we could do bit by bit as we raised the necessary cash, and this seemed ideal. Glena particularly liked the warmth and organic feel of mud-brick buildings, because they felt more homely.

We set to work. As much as we could we used talent from within our own community, and it was surprising what we found. Ted Adams, a farmer in our community, provided the trees for the beams. Mike Peele also knew how to adze timbers, so he did a lot of the work on the timbers and our two magnificent twelve-foot-high wooden doors. We had a smith who made wonderful cast-iron light fittings and splendid hinges for the massive doors, which were hung so well that even a three-year-old could push them open.

George Harvey was an experienced site foreman-cum-overseer, so he and his wife Joy organized much of the work, from the mud-brick production to the making of windows. We used the mud from the back yard and at first pressed it by hand into moulds. We got hold of an asphalt-making machine that was laying idle and converted it into a mud-brick manufacturer. We called it L. E. Phant, because the big bricks fell out of the back of the machine rather like elephant's droppings!

The work was useful therapy as well as necessity. It enabled large numbers of people to get their hands dirty, to get to know one another in the process and to feel they had a part in the place. It wasn't an easy job. Hand winching 35-foot beams up to the roof and then coach bolting them in place was difficult and dangerous work. Although the men did much of the heavy labour, it was the women who put in much of the hard work. Their weekly work parties kept the project moving when enthusiasm flagged.

It took the best part of five years to complete, though we were able to use it before then. Glena and others had chased up some more old theatre seats, which are so much more comfortable and less formal than normal church furniture. These were placed in curved rows lengthways so the congregation was facing one of the long walls. By this device, each member was able to feel part of the gathering; you could see people's faces, not just the back of their heads. Set in the walls before them were two enormous kitchen fireplaces, a feature Glena had insisted on. In winter they burned logs and lent a real atmosphere to the place. Glena was determined that coming into a church should be as easy and welcoming as walking into someone's lounge room.

It was a magnificent building. It didn't have the coldness of more orthodox church architecture, yet it definitely had its own dignity. It could seat over 500 people and also had space for offices, a large kitchen and a sizeable eating area. It cost probably one-fifth or less of the price it would have been to build commercially, but only because of the mammoth efforts of the community. When it was first built it was recognized as the largest mud-brick building in Australia. The record has since been broken by a Baptist church inspired by our efforts, but it remains a monument to everyone who made a brick, chiselled a window or carried in a cinema seat.

It was a family home for the many of hundreds of people who poured through its doors.

With the people came their problems and hangups. We were attracting people who needed a lot of help and that took time. We adopted a policy from the very start of counselling and providing practical help to anyone we thought required it, regardless of whether they were really part of our church community or not. Word went round and we used to get phone calls from all over the country, made by desperate individuals who'd often say, 'Are you the people who help people?' before launching into their story.

It has too often been said that the church attracts the weak because they need a psychological crutch of faith to make up for their inadequacy. This is a myth. It is often only when they are in pain that people realize their former, apparently healthy condition was actually a fraud. It was in fact their success, friends or family which were their props; when these disappeared there was nothing left to rely on.

As superintendent minister, many of these calls came to me. After a while, I couldn't cope. I'd try to talk to as many people as I could, but I was beginning to get strung out with the many demands on my time. I love talking to people face to face. The one thing I regret is that the more I have been called to speak and preach, the less time I've had for individuals. We needed an experienced counsellor on the team. So I talked to Ian Clarkson, a Uniting church minister I'd met on my epic journey to Perth. He was happy to join us and made a tremendous difference.

The catalogue of problems was enormous. We had broken and breaking marriages. We had kids on dope and adults on drink. There were manic depressives, people crippled by guilt and others who were just plain lonely. Incest, domestic violence and schizophrenia were almost daily challenges.

We also took a supervisory role for churches beyond Melbourne which shared our vision. John and Ma Sutherland in Brisbane felt very deeply for the street kids in their part of the city. John was an older man, a retired electrician. He and Ma started a club for kids called 'Crossroads'.

Then Dave Peake, a veterinary surgeon, who was also from Brisbane and was eventually to become the Vice President of a Brisbane chapter of God's Squad, spent time with us and observed our approach at T&LC. He and his brother, Graeme, did the spade work for one of the most outstanding university missions we ever had – two weeks of large, responsive audiences. In Brisbane, with our help, he planted a church called 'Signposts', in the suburb of Inala, a working-class, housing commission area with enormous social problems. He did a tremendous work there, until the mission closed in 1982. The leaders then scattered into other fruitful ministries.

One of the first situations Ian had to deal with was a woman with severe psychological difficulties, who used to burn herself with cigarettes. When she was in this state she could feel no pain. In her broken daze, she once said, 'At least if I'm sinful, I'm something.' At one time in her history she had crushed a drinking glass under her bare heel as if it were cardboard, severely lacerating her foot. Ian and his wife Rosemary worked closely with her for a long time, and the process of healing began. We noticed the change one day when she shoved a cigarette butt into her body and jumped. Reality was emerging. It was a long battle, but gradually her life was transformed.

I am convinced that while schizophrenia may often be chemically based, like many other broken human conditions, rejection may be the last straw which breaks the camel's back. If so, it is not surprising that vulnerable accepting love so often brings amazing healing. For all its weaknesses, there is no human association more effective than those genuine, loving church fellowships scattered all over the world.

Looking back, some of the events and experiences were bordering on bizarre. On one occasion a criminal on the run from horrendous connections came to our house in terrible disrepair. He had worn through not only the soles of his shoes but also through successive layers of skin. His feet were worn through to bare bleeding flesh. His Sydney-based mates were involved in the torture of other criminals; thieves preyed upon thieves to obtain the profits of robberies. Here was a man who had once listened mercilessly to the screams of others, now desperate and on the run. I am not sure if the contract out on him by the gang was $5,000 or $10,000, but he was worth a tidy pocketful of money — dead.

I gave him one of only two pairs of shoes I possessed at the time. He stood in the lounge room and wept. His recent experience of faith had certainly softened a once-brutal heart. But his fears were very much alive. We offered to mediate with the gang, but he fled, fearing recriminations against me and my family if I were to enter into the situation directly. We pleaded with him that the Old Book calls us, if necessary, to lay down our lives for our brothers and sisters. But he had moved on by the next morning.

There were many less dramatic stories of healing and transformation. As the church grew, we found we were beginning to see more mature people coming to us. There were housewives with barbiturate and alcohol problems. Also there were men who could no longer communicate with their wives or children. We were still predominantly a young church, but the social and age mix was widening.

Psychologists and psychiatrists have an important role to play in our disturbed and fragmented culture. The insights that have been gained into the diagnosis of neurosis and mental illness are important. But often these professionals have to work in a vacuum. They often find it takes patients a long time to get back on their feet, because they have to struggle with their problem alone.

One of the most significant things we have seen in the life of our community is the power of the gospel to heal people. I don't mean that this hasn't taken place alongside sound counselling. But again and again we have seen people's lives transformed.

When a person is loved and made to feel genuinely at home

in a community of people, the process of healing has already begun. And when people realize that there is a father God who loves them, and whose Son was prepared to die for them, it gives them a completely new dimension to their lives and to their problems.

There were professionals who came to see this too. One of the members of our congregation, an ex-policeman, became a prosecutor in the Children's Court. Having seen the work we were doing with hard street kids, he would sometimes recommend that youngsters who'd had a brush with the law be sent to us.

This brought us to the attention of the chief psychiatrist of a State Children's Court. This man, a Sri Lankan by birth, called me in and asked me about the nature of our work. I began defensively, not wanting to sound like an irrational Christian, dispensing cheap spiritual solutions to deep social and emotional problems. But he stopped me.

'You don't have to defend yourself to me. I'm not a Westerner, I'm not a materialist like most of you Australians. I'm observing in this country a breakdown in the culture that is so severe, that if you can't reverse it by finding some kind of foundation, then you are finished. You are a civilization that is dying from within. Don't be tender about the faith aspect of your work. The kids who are coming to these courts are often in a frightening state of disrepair. They get younger and their problems get worse year by year. So serious is their state of breakdown, the only person who can help them now is an evangelist.'

He wasn't a Christian. He was probably Hindu. But he understood that there are spiritual causes to social problems as well as psychological and environmental ones. We were finding that if you tackled all three causes in an integrated way, then people were able to change.

Homelessness was another question we had to face from the very start. As T&LC developed, it soon became obvious that we could no longer have people crashing out all over the floor in the main meeting area. They were often homeless because of problems with money, relationships, incest, drugs, drink — or a complex of reasons.

So we bought a place called Montrose House. It was situated in Melbourne's outer suburbs, but it was surrounded by fields, so it felt less like the city. The several caring couples who took on the task of leadership at different times deserve a particular mention for their courage and commitment. They brought up their families of small children among people who many in our society would call undesirable. On one occasion, a child molester was loved and nurtured by one of the families.

It can be tough facing people's traumas and problems day in and day out. And there are risks. Again and again I have seen psychologists and welfare workers burned out. Dealing perpetually with people's distress can not only warp your view of the world, it can also attack your own sense of identity. It's like sucking the poison out of a snake bite. You can save a person's life but, if you've got an ulcer or broken skin in your mouth, then the venom can enter your own bloodstream.

I've watched so many idealists start this kind of work with compassion and enthusiasm, and then retreat into cynicism or else break down themselves — all because they hadn't adequate defences to deal with the weight of the world's problems. If people haven't a strong sense of identity or self-worth, and some kind of belief which gives them a healthy overview of the world, then burn-out can easily occur.

I am fascinated by the Old Testament story of the burning bush. Moses was out looking after his sheep one day when he saw a flaming bush out there in the scrub. It burned, the Bible puts it, 'without being consumed'. God spoke to Moses from that bush. There is a strong symbolism here. The bush wasn't scorched because it was flaming from God's perpetual fire. This, I think is how I and many other Christians working with our nerve ends constantly exposed to people's

229

feelings, carry on without collapsing.

While in Israel, I discovered a medallion celebrating Israel's identity. It featured a stylized burning bush circled by words in Hebrew and English — 'And the bush was not consumed'. Strong identity — personally or nationally — is based on a sense of destiny, meaning and calling in life.

I have a fire in my belly, which I believe will not burn out. What sensitivity I have to people is strengthened by a call from God to tackle their needs. But my identity is not bound up with my ability to perform, but in the dignity of being a child of God. Intellectually, spiritually and emotionally, I know that I am worth something because God made me. My value was set by Jesus' willingness to die for me. Whatever the world throws at me, that central core to my identity cannot be shaken. I am his and he is mine. If I didn't know that, I don't think I could cope.

Much more could be said about the growth of our community church. There are hundreds of stories of people arriving, lost and hurt, and finding in God's infinite love a reason for living. The ten years it took were hard. Glena and I didn't see a lot of each other. Often the pressures of the work brought argument and conflict in the family. I was often to blame, failing to turn up when promised and on occasions putting my family second when they should have been first.

At times our own home, and the homes of other staff members, were centres of costly care and ministry. One day a woman rang in desperation.

'Are you the people who love people?' she asked. 'I don't want a —— appointment next Wednesday with a —— psychologist behind a —— desk. If you don't talk to me now I'll —— well kill myself!'

Coming from a fine home, somehow she had lost her self-worth. She was attractive, in fact she was positively sexy. She claimed to have seduced a number of big name counsellors, including celebrated ministers and a talk-back radio counsellor. She was a capable, highly qualified nurse and she was an alcoholic.

Two staff members carried her into our home, hopelessly drunk. We promised to pay her wages personally for as long as it took for her to dry out.

Well on into the first evening soon after retiring to bed, I heard a plaintive cry from her. Glena said to me, 'You had better go to her and see what she wants.' I went.

She began a cunning line. 'Do you find some of the people you help are more attractive than others? Do you find *me* attractive?'

I played dumb. The conversation became obvious.

Suddenly she stopped, looked intently at me and said, 'You know exactly what I'm doing, don't you?'

'Yes', I replied.

'And you're not going to come on, whatever I do, are you?'

I assured her she was most attractive, but we were not about to exploit or be exploited.

She broke down, weeping, and cried — 'You really do love me, don't you.' She had tested and found wanting a number of vulnerable counsellors, only to be used and dehumanized again and again. The story ended with a healed life, deliverance from alcoholism and low self-image. Her marriage was restored and strengthened.

I shudder in horror at the exploitation of such broken people by professionals. Experts and professionals can, in our culture, live in public mystery and beyond public answerability. Lawyers, psychiatrists and psychologists can often leave the ordinary person feeling as helpless as if in the hands of witch-doctors. I believe in professional care and expertise. But there is one thing I don't believe: that professionals are any more moral than labourers.

These were some of the most exciting years of our lives. When God gave me a calling to be an 'apostle to the Gentiles', I never expected I would end up swathed in leather on the seat of a Harley Davidson. (I did eventually get one of those magnificent machines.) Nor did I imagine pastoring a church full of people — for many their first and only church

— and whose attendance some days topped 800. It wasn't my skill, or my personality. It was obedience to God's nudgings. I can't explain it any other way. And the story wasn't over yet.

CHAPTER SEVENTEEN

As a movement, we were into everything. As God's Squad we would still set off on our runs to meet with our outlaw mates, or to visit prisons, high schools and universities. Meanwhile, back at the church we continued to care for homeless people, deal with individual problems and run a club for younger kids under the leadership of Quince. The challenge of our weekly Bible studies maintained its sharpness, and as a result, a social justice group was formed.

We believed that this was a significant time in the history of Australia, with the election of a socialist government under Gough Whitlam, and our hopes were high. We believed, in our idealism, that we were going to see a period when the state would take seriously its responsibility to the poor and disadvantaged. In the early days of his government, Whitlam looked as though he was going to bring to the country some sense of fair play.

We supported this, but felt concerned lest he apply purely secular solutions to the country's social problems and neglected the spiritual causes behind them. And so around 2,000 Christians, from different groups, gathered together in the country's capital city of Canberra to serve notice on the government. We silently surrounded the entire National Parliament, holding hands, praying for Whitlam and for national justice. I gave a speech, based on Jesus' liberation address in Luke chapter 4, from the steps of the Parliament building expressing support for Whitlam's concern for people, but warning him that a re-distribution of wealth did not answer all the questions posed by people's poverty and pain.

The Whitlam experiment foundered in confusion and controversy, and we returned to a system which encouraged the rich to get richer at the expense of the people at the bottom. Despite our relative affluence in the Western world, there are many who, because of their circumstances, their background or their racial origins, find themselves with no voice and little influence to improve their lot in life. The unemployed, inner-city families, Aborigines and ethnic minorities, for example.

I remember our discovery of a deserted urban aboriginal wife, who had lived for weeks on dry cornflakes. She had applied for welfare for herself and her children. The government officer sent to investigate accused her of being a black whore. He accused her of having a husband in the cupboard. Dehumanized and humiliated, she slammed the door in his face. She ran into the shower fully clothed, and screamed as the water poured over her. She vowed not to seek help again, even if she starved. It was a privilege to be able to help her.

The poor and weak are dependent on the wealthy, the powerful and the articulate to speak for them, but they get precious little help. The services such people get from doctors, lawyers and social workers are too often inadequate. Those who suffer don't have the confidence or the clout, and they don't know the system well enough, to demand satisfaction.

Poor one-parent families often get a raw deal. These are the modern equivalent of 'the widows and fatherless' that the Bible constantly commands God's people to protect. One woman we looked after for a while illustrates starkly the predicament of such people. Her wrists looked like crossword puzzles, they'd been slashed so many times. The court understandably removed her children because she could no longer cope. Under our care she recovered substantially, but the courts wouldn't budge on their judgment.

After many attempts to get her kids back, she broke down again and attempted suicide, and was placed with a psychiatrist. At the start of one of her half-hour sessions he asked if she'd mind if he rang his colleague. After a 25-minute conversation setting up a weekend's golf, he then put the phone down and said, 'Well, I see we only have five minutes left. Never mind. Have you still got some of the tablets I prescribed last week?'

If you're weak and vulnerable, it's difficult to know how to respond. Someone in the psychiatrist's position holds all the cards. This woman went home and in despair she slashed her wrists — again.

There are too many professionals making themselves fat and famous on the backs of the poor. There is corruption and cynicism amongst this intelligent and supposedly compassionate élite. I believe the wrath of God will fall upon those who abuse their privilege, power and status. They will one day face God Almighty, and then they will see true justice. People in the professions, and those in politics and business, are too protective of one another. Their best interest is served in integrity and in the trust of ordinary people, not in cover-up.

Cruelty, insensitivity, selfishness and cheating, are all human traits. Being an expert can simply be a great disguise. The mystique and myth of intellectuals and professionals needs to be stripped away. As my Grandad used to say, 'If you educate a devil, you don't have an angel, you have a clever devil'. A need for integrity, morality and compassion is as important for those of us in the caring professions as for anyone else.

God help us if social work and counselling become another lucrative growth industry. How obscene to see experts become wealthy and powerful on the backs of broken and vulnerable people. People are the one asset we must value. We must treat them with dignity and sensitivity.

I hate the double standard which exists in the West, which approves of extravagant excess among the rich jet set, yet which despises the lonely drunk on the street. There are revealing verses in the Old Testament book of Proverbs which show that God has his own way of balancing the books. Except that his standards favour the poor. God

235

understands the causes of people's problems. He says that it is 'not for kings to drink wine, not for rulers to crave beer, lest they drink and forget what the law decrees, and deprive all the oppressed of their rights.'

Then the passage continues, 'Give beer to those who are perishing, wine to those in anguish; let them drink and forget their poverty and remember their misery no more.'

The homelessness issue was something we felt keenly about. In co-operation with a number of other Christian groups, we took our sleeping bags and made our home for a week under a canopy in Melbourne's city square. Glena and the kids, who were still quite small, volunteered to come too. It was a revealing experience for us all to spend that time on the cold pavement, with the rain running down the steps and soaking our sleeping bags. On a placard we wrote a verse from Proverbs: 'Speak up for those who cannot speak for themselves'. It captures exactly the Christian responsibility to our neighbours. We are not called to demand our own rights, but we should agitate for the rights of others.

News got around that this was going on. It also became known that the authorities weren't moving us on because that would create publicity and so aid our cause. So we were joined by a number of homeless people of all ages who took refuge in the safety of numbers. You can read about sleeping on the streets in books and preach it on the platform, but now and then you have to experience it — even if you know you have the luxury of a bed and a bath to return to. It's the only way to catch something of the hardship some people face every day of their lives.

It's all very well rattling on about the need for justice in the courts and between nations, but this is only a magnification of what goes on in homes every day. There are husbands who use their wives like slaves, mothers who ill-treat their children, adolescents who despise their parents and elder brothers or sisters who put down their juniors.

This need for common justice in the family was brought

home to me by my own children, in an incident some years ago. We were travelling on a long journey in the car. We were late and I was tense. The kids were stroppy and began fighting. Eventually I lost my cool and said, 'If there's any more trouble, then I don't care who started it, you all get a hiding.'

Seconds later there were more yells and thumps. I jammed on the anchors, leaped out of the car and walked into the scrub by the side of the road. I broke off a thin piece of mallee scrub branch, stripped it of leaves and called them out of the car. I lined them up and whacked them on their backsides, one, two, three. We drove on.

I didn't think much more about it. Then some weeks later we had a rare evening to ourselves and had a time of family devotions. Normally we'd read the Bible, talk about it and pray together. But that night I said, 'Right, you can ask me any question you like.'

Quick as a flash, Paul asked, 'Dad, when we were in the car, why did you hit me when I hadn't done anything wrong?'

I cried. I realized what it must be like to have a Dad who's always raging on from the platform about justice, yet who was himself guilty of making poor judgments. It was as if he'd been watching me in the intervening weeks and was saying, 'You're a fraud'. I certainly felt like one. How imperfect we all are, and tragically we seem worse in our own homes. Justice is primarily not a political or international issue — it's a personal one. How obscene is the fact that the worst violence in many Western societies is *domestic* violence? Many battered wives long for the phone call which will announce, 'Your husband is dead!'

In our family, we have had to face many pressures and problems. Having gone through my own struggles because I was the son of a minister, I know something of what it must be like to be my children. It hasn't been an easy upbringing for them. They haven't seen as much of me as they would have if I had had a normal job. And when I'm home, I'm often tired and can be ratty. They've had their toys and

237

favourite objects broken by the kids of our many visitors, and they've lived in a glass house where everyone expects them to be better than anyone else.

I know I'm biased, but I think they've done really well considering what they've had to put up with. They're not wimps. They're rebels and they sometimes give their old man a hard time — quite often, in fact. But I wouldn't want them to be dull and conformist. That's no way to cope with this world. They're going to have to fight to achieve their own identity. But they've got the strength of mind and the guts to do it. I love them to bits and I'm very proud of them.

And Glena too. She's had to bring up Paul, Kathy and Lyndal single-handedly at times. She's had to deal with my insecurities and vulnerabilities and my chauvinism of earlier years. She's had to budget on a shoe-string, lose the privacy of her home and fight to keep some sanity in a marriage which I've seldom made easy. I love her every bit as much as I did the day we were married. She's the one person who's kept me together when I've threatened to fall apart.

Together, as a family, we saw Truth and Liberation Concern grow from nothing into a thriving congregation. By the 1980s, it had established a name for itself as a very unusual place, a kind of alternative church. It was an incredible collection of people: doctors, lawyers, some university students, together with bikers, manual workers, skilled tradespeople as well as those without jobs. We baptized hundreds, married scores and saw a great many come to a strong and informed faith.

But then it began to go sour. Internal leadership problems raised their heads. These were largely invisible to the membership, but they were real enough. The reasons behind the tensions are complex and not really the subject of this book. The sad fact is that we were unable to sort them out.

It broke apart. The building had been Glena's vision. More than anyone else she had dreamed it into existence. To lose it almost cost her her emotional survival. I remember

238

months of broken nights — hearing her at 3 a.m. walking around the house in tears. Not able to understand what she saw as the injustice of it all.

We were a frontier organization with a distrust amounting at times to paranoia of anything which smacked of authority and rigid structure. Also we had grown out of a decade of unprecedented idealism, so that when our high expectations of people and events weren't fulfilled, it led to disillusionment and bitterness for some people. And because we were independent, we didn't have access to external arbitration and discipline which might have helped heal the rift. These were all lessons that were to be useful for the future.

We were so busy doing so many things in so many places that we didn't recognize the significance of our differences until too late. In the end, with great sadness, I felt I had to resign. In November 1982 I left Truth and Liberation Concern, just over ten and a half years after it had all begun.

Leaving T&LC broke me up. I left with a sense of bereavement which is still with me. But I'm most sorry for the members of the congregation, many of whom felt hurt and betrayed by this family breakup. A number stayed, some left and joined with me in the inner-city community church that we eventually established. Others scattered to other churches around the city, but some have felt so badly about the breakup that they can't bring themselves to go anywhere. It was a tragedy, and I can't disguise the fact. Nevertheless, nothing can wipe out entirely the reality of transformed lives during those ten years.

As with all tragedies, we had to pick up the pieces and carry on as best we could. About a hundred of us, including nearly all of God's Squad, spent a year or so in limbo church-wise, moving from hall to hall, looking for a permanent place to settle. Finally, we found a large, disused Anglican church near inner-city Melbourne in Carlton. We kept its original name: St Martin's Community Church. I was pleased that we'd found an urban location, because so much of our work was directed towards the urban community. I

239

was inducted as Superintendent Minister in 1984. God's Squad continued to operate from St Martin's and has a special place in the congregation. We're still rolling. In fact, our wider work never really slowed down. We continued, right through the period of separation, to work in schools, universities, prisons, and on the streets. Our overall organization is now known as 'Care and Communication Concern'.

Schools have always been a special concern of mine. I had been involved (as an ex-'chalkie') in schools seminars for many years. Now I became involved in a major initiative among high school students in the state of South Australia.

The idea was a simple one. To educate children in this part of Australia about Christianity. We weren't going into schools to hit them over the heads with propaganda, but to show them that Christianity was a real option and not something to be dismissed in an off-hand kind of way. It was organized and run in such a way that it had real educational value as well as something to say. We addressed some 500,000 students across Australia.

The idea grew out of a concern for the disintegration of Australian society. Most of our social statistics match (and in some cases are worse than) comparable Western societies. One child out of every five lives on or below the poverty line. We used to have the highest rate of declared rape in the world. We have a terrible record of alcoholism, and an extraordinarily high rate of suicide among young men between the ages of twenty and twenty-nine.

It seemed as if our kids had been dumped in a hostile world without any real moral guidance on how to handle it. Years ago a first-form girl told me of a school visit to see the nude revue *Hair*. She maintained the class had an 'orgy' at the hotel after the show. She said with unbelievable intensity, 'Sir, we want to ask you a question, because we felt guilty afterwards. Is sex any different for two human beings than for two dogs doing it on the grass outside?'

There is a crisis amongst many kids who are adrift in

240

relationships in what can only be called a moral vacuum. Take the case of one girl who was only fifteen. She had gone out one evening, got totally drunk and allowed two guys to 'have' her. She told her mother, 'Mum, I didn't even know the two guys who did it. Have I just become like an animal or something?'

But her mother replied, 'Your grandmother was a randy lady; your dad and I split up because of this kind of thing, and I guess that's just the way you are. You might as well just lie back and enjoy it!'

As the tears ran down her face, she said to me, 'I asked my mother for moral guidance and that's all I got.'

If you ask the average kid who taught them their relationship skills, or about values in life, tragically you will find that it is Mum and not Dad. And furthermore, the breakdown of the family means, of course, the average kid is not getting any guidance. One girl told us of a savage rape by a 45-year-old who had so damaged her at thirteen, that at sixteen she discovered she could not have children. She told her parents she fell off the house to explain broken bones and other injuries.

At a very posh private school I was once ushered into the pain of the children of the rich. One first year high student was crying because of the loss of $20. It was a special weekly payment from his dad — a prominent doctor. He said, 'Dad gives me $20 to keep my mouth shut. Mum thinks Dad is taking me for a walk but he's going out to perve on the girls on the nude beaches.'

What loneliness in the heart of the professional. And what confusion for the thirteen-year-old son.

One son of a rich and prominent businessman on the Gold Coast said — again with tears in his eyes — 'My Mum and Dad can send me to the Bahamas for a holiday, but I don't know if they love me and I have no idea who I am.'

The stories of teenagers in distress are commonplace. Almost every schools programme we do now brings to light at least one horrendous story of incest, domestic violence or

241

dire consequences of a personal, sexual nature.

I'm not a right-winger at all on this issue, but our society is giving almost no guidelines in this important area of life. What we thought would bring freedom and creativity, is in fact limiting the possibilities of being human. The secularists have some profound questions to answer. The age of reason has become an age of darkness and confusion. The age of rationality has become the age of irrationality in practice. The age of communication has become the age of divorce, widening generation gaps, aloneness and fragmentation.

Having mentioned high schools, I should add that I also love to spend time with university and college students. I am not in the least scared of intellectual debate. Christianity can stand on its own against the most fiery attacks from the most brilliant minds. I have spoken now at every university in Australia except one and love the opportunity to grapple with bright young minds who are wrestling with the big questions of life. My mind hasn't been academically trained, but I am a voracious reader still and my library currently contains about 6,000 volumes. I try as much as I can to keep track of the shifts in literature, music and art. All of which is valuable exercise for my ageing brain cells.

Over the last decade or so, I have become progressively more Australian. That's not to say I'm in any sense a nationalist. I am passionately an internationalist. Einstein once said that nationalism is the most venomous disease ever to inflict itself on humanity. It has been the cause of more violence, hatred and bloodshed than can be conceived of. The nation should never come before truth.

But since I live in Australia, I have tried to soak myself in its history and culture, the better to understand why my countrymen are like they are and therefore how best to be understood by them. Jesus came down to earth and lived in the same dusty places as the people of Palestine. Since he is my one living example, I feel I should make every effort to appreciate every aspect of my environment.

My awakening fascination for my country coincided with

the time I broke out of my self-centred, holy cocoon and began looking around me at the real world. As I discovered Australia, it opened up a whole arena of life. This inevitably led me to re-think my dismissive and racist attitude to Aboriginal people.

Once I spent time with Aboriginals and talked with them, my respect and affection for these dignified people grew immensely. And as I explored their history and culture, I grew deeply ashamed at the brutal treatment white people had inflicted on them in their past. I was also shocked and angered at the level of prejudice, hatred and injustice they still have to face, day in, day out. Past and present governments have systematically ignored their legitimate rights. I became a vigorous supporter of their claims to land rights, and for the protection of their culture.

I still ride a motorcycle and I'm still President of God's Squad. I'm currently piloting a Harley Davidson FLST Heritage, a beaut machine generously bought for me by a businessman who supports our calling (do you really think I could afford one myself?). I guess I'm·a bit long in the tooth to be haring around on a bike, but I'm a long way from being the oldest on the scene. There are several vintage bikers around, and one of them, Bingo of the Black Uhlans, must be sixty-four. He still rides a big black Harley, wears his colours on his back and his war medals on his chest. He's reputed to be the oldest living outlaw biker in Oz.

I'm also a lot wiser in the ways of the outlaws than I used to be. The language and the filthy jokes used to bother me at first. I had come from a background where you corrected someone the moment they dropped a profanity. Do that when you're with the outlaws and you'd never get a chance to talk about anything else. All these years on, it would take a lot more than cursing to catch me off balance. Most important, I've learned to look beneath the surface of the outlaw style, which is often bravado, and deal with the men behind it.

Before I became a part of all this, I'd heard a lot about the dangers and the violence among bike gangs. I've seen some nasty incidents, but so far I've been protected. And in any case the violence of bikers has been greatly exaggerated by the popular press. It's rare for members of the public to get caught up in anything, though there are some psychotics who are attracted by the scene, and they'll do anything.

At the Calder races on one occasion, I noticed that two bikers had nicked a small child's tricycle and were riding around on it. The child was crying, so his father, an ordinary bike race spectator, asked politely for the trike to be returned. With lightning reactions, one of these thugs gave the man a bunch of fives in the face while the other smashed a bottle and ground the jagged end in the back of the man's head. It was a horrifying incident and there was nothing their victim could have done about it. But then psychotics, whether they're in leathers or in suits, will always act irrationally.

The nearest I got to having my head kicked in was by another character of a similar persuasion to these two. After I crashed my Honda Four on the way back from Perth, Eddie Pye, who ran a bike shop at the time, sold me a Kawasaki 900. I'm now very much a Harley man, but that Kwacka was a ripper. I drove it into the ground, but it still had equal pressure in all four pots the day I sold it with 87,000 miles on the clock.

The gent in question didn't share my enthusiasm for the Kawasaki. We'd been to a big biker funeral and had retired to a pub, as was normal practice. This guy had been drinking for a while and he was a mean drunk. He walked over, grabbed my shirt and demanded, 'What's this Jap crap you're riding?' It didn't make a lot of sense to answer. Out of the corner of my eye, I could see Quince bristling, and I was worried in case he stepped in. I was worried that my mates might lose control, but I stood there. I couldn't do much else because he had my shirt. Fortunately, a couple of his mates we were on friendly terms with put their arms around him and eased him out of the way. I breathed again.

Only moments later, this same bloke walked over to a table at which some bikers from another (friendly) club were sitting. He took a schooner of beer, poured it on the table then smashed the glass. With the other hand he flipped the table over on its side, leaped over it and landed on another guy's head. Then he started putting the boot in. It was all over in a few seconds. His mates carried him out spitting blood. It had been a close call.

If there is violence on the bike scene, as I've said, it's usually between one club and another, and usually because a code has been transgressed. In one such case the Squad, through the skills of Norm Briddock, was able to save a life. Even at a place as anarchistic as the Hell's Angels rock concert, which is held every year on the Angels' own property at Broadford, north of the city, it's useful having someone around you can trust. The Angels had arranged for a doctor to be on site to look after the inevitable scratches and scrapes which happen when blokes have had a few beers too many. Unfortunately, on the first day a biker came riding through the crowd and cleaned the doctor up with his Harley. He knocked him right up in the air, and the festival's medical representative went back to hospital in an ambulance with an injured back.

That's where Norm, ambulance man extraordinaire, stepped in. He spent almost all of each day and much of the night bandaging people's cuts, splinting people's fingers and treating burns and abrasions. But in the middle of one night, he was faced with a more serious problem. One club believed that a member of another had had his way with one of their women. Their response was to attack him while he was asleep and beat him senseless with an iron bar.

Norm was called over with his first-aid kit, only to find the victim had a badly fractured skull and was near to death. When someone's life is at stake, Norm is absolutely fearless and very professional. He ordered outlaws much larger than himself out of his way and commanded a particularly fierce biker to send for an ambulance. When the ambulance arrived it had no attendant, but Norm knew the driver and went with the injured man to hospital. Norm had to resuscitate him twice before he reached there, without question saving his life. Prompt and selfless action of this kind makes a lot of friends, and this was another of those instances which have now become part of the history which adds up to the Squad's good standing among bikers.

It was because we're always ready to help that Ball Bearing (so called because of the chrome helmet he used to wear) who has been at various times Secretary and Publicity Officer of the Melbourne Angels, asked me to officiate at a wedding. The couple were two mates of his, Rob and Haley. They wanted to get married on the stage at Broadford. I wasn't sure. They'd been living together and Haley was pregnant. But this was a serious request.

I asked Rob and Haley lots of questions. Many outlaw weddings are very secular affairs, done over a Harley Davidson manual instead of a Bible. So I wanted to know why I'd been approached. It turned out that they were serious about marriage, that they both believed in God and wanted his blessing on the union. They wanted the wedding to be at the festival, because all their mates would be there. I visited them at their little weatherboard home for some pre-marriage counselling, only to find they had a group of their mates there too. Did they want to go to another room for privacy? No their friends all wanted to know what I had to say as well!

Having agreed, I didn't relish the prospect of standing up in front of 7,000 mostly drunk bikers, many with a can of beer in hand, and trying to say something serious. Ball Bearing was Best Man and I hoped an official Hell's Angel presence would help. In the end it went well. There were a good few catcalls and boos whenever I said anything connected with goodness, but for Rob and Haley's sake the crowd were pretty well-behaved. It was an odd experience reading a famous passage from the New Testament which reads, 'Love is gentle, love is kind,' to this beer-swilling crowd and with a twenty-foot-high Hell's Angels death's head behind me. It was an uneasy peace, though, until the final prayer. For this there was a total and complete silence. It was remarkable. Rob and Haley are still together and still doing well. Even in that unlikely setting we were able to speak of the need for a deeper meaning to life.

Ball Bearing, who had made the initial approach, has become a good friend. He doesn't agree with my beliefs, but he won't stand in my way. It's a relationship of mutual respect. He has done a great deal to give the Squad credibility among bikers. For my part, I once defended him in court on a drugs charge. Not just out of friendship. I believe he was innocent.

A few years later I was asked by another couple if I'd baptize their two small children at Broadford. That wasn't nearly so easy a decision. Marriage is something God intended for people and therefore it's fine to marry them if they request it. But with baptism you're really talking about something which relates to the church. I didn't want to prostitute either this precious sacrament nor my own integrity.

I talked to the couple, who had both come from church backgrounds in one way or another. They both wanted their children to be given God's blessing and were firm in their commitment to provide them with the opportunity of discovering the Christian faith. That was fine, but then I found out that there were to be five godparents, all of them from the bike scene.

I talked to the chief godparent (if there is such a thing) and said, 'Your responsibility as godparents is to make sure, if these kids' parents die, that they get every opportunity to hear and respond to the Christian gospel and to find their own place of faith. If you aren't prepared to agree to that, then the baptism's a farce and I can't go through with it.'

To my surprise he agreed, saying, 'I don't want to stop any kid from having the chance of finding God.'

The baptism went ahead, but not from the stage this time.

247

It was a more discreet gathering round the back of the Squad bus from which we serve free coffee twenty-four hours a day during the Hell's Angels rock festival.

It was an attentive crowd, and a moving experience. Tough old bikers stood sniffing back the tears. I spoke about the importance of family life, very much aware that guys on the bike scene often neglect their wives and children in favour of their clubs. I also took this opportunity to speak about the need to give each other the room to find faith, despite the fact that among bikers it's seen as very uncool. A lot of deep and serious conversations came out of that little ceremony both with bikers and their wives. I was treading a fine line to do it. But then I've often had to do that in order to reach people with the good news of Jesus Christ.

Since I came to belief in Jesus, it's what I've wanted to do most of all. That's why I sat on a motorcycle in the first place and it's the reason I ride one still.

This book isn't called *On the Side of the Angels* because I have defended Hell's Angels in court. I can't unconditionally endorse the Angels or any of the other outlaws I've met and made friends with. But the pun is intentional. I want bikers to get a fair deal from the police, the courts and the public. They are citizens like anyone else, with the same rights as anyone else.

Above all bikers are human beings who deserve to be treated as such. They also deserve the chance to hear the case for Jesus Christ, Son of God just as much as Mr and Mrs Average next door. In this respect I am most definitely on the side of the Angels.

And I'm also on the side of the other kind of angels in the sense that I believe in goodness, freedom, peace and justice. For students, single people, those managing to maintain their marriage. For the 'up and outs', the intellectual and creative people, the lovers of art. For the elderly, the oppressed, the lonely, the illiterate . . . and for bikers. Whatever their home background, beliefs or race. I want this world to be a better place.

Jesus said something once which always moves me deeply. He was teaching his disciples to pray and he told them to ask, 'Your kingdom come, your will be done, on earth as it is in heaven'.

That's what I want to see. God's justice and God's love made real in this broken world. I long for a better world. And as best I can, I intend to be part of the answer rather than part of the problem.

ACKNOWLEDGEMENTS

God knows that many people have been influential and helpful to me in my journey. To name each individually would be an enormous task. Let me simply record my thanks to the following people:

Malcolm Doney who, as a biographer, has shaped and compiled this account faithfully and sensitively, and given written form to the majority of this story.

Care and Communication Concern Board of Directors, staff and schools team. St. Martin's Community Church leadership team and members. My mates in God's Squad Motorcycle Club. The many individuals who have consistently supported my ministry and my family.

John U'Ren, of Melbourne's Scripture Union, whose remarkable ability to put other than his own ministry first, has made him my most frequent counsellor and friend in crisis.

Hank Petrusma, who apart from being a good friend and advisor over many years, has inspired me to believe that leadership, power and entrepreneurial gifts do not have to corrupt a person, but rather can be used in service of all.

Steve Drury, without whose organization, encouragement and faith in the project, I would never have been able to ignore the tangled web of demands long enough to finish this book.

Trevor Chambers, who has tirelessly assisted me for years with research and now, in a full-time capacity, also with administration.

Mike Rule, whose commitment, not only to me but to the kids of working-class Melbourne, has long been an inspiration to dogged determination and faithfulness.

John Curtis, whose ability to keep moving with the times and whose desire to be immensely practical has inspired me to believe that the gospel is valid in the real world.

Mandy Halsall, Rosemary Spillane and Ruth Duck, who spent the many, many dedicated hours typing up the draft for this text.

To the staff of Truth and Liberation Concern and the people of that movement. The measure of disappointment and disillusion-ment with some cannot erase the gratitude I feel for those who were part of the inspiration of those heady counter-culture days. We did many great things together for which I thank God.

Organizers like Paul Wightman and comperes like Fuzz Kitto. Robert Timms, Tony Williams and Trisha Watts and other musicians who have helped stage some extremely exciting outreach missions across Australia. All the evangelists and preachers who tenderized me and made me aware of that 'other reality'. Graeme Smith who taught me the rudiments of warm-hearted communication of the gospel to Australian audiences.

The congregation of the Glen Forbes Methodist parish who, in their maturity, suffered with grace and love my early efforts at pastoral ministry. All my colleagues who worked with me in the other place in the foundation of God's Squad and its associated ministries. Ken Medema, musician extraordinaire, whose creative excellence and friendship has, in recent years, encouraged me in the pursuit of meaning in art and music.

Melbourne Anglican Archbishop David Penman who has given encouragement and advice of much value. And to hundreds of hosts, both clergy and others, who have accommodated me in their homes while I've been 'on the road at mission'.

To all those whose wisdom has gone before and helped me shape a complex, satisfying, but ever-moving and growing understanding of the Universe and humanity's place in it: Martin Luther King, John Wesley, Francis Asbury, Desmond Tutu, Steve Biko, Jacques Ellul, Helmut Thielicke, C. S. Lewis, Os Guinness, Manning Clark, Viktor Frankl, Henry Lawson, Arnold Toynbee, Allan Boesak, Oscar Romero, Henri Nouwen, Billy Graham, John Pilger, Robert McAfee Brown, Mother Theresa, Paul Tournier, Woody Allen, Leo Tolstoy, William Shakespeare, Charles Dickens, Victor Hugo, and above all others Jesus of Nazareth, Saviour and Lord, whose life and teaching are like the Sun itself in the presence of which all other lives and writings are a mere shadow of the substance of reality.

Few things have traumatized me as much as the writing of these credits. If you are not named, and knew you should have been, it is only because publishers demand an immediate response for a dead-line, which is yesterday. Tomorrow morning, I shall regret that, in the imperfection of human memory, I failed to remember you. I have nothing which I have not received either from God or from someone else. I have been impacted, inspired, instructed, educated,